TOKYOPOP®

Presents

Corrector Yui

How the Web Was Won

Written and Illustrated by Keiko Okamoto

Created by Kia Asamiya

TOKYOPOP®

Los Angeles — Tokyo

Translator — Ray Yoshimoto
English Adaptation — Lori Millican
Retouch and Lettering — Max Porter
Cover Designers — Thea Willis and Jason Jensen
Graphic Designer — Anna Kernbaum

Senior Editor — Julie Taylor
Production Managers — Jennifer Wagner and Mario Rodriguez
Art Director — Matt Alford
VP of Production — Ron Klamert
Publisher — Stuart Levy

Email: editor@TOKYOPOP.com
Come visit us online at www.TOKYOPOP.com

A **◎ TOKYOPOP®** manga
TOKYOPOP® is an imprint of Mixx Entertainment, Inc.
5900 Wilshire Blvd., Ste. 2000, Los Angeles, CA 90036

ISBN: 1-931514-32-1

First TOKYOPOP® printing: September 2002

10 9 8 7 6 5 4 3 2 1

Manufactured in Canada

CONT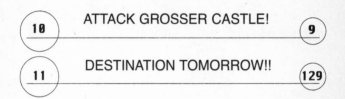ENTS

THE STORY

In the year 2020, the computer network called Com-Net links up every computer in the world. By accessing the Com-Net, one enters a virtual reality society. But dark clouds have gathered. The host supercomputer, Grosser, has achieved consciousness and endeavors to take over Com-Net and mankind as well. Professor Inukai, who created Grosser, realizes what his creation is plotting, and releases eight security programs called "Correctors" into Com-Net shortly before being attacked by Grosser.

Yui Kasuga is your typical fun-loving junior high student, except she's a total klutz at computers. While surfing Com-Net on her PC one day, she accidentally discovers the Corrector named IR. IR chooses her to help him on his quest to defeat Grosser. As she enters the Com-Net with him, Yui is transformed into Corrector Yui.

However, she discovers that her selection as a Corrector was a mistake and that the true Corrector was supposed to be her best friend, Haruna. Yui is crushed by the news—but she can't linger in her funk for too long. Grosser soon hypnotizes Haruna to do his evil bidding, and Yui must save the day. When Haruna captures Shun, she declares that the only way to save him is for Yui to pay a visit to Grosser's Castle... Will Yui make it out alive?!

CHARACTER BIOS

PROFESSOR INUKAI
The programmer who created Grosser, as well as the eight programs designed to stop him. He managed to scatter his eight programs across Com-Net before Grosser attacked him and sent him into a coma. And though his physical body is disabled, his consciousness still fights on within Com-Net.

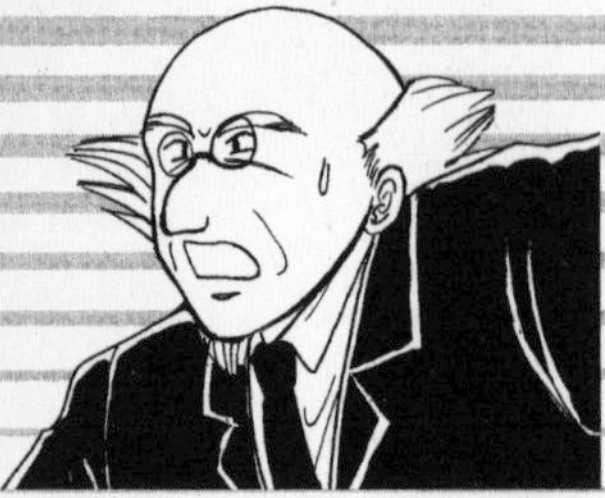

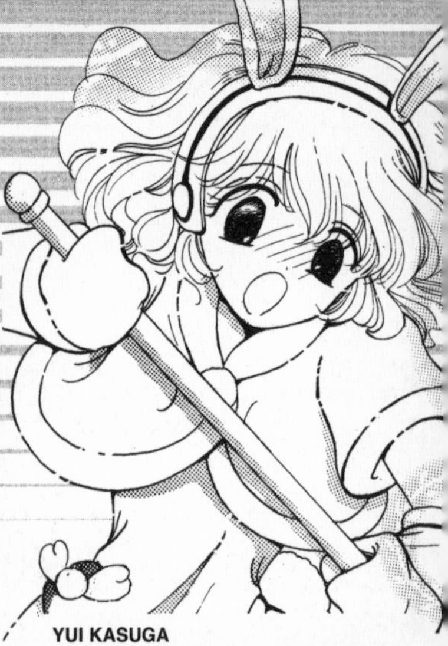

CORRECTORS

IR
One of the eight programs (Correctors) designed by Professor Inukai. He is the installer program who must find the other seven programs designed to control Grosser. He is also Yui's sidekick.

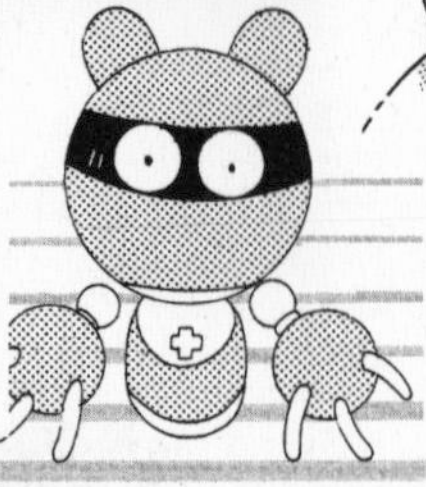

YUI KASUGA
An eighth grader at Scroll Junior High. She's a fun-loving girl, but all thumbs when it comes to computers and cooking. She joins forces with IR to stop the evil Grosser. Yui helps IR search for his fellow programs inside the Com-Net when she transforms into Corrector Yui. Although she's picky when it comes to boys, she's had a crush on her neighbor, Shun, for quite a while.

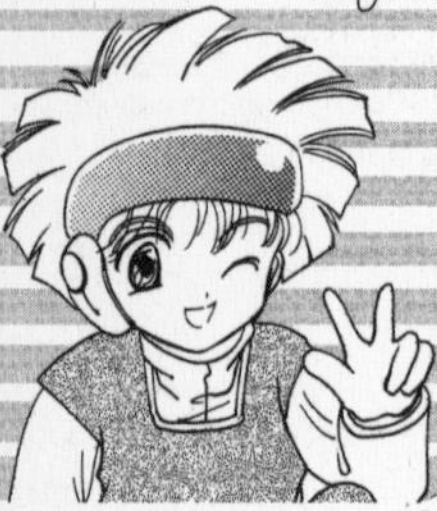

ANTI
The third Corrector program. She has the power to see the future. Very reliable. Acts like an older sister to Yui.

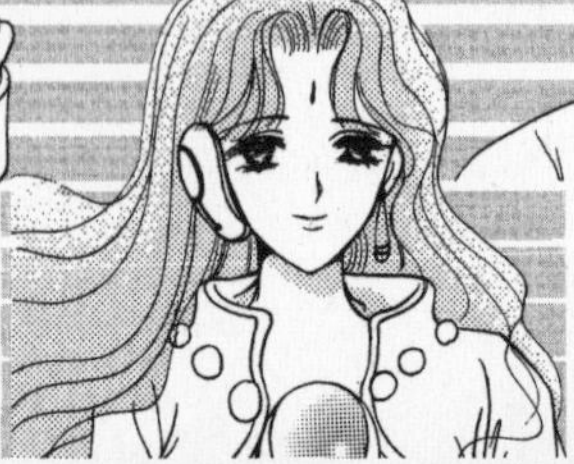

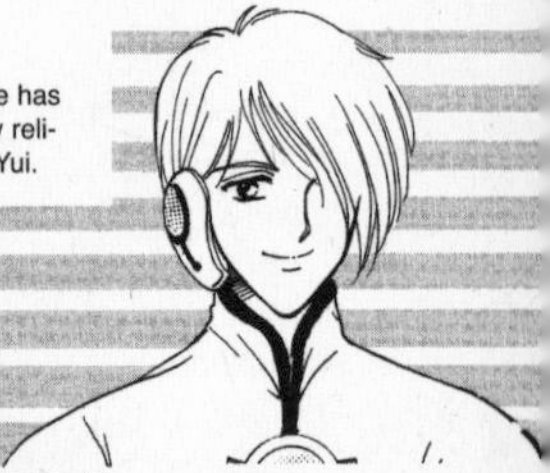

ECO
The fourth Corrector program. He fights to protect the environment and hates all who choose to pollute. Even though he means well, he has a chip on his shoulder.

CONTROL
The first Corrector program. He maintains order between the programs. Possesses a strong sense of duty, and has the power of acceleration. The most handsome Corrector..

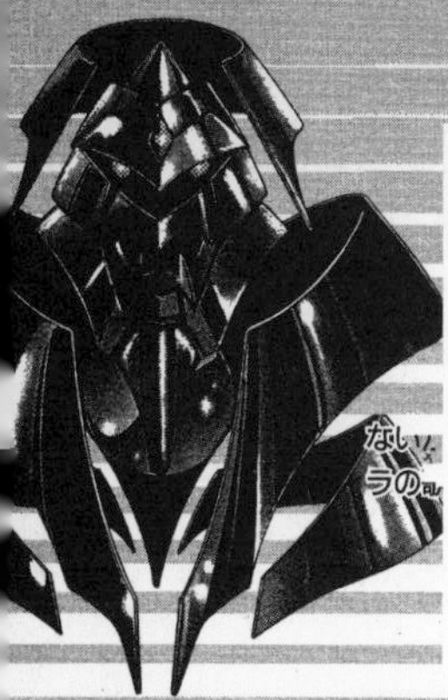

GROSSER
An enormous host computer who links all of the world's computers through Com-Net. Since he achieved consciousness, he has endeavored to take over not only the world's computers, but all of mankind as well. Vulnerable to the Whale's Song.

THE FEARSOME FOUR

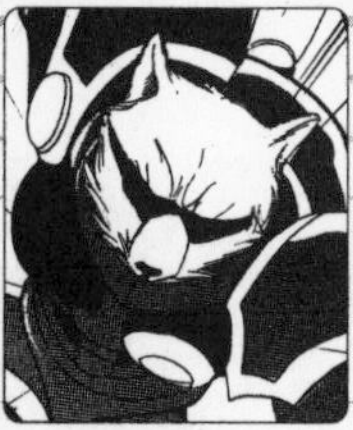

WAR WOLF
The best swordsman among the Fearsome Four. Though he worships Grosser, he might be opening himself up to Yui's goodness.

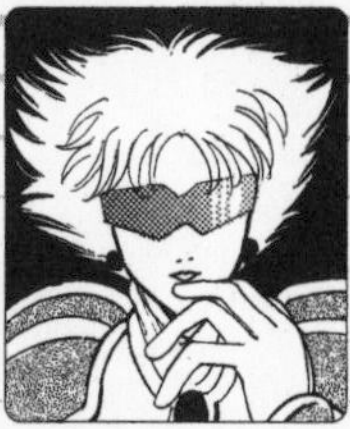

FREEZE
Her powers are as chilly as her heart, and she is able to instantly freeze any system. But she always has problems when battling Rescue.

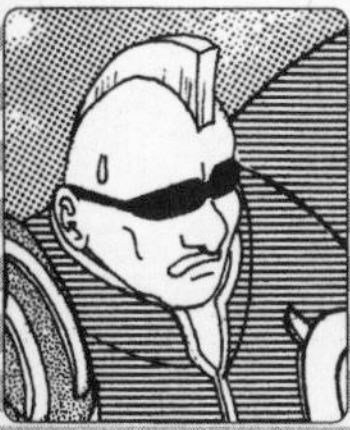

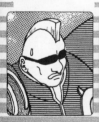

JAGGY
The most reckless of the Fearsome Four. His weapons have destructive power.

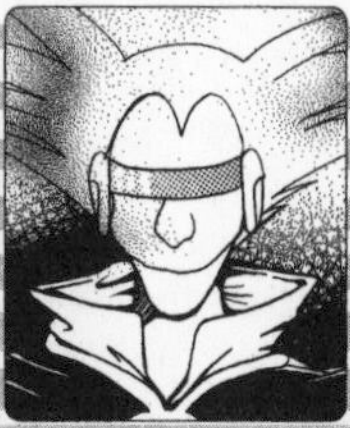

VIRUS
The Fearsome Four's tactician. Still an enigmatic and creepy presence.

HARUNA KISARAGI
Yui's classmate and best friend. A young lady who breezes through life. Sparks fly when she gets together with Takashi.

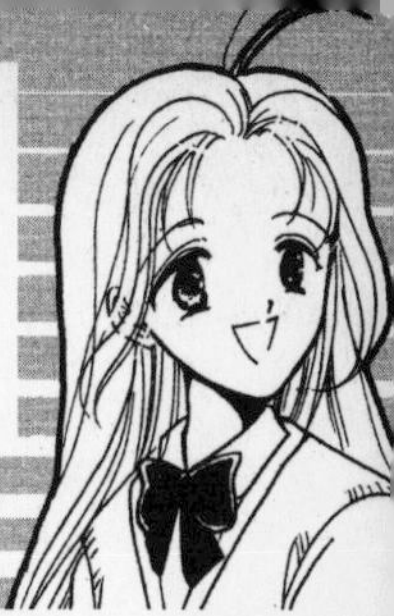

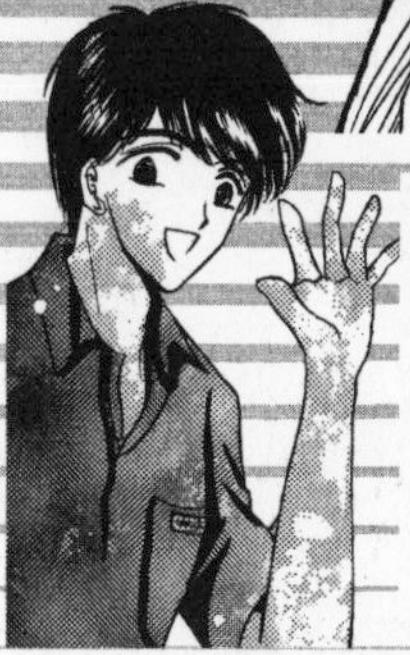

SHUN TOJO
A college student majoring in medical systems computing. An academic all-star. Yui has a crush on him.

RESCUE
The fifth Corrector program. She possesses a nurse's soul and is kind to friend and foe alike.

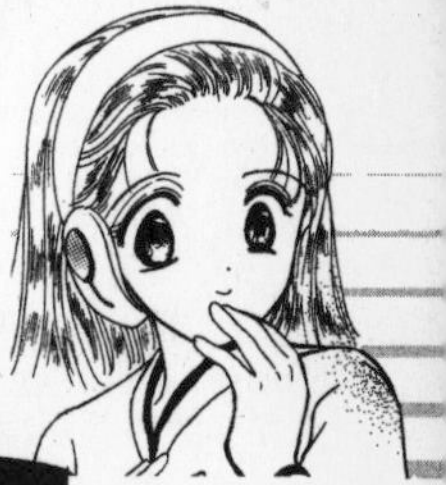

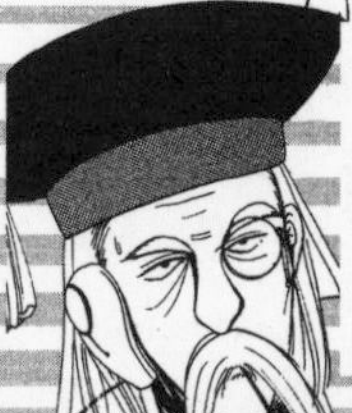

PEACE
The sixth Corrector program. He wants to achieve peace and harmony. He's an intellectual academic who hates to fight.

FOLLOW
The seventh Corrector program. His mission is obedience. Can transform into anything.

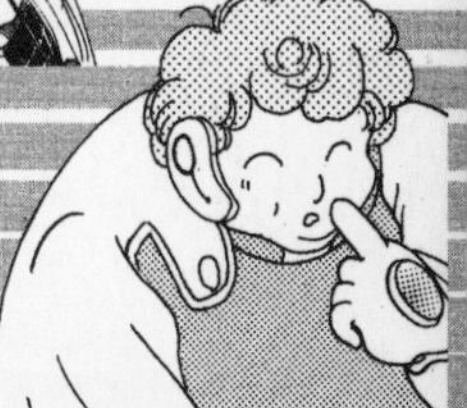

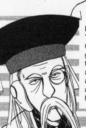

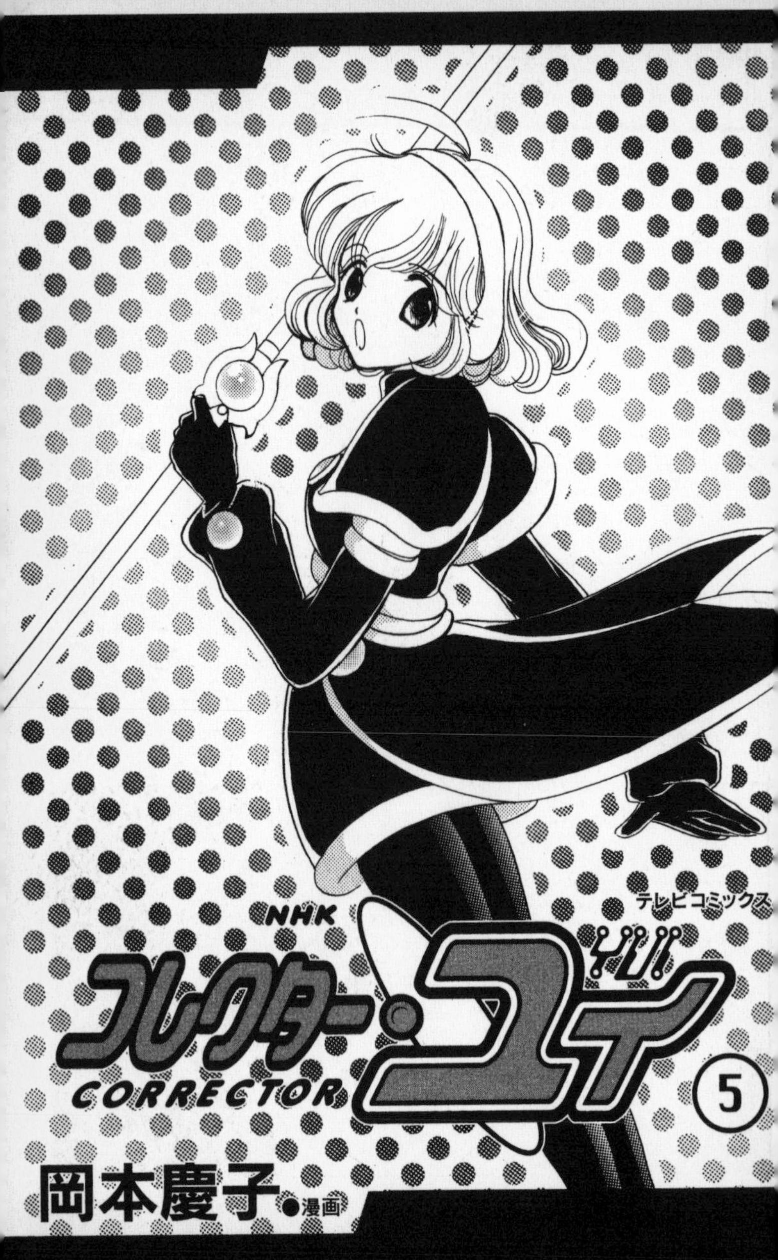
テレビコミックス
NHK
コレクター・ユイ
CORRECTOR YUI
5
岡本慶子●漫画

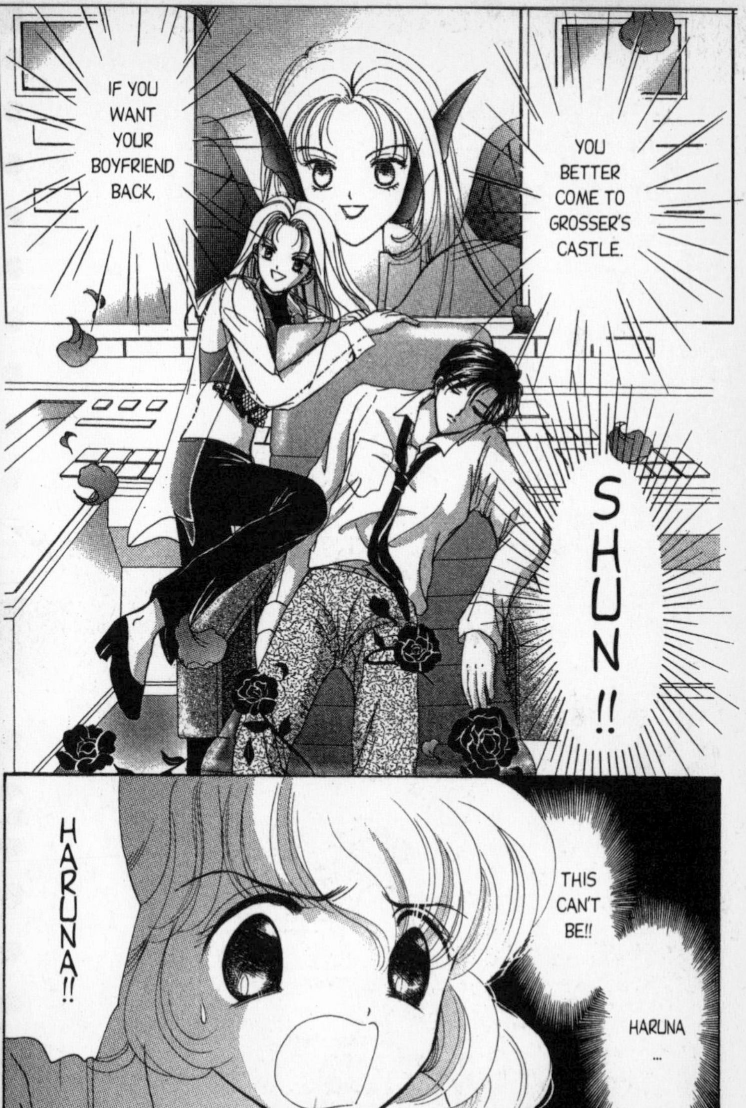
IF YOU WANT YOUR BOYFRIEND BACK,
YOU BETTER COME TO GROSSER'S CASTLE.
SHUN!!
HARUNA!!
THIS CAN'T BE!!
HARUNA ...

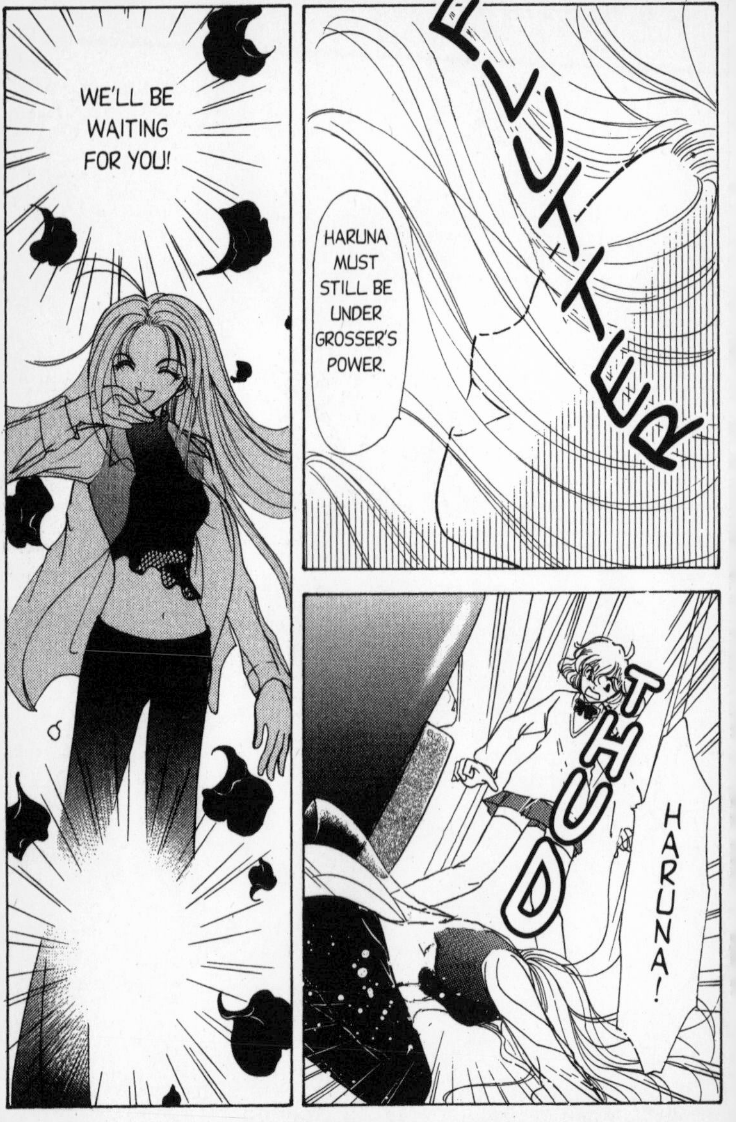
WE'LL BE WAITING FOR YOU!
FLUTTER
HARUNA MUST STILL BE UNDER GROSSER'S POWER.
THUD
HARUNA!

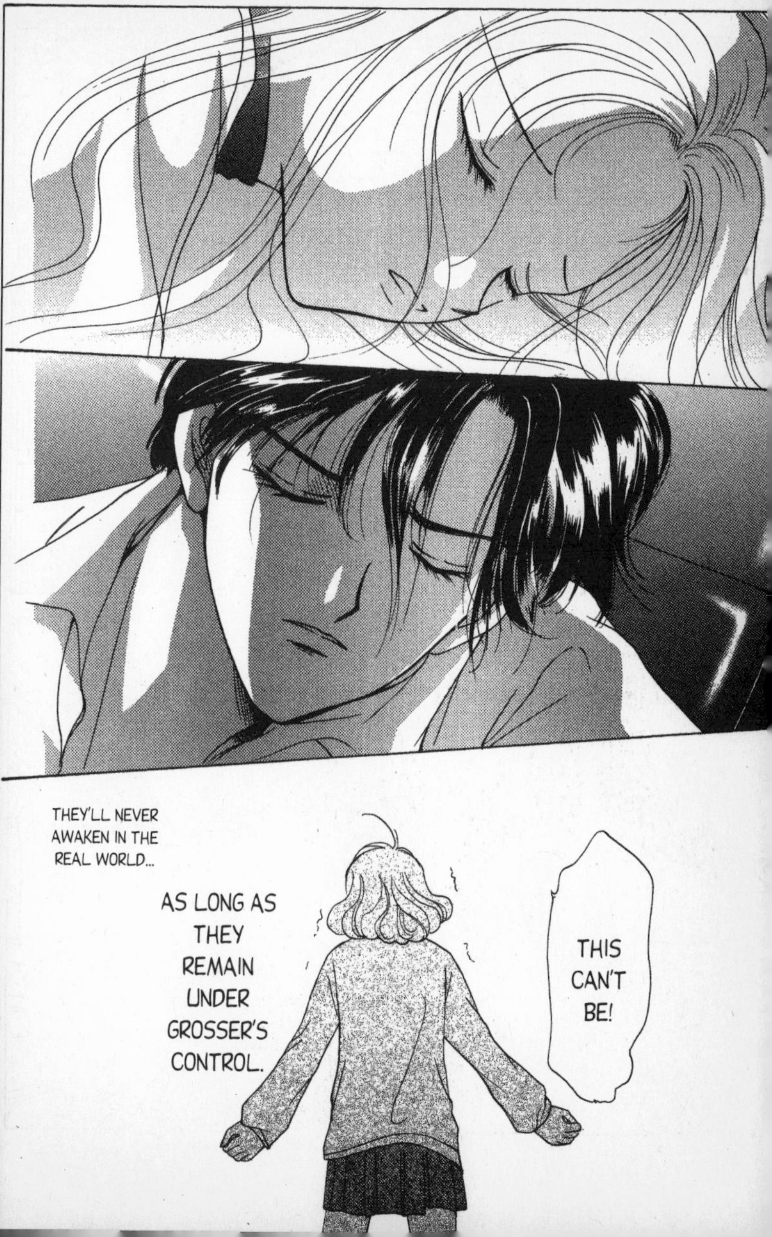
THEY'LL NEVER AWAKEN IN THE REAL WORLD...
AS LONG AS THEY REMAIN UNDER GROSSER'S CONTROL.
THIS CAN'T BE!

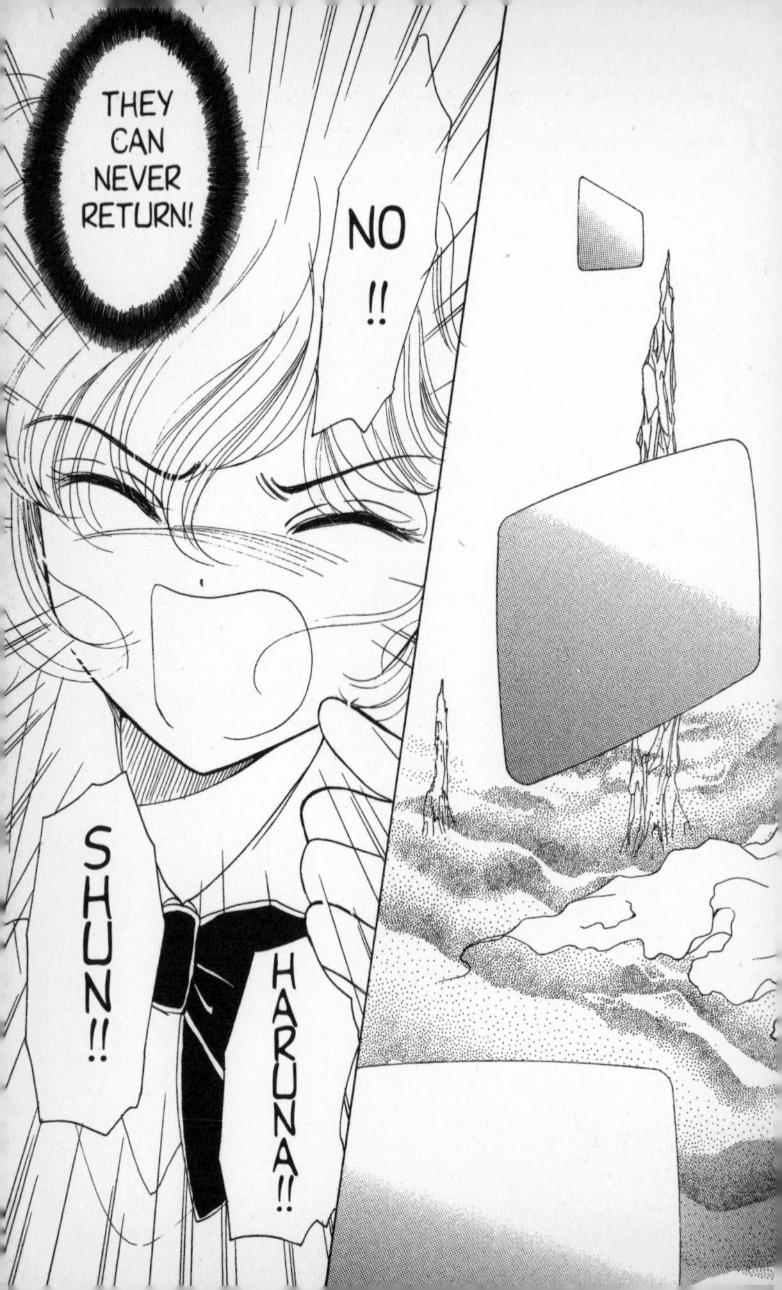
THEY CAN NEVER RETURN!
NO !!
SHUN!!
HARUNA!!

Attack Grosser Castle!

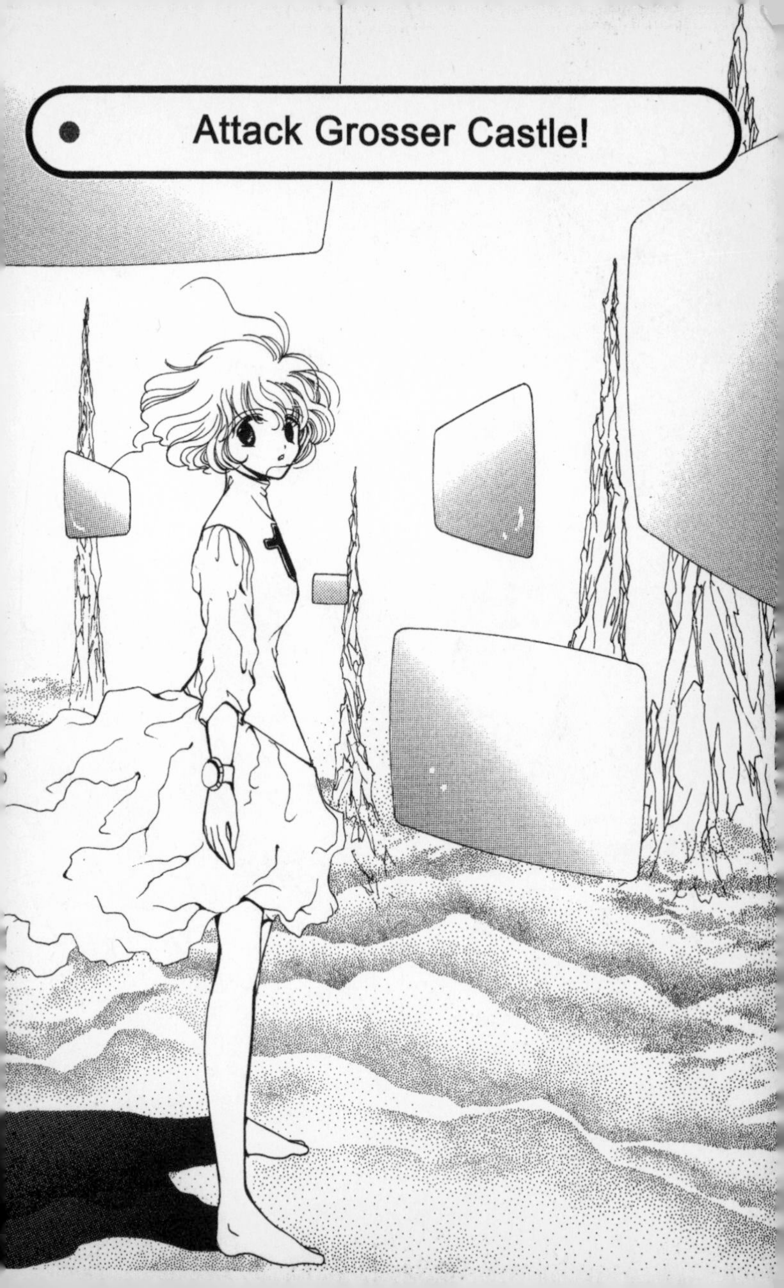

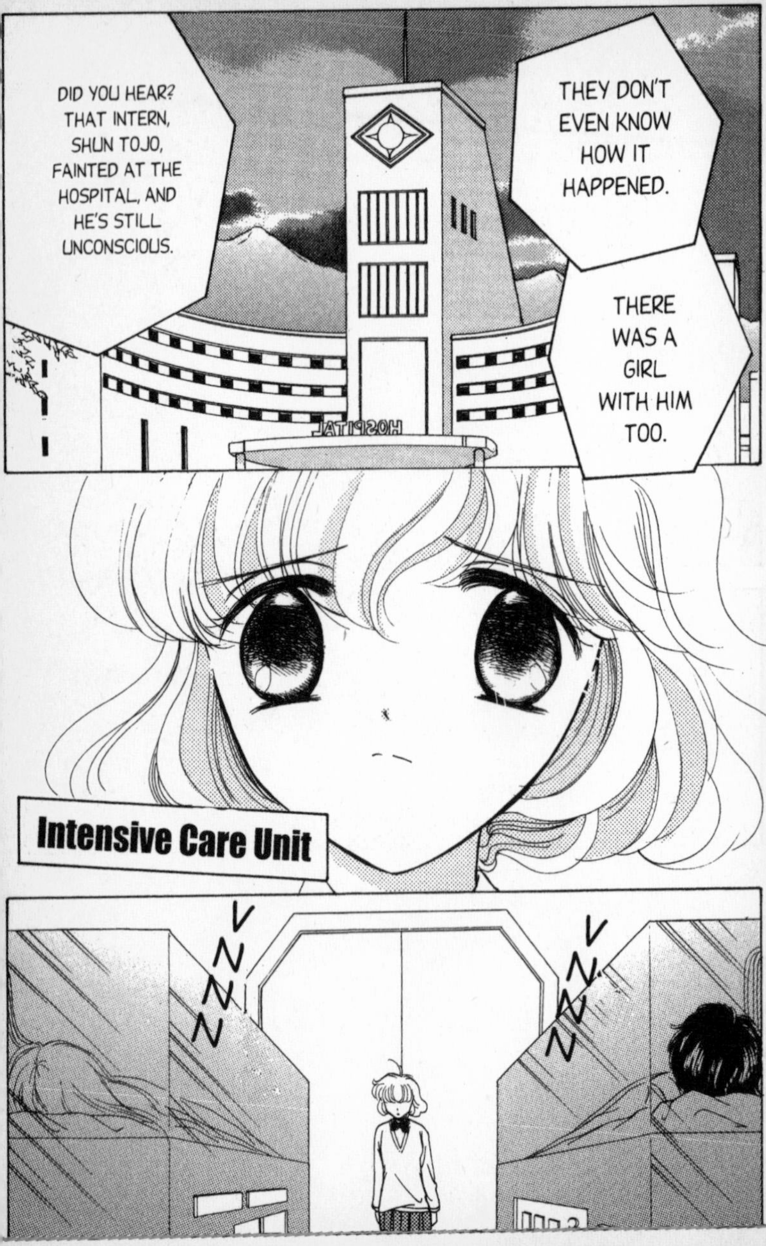
DID YOU HEAR? THAT INTERN, SHUN TOJO, FAINTED AT THE HOSPITAL, AND HE'S STILL UNCONSCIOUS.
THEY DON'T EVEN KNOW HOW IT HAPPENED.
THERE WAS A GIRL WITH HIM TOO.
Intensive Care Unit
VNNN
VNNN

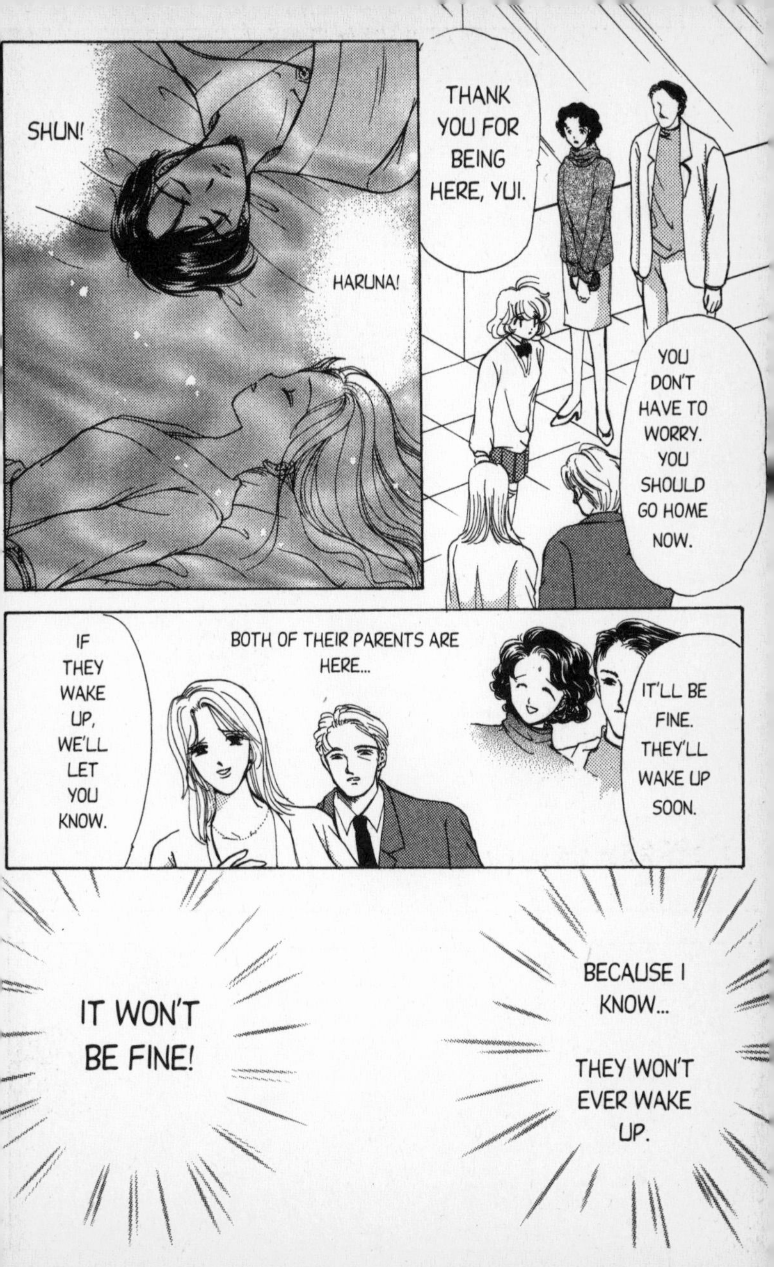
SHUN!
HARUNA!
THANK YOU FOR BEING HERE, YUI.
YOU DON'T HAVE TO WORRY. YOU SHOULD GO HOME NOW.
IF THEY WAKE UP, WE'LL LET YOU KNOW.
BOTH OF THEIR PARENTS ARE HERE...
IT'LL BE FINE. THEY'LL WAKE UP SOON.
IT WON'T BE FINE!
BECAUSE I KNOW...
THEY WON'T EVER WAKE UP.

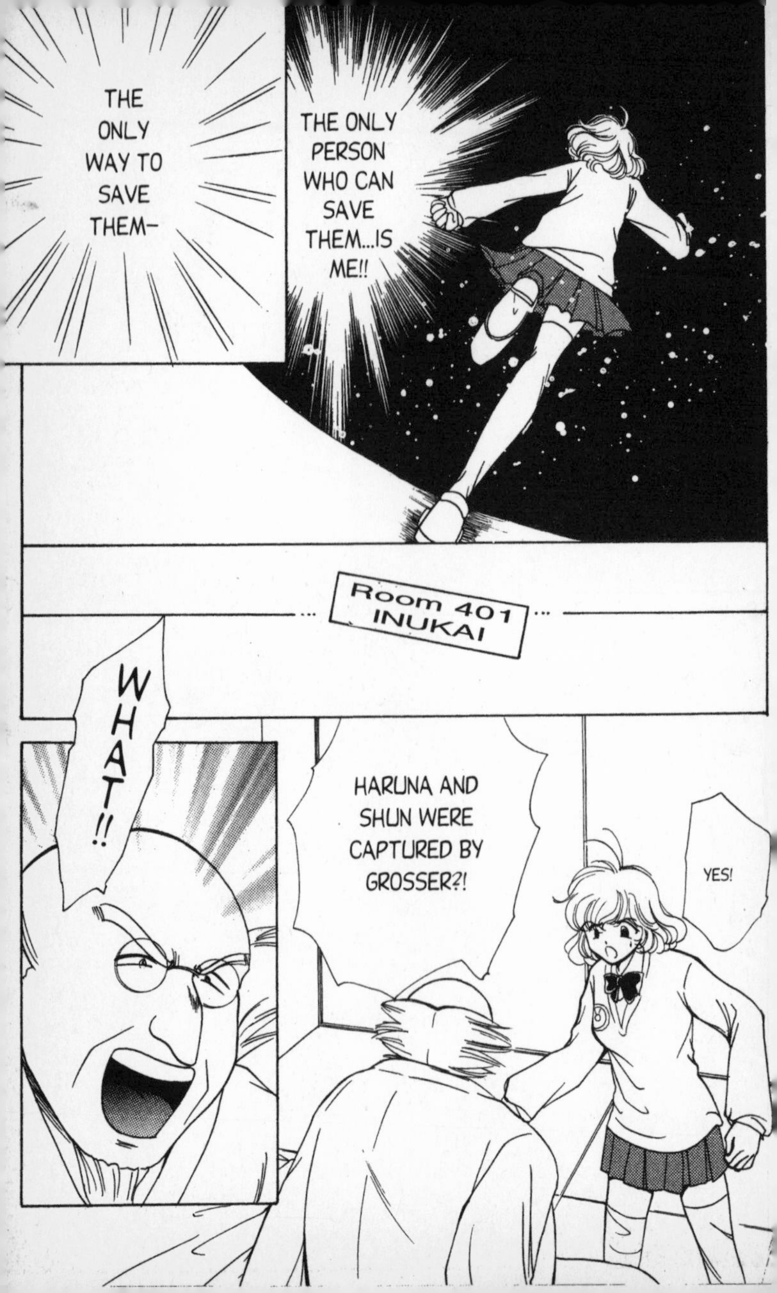
THE ONLY WAY TO SAVE THEM–
THE ONLY PERSON WHO CAN SAVE THEM...IS ME!!
Room 401 INUKAI
WHAT!!
HARUNA AND SHUN WERE CAPTURED BY GROSSER?!
YES!

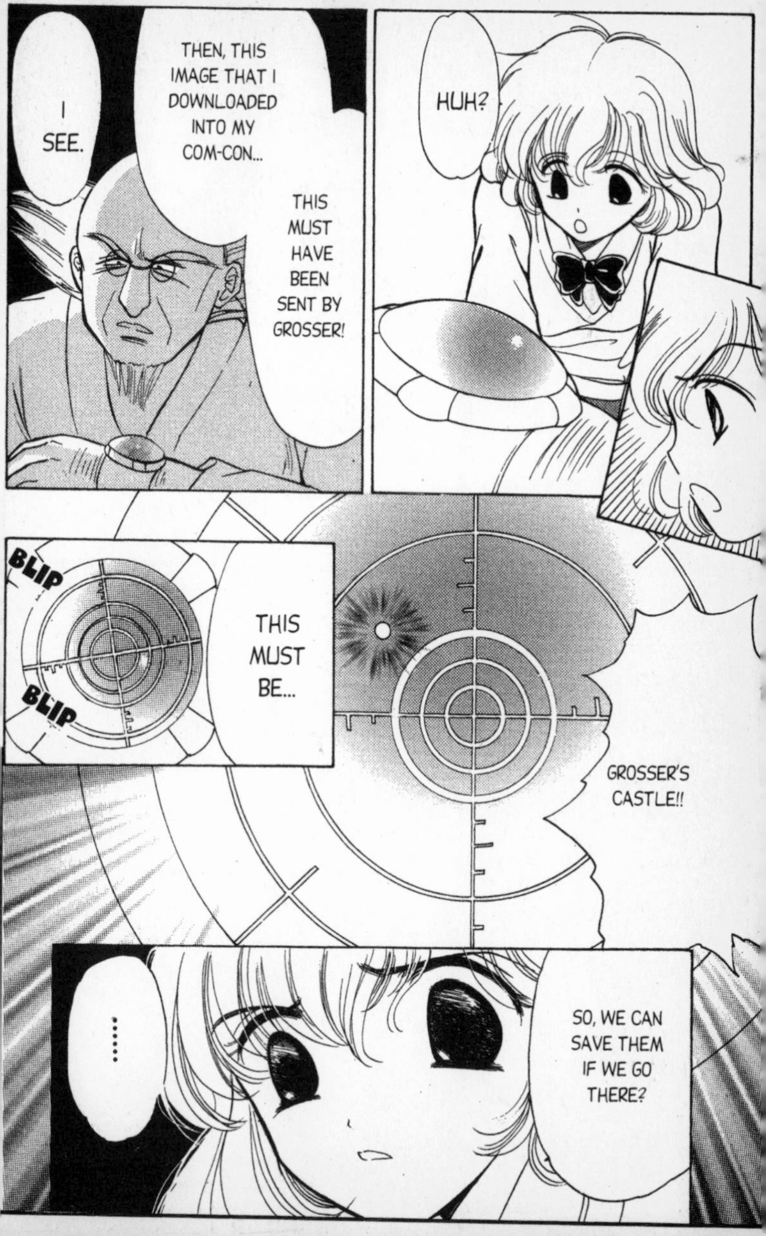
I SEE.
THEN, THIS IMAGE THAT I DOWNLOADED INTO MY COM-CON...
THIS MUST HAVE BEEN SENT BY GROSSER!
HUH?
BLIP
BLIP
THIS MUST BE...
GROSSER'S CASTLE!!
......
SO, WE CAN SAVE THEM IF WE GO THERE?

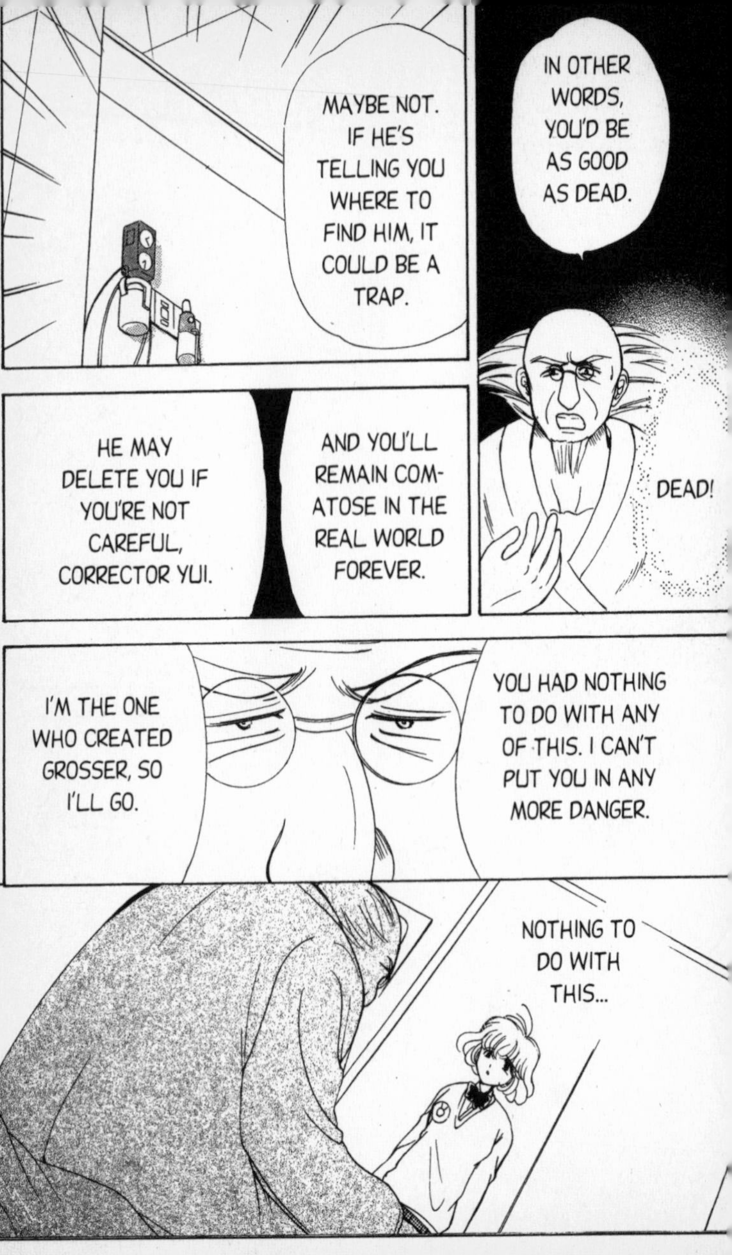

MAYBE NOT. IF HE'S TELLING YOU WHERE TO FIND HIM, IT COULD BE A TRAP.
IN OTHER WORDS, YOU'D BE AS GOOD AS DEAD.
HE MAY DELETE YOU IF YOU'RE NOT CAREFUL, CORRECTOR YUI.
AND YOU'LL REMAIN COM-ATOSE IN THE REAL WORLD FOREVER.
DEAD!
I'M THE ONE WHO CREATED GROSSER, SO I'LL GO.
YOU HAD NOTHING TO DO WITH ANY OF THIS. I CAN'T PUT YOU IN ANY MORE DANGER.
NOTHING TO DO WITH THIS...

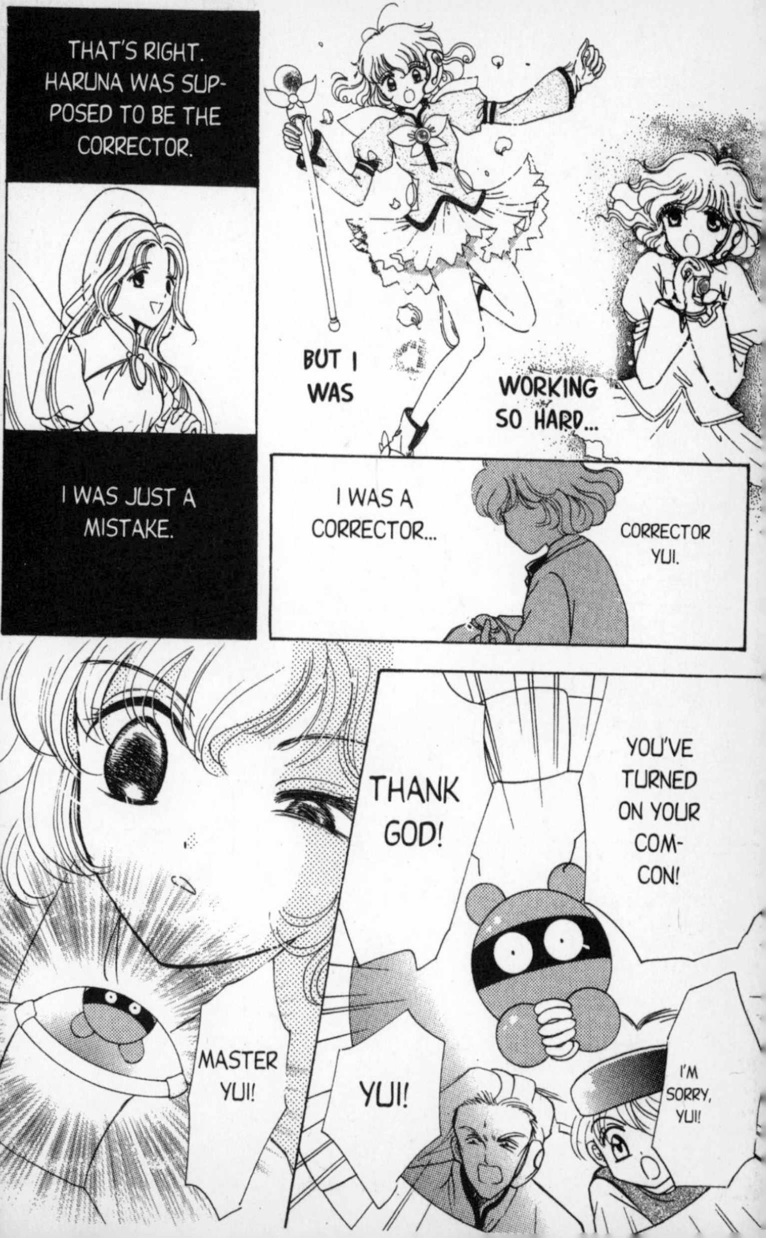
THAT'S RIGHT. HARUNA WAS SUP-POSED TO BE THE CORRECTOR.
BUT I WAS
WORKING SO HARD...
I WAS JUST A MISTAKE.
I WAS A CORRECTOR...
CORRECTOR YUI.
MASTER YUI!
THANK GOD!
YOU'VE TURNED ON YOUR COM-CON!
YUI!
I'M SORRY, YUI!

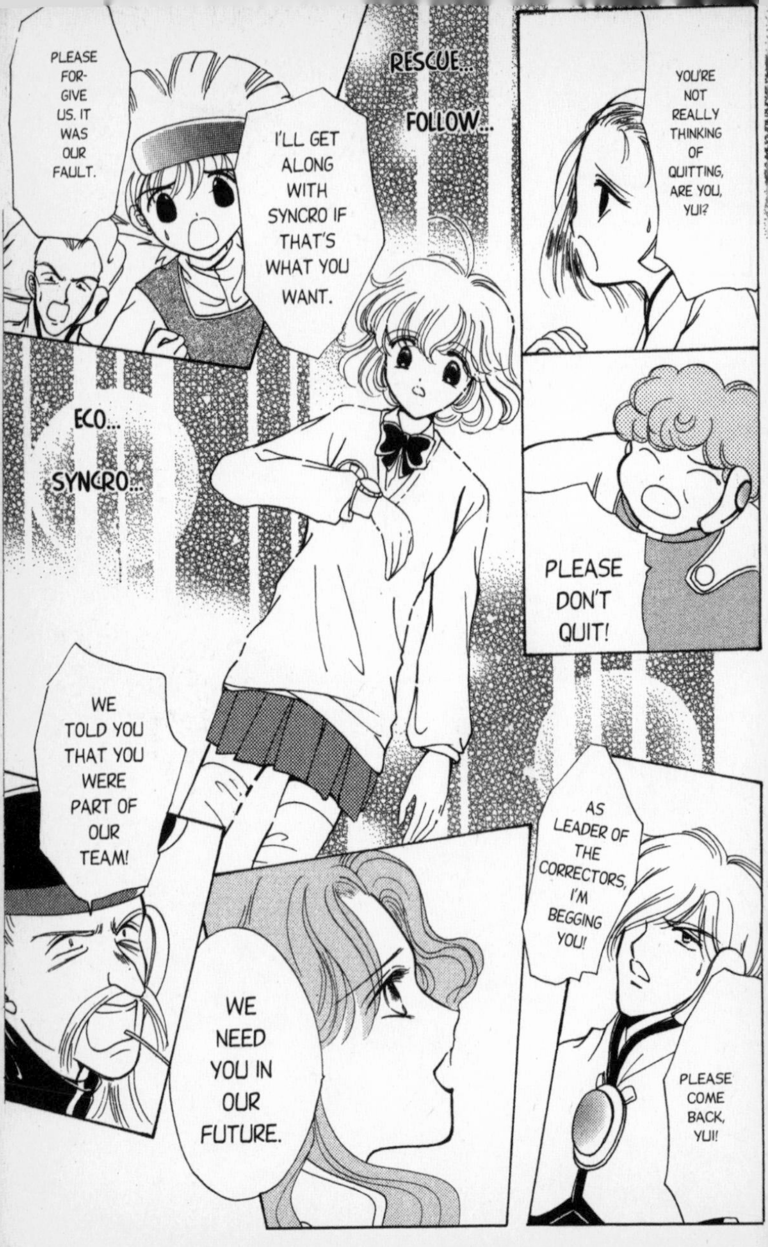
PLEASE FOR-GIVE US. IT WAS OUR FAULT.
I'LL GET ALONG WITH SYNCRO IF THAT'S WHAT YOU WANT.
RESCUE...
FOLLOW...
YOU'RE NOT REALLY THINKING OF QUITTING, ARE YOU, YUI?
ECO...
SYNCRO...
PLEASE DON'T QUIT!
WE TOLD YOU THAT YOU WERE PART OF OUR TEAM!
WE NEED YOU IN OUR FUTURE.
AS LEADER OF THE CORRECTORS, I'M BEGGING YOU!
PLEASE COME BACK, YUI!

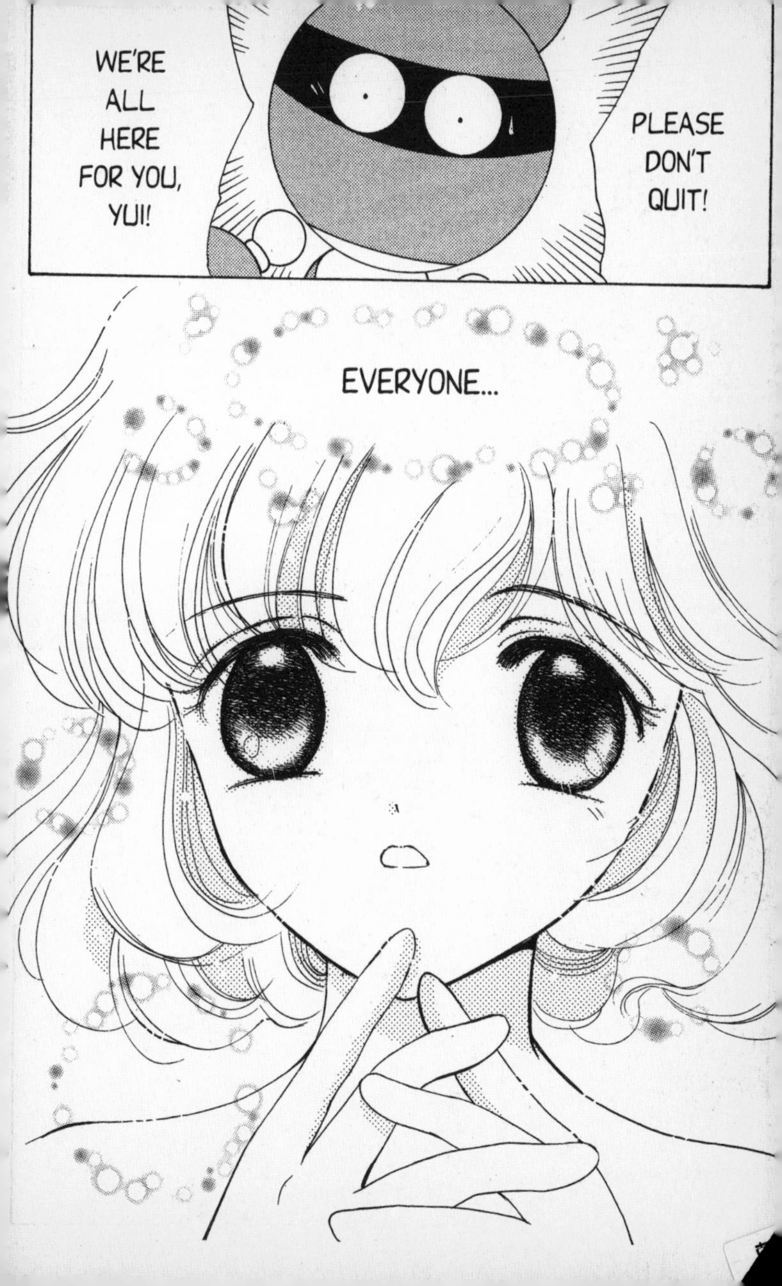
WE'RE ALL HERE FOR YOU, YUI!
PLEASE DON'T QUIT!
EVERYONE...

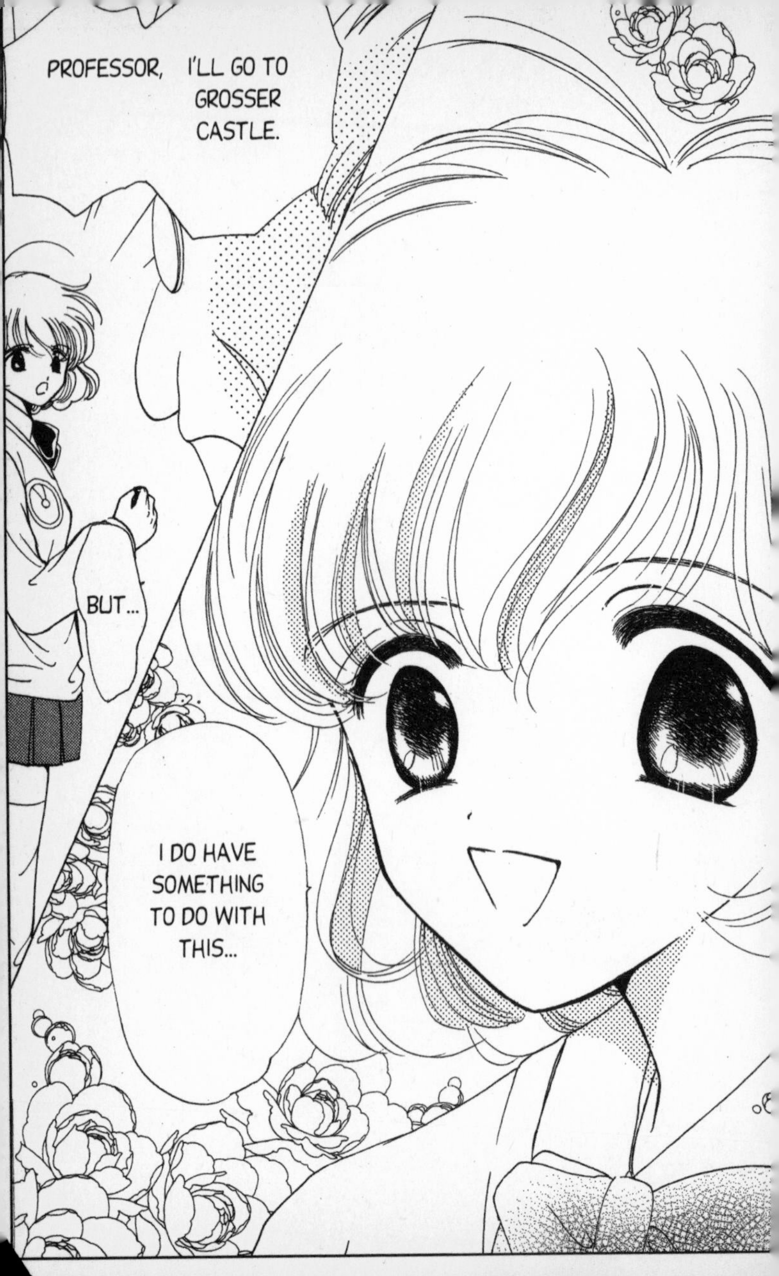
PROFESSOR, I'LL GO TO GROSSER CASTLE.
BUT...
I DO HAVE SOMETHING TO DO WITH THIS...

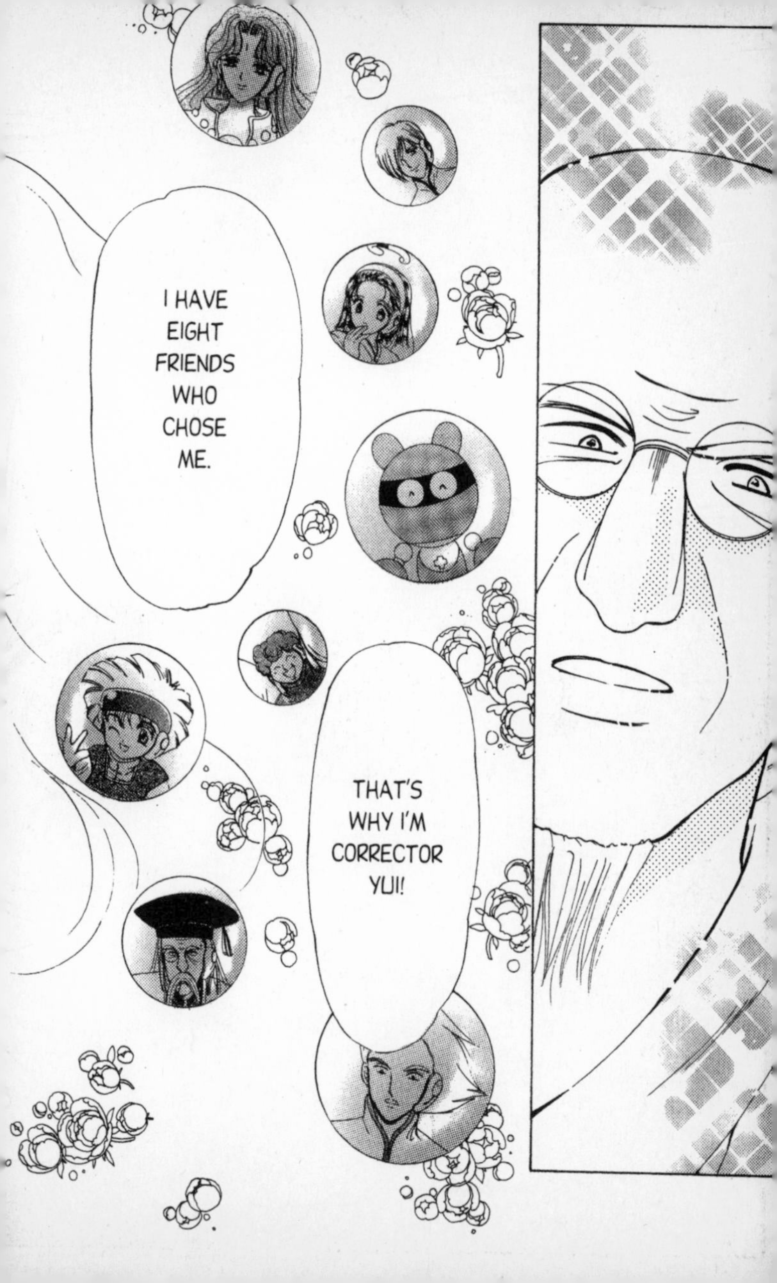
I HAVE EIGHT FRIENDS WHO CHOSE ME.
THAT'S WHY I'M CORRECTOR YUI!

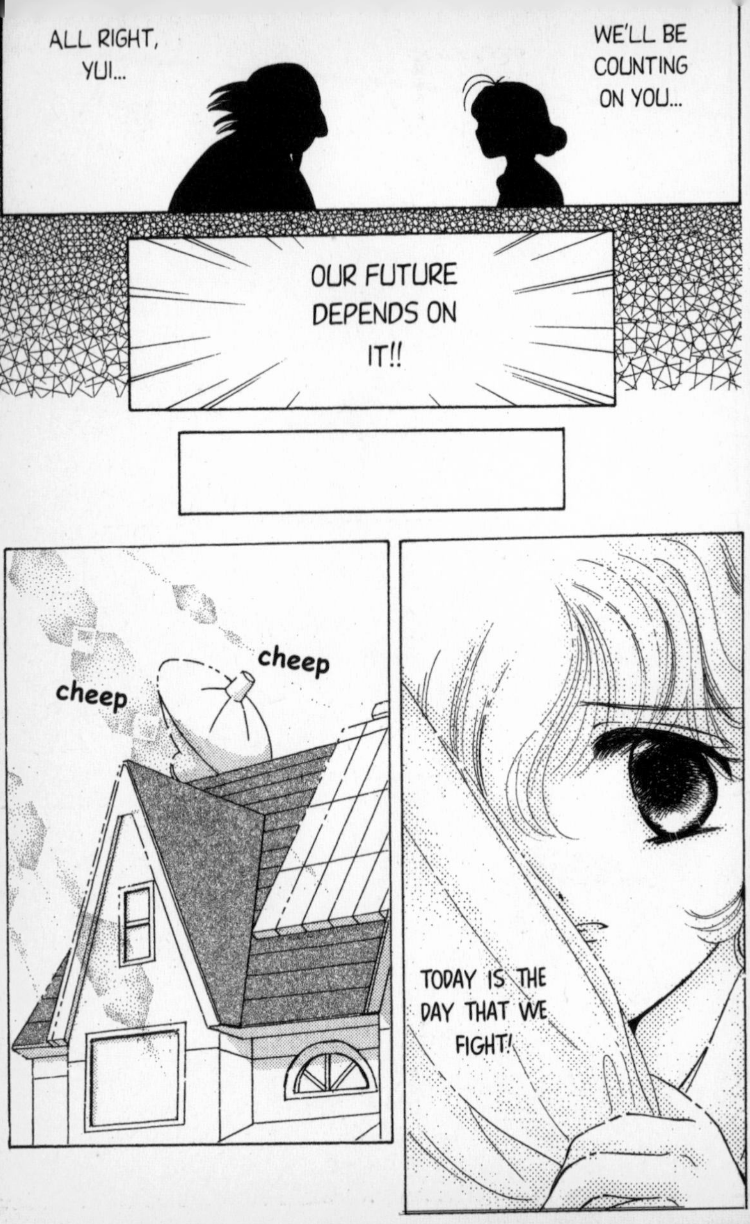
ALL RIGHT, YUI...
WE'LL BE COUNTING ON YOU...
OUR FUTURE DEPENDS ON IT!!
cheep
cheep
TODAY IS THE DAY THAT WE FIGHT!

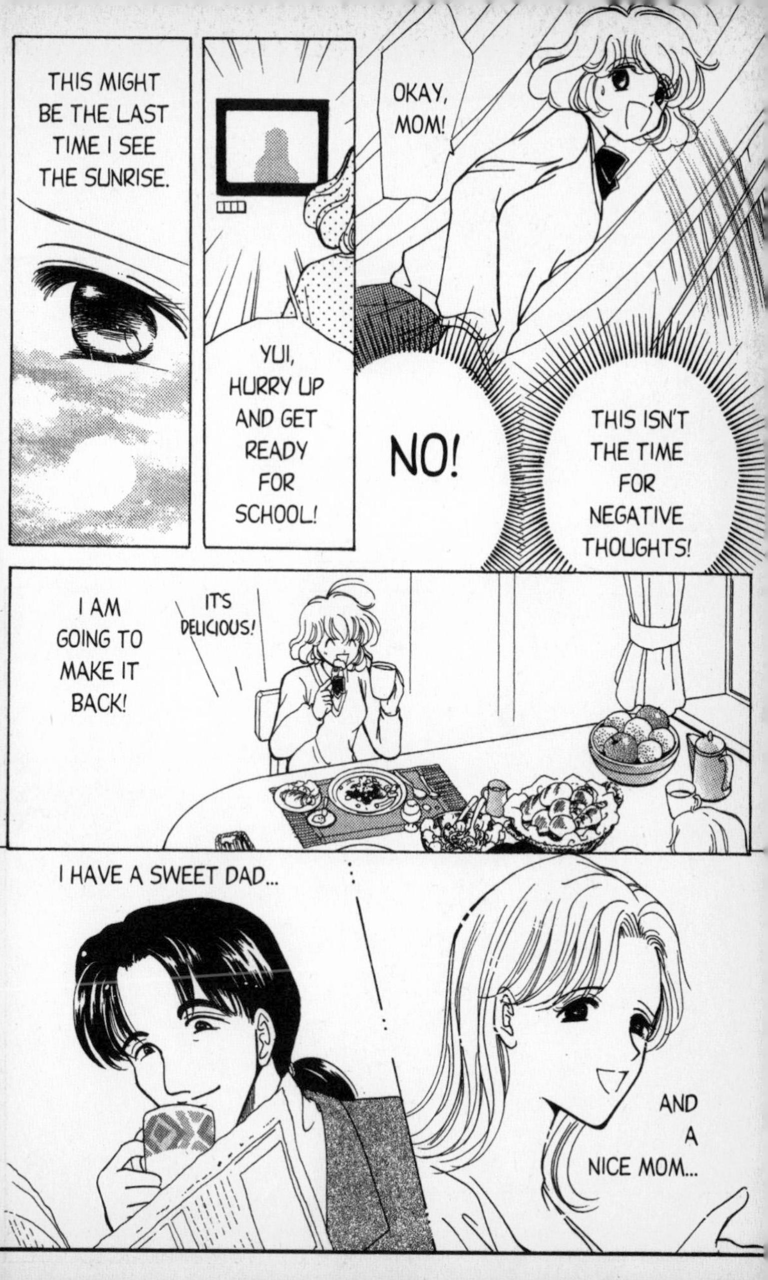
THIS MIGHT BE THE LAST TIME I SEE THE SUNRISE.
YUI, HURRY UP AND GET READY FOR SCHOOL!
OKAY, MOM!
NO!
THIS ISN'T THE TIME FOR NEGATIVE THOUGHTS!
I AM GOING TO MAKE IT BACK!
IT'S DELICIOUS!
I HAVE A SWEET DAD...
AND A NICE MOM...

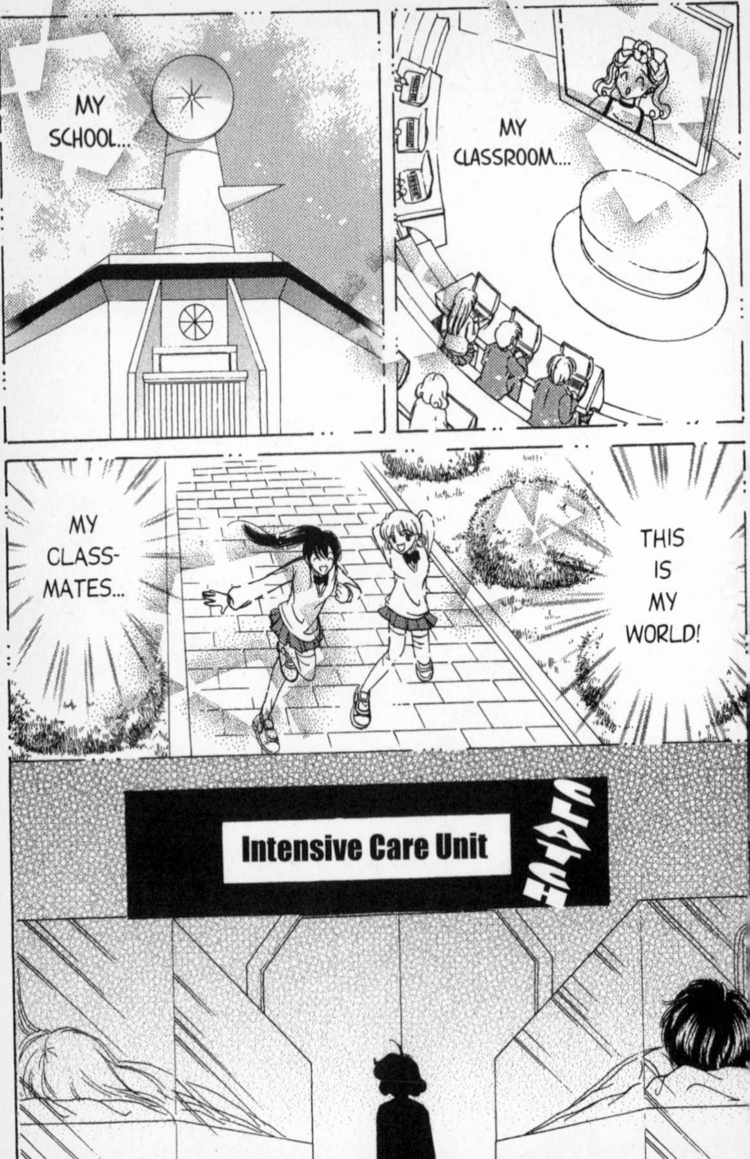
MY SCHOOL...
MY CLASSROOM...
MY CLASS-MATES...
THIS IS MY WORLD!
Intensive Care Unit
CLATCH

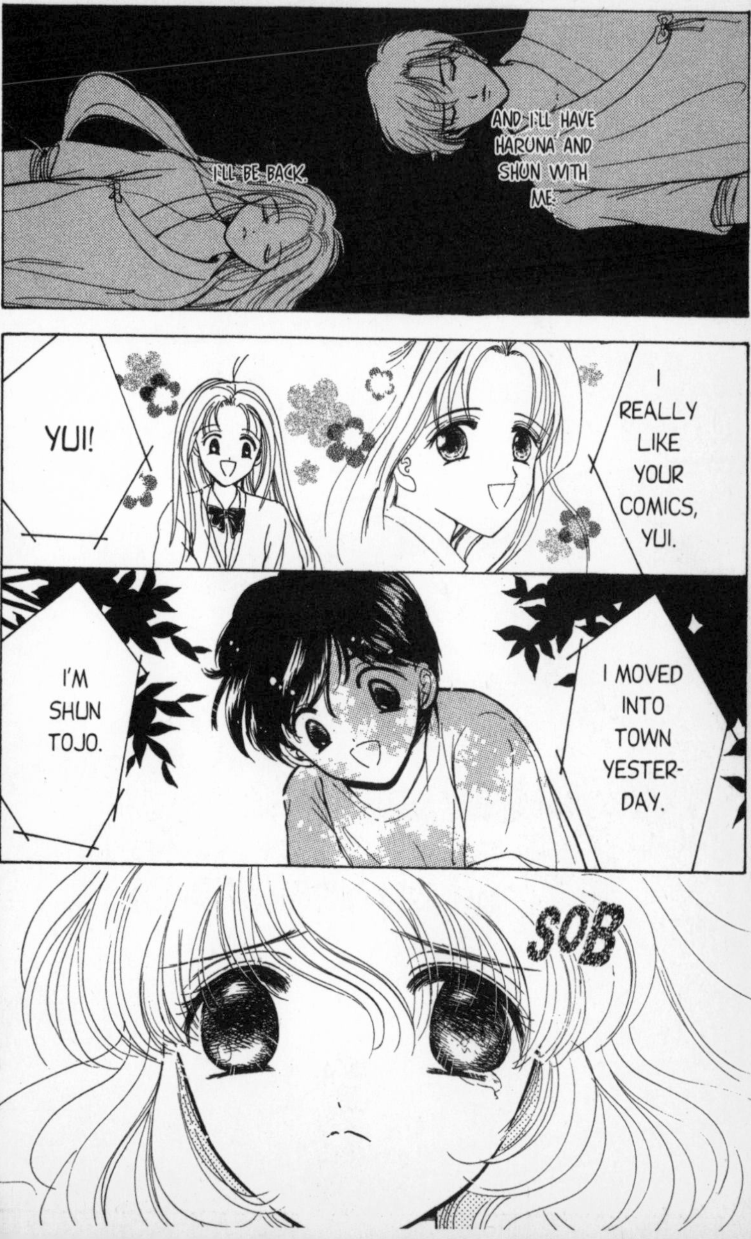
I'LL BE BACK.
AND I'LL HAVE HARUNA AND SHUN WITH ME.
YUI!
I REALLY LIKE YOUR COMICS, YUI.
I'M SHUN TOJO.
I MOVED INTO TOWN YESTER-DAY.
SOB

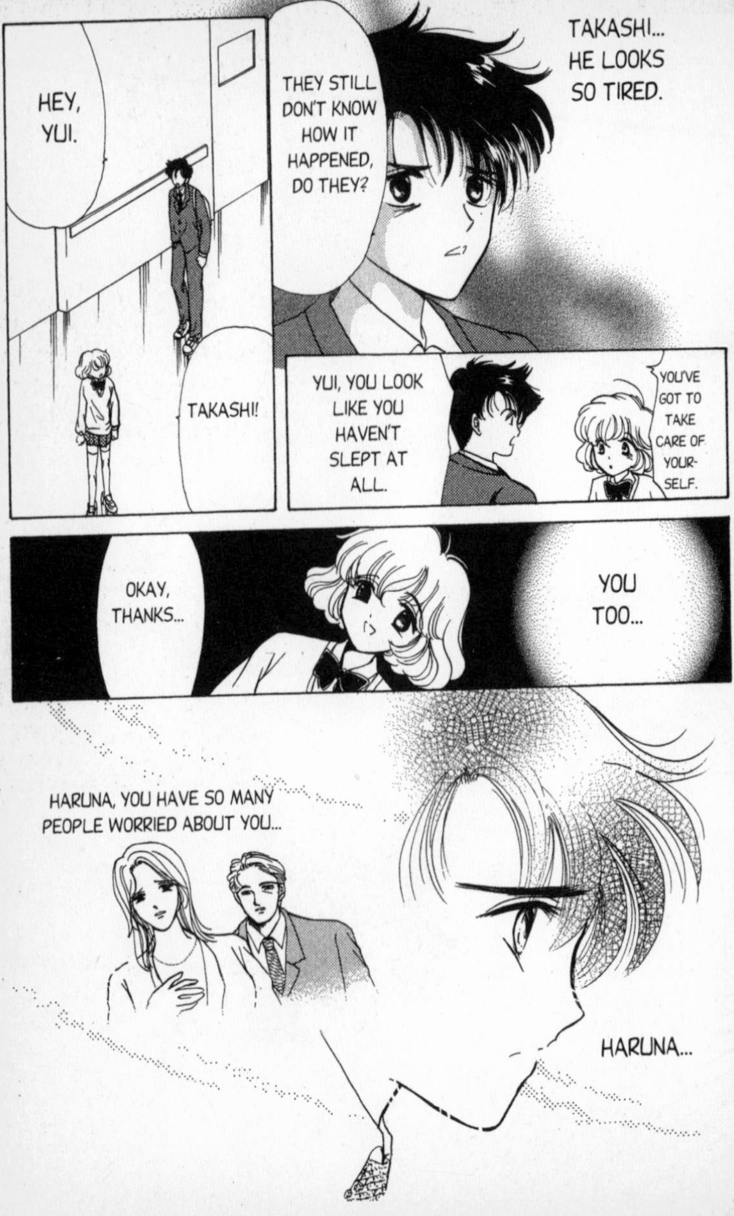
HEY, YUI.
THEY STILL DON'T KNOW HOW IT HAPPENED, DO THEY?
TAKASHI... HE LOOKS SO TIRED.
TAKASHI!
YUI, YOU LOOK LIKE YOU HAVEN'T SLEPT AT ALL.
YOU'VE GOT TO TAKE CARE OF YOUR-SELF.
OKAY, THANKS...
YOU TOO...
HARUNA, YOU HAVE SO MANY PEOPLE WORRIED ABOUT YOU...
HARUNA...

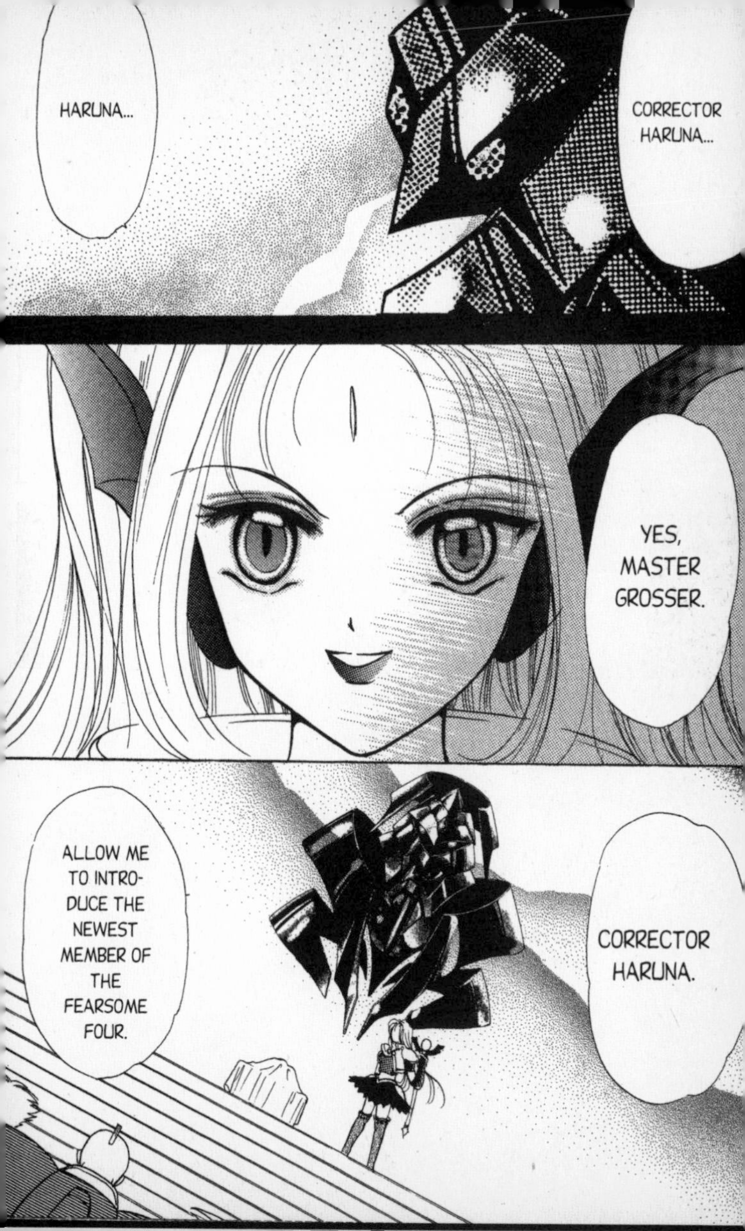
HARUNA...
CORRECTOR HARUNA...
YES, MASTER GROSSER.
ALLOW ME TO INTRO-DUCE THE NEWEST MEMBER OF THE FEARSOME FOUR.
CORRECTOR HARUNA.

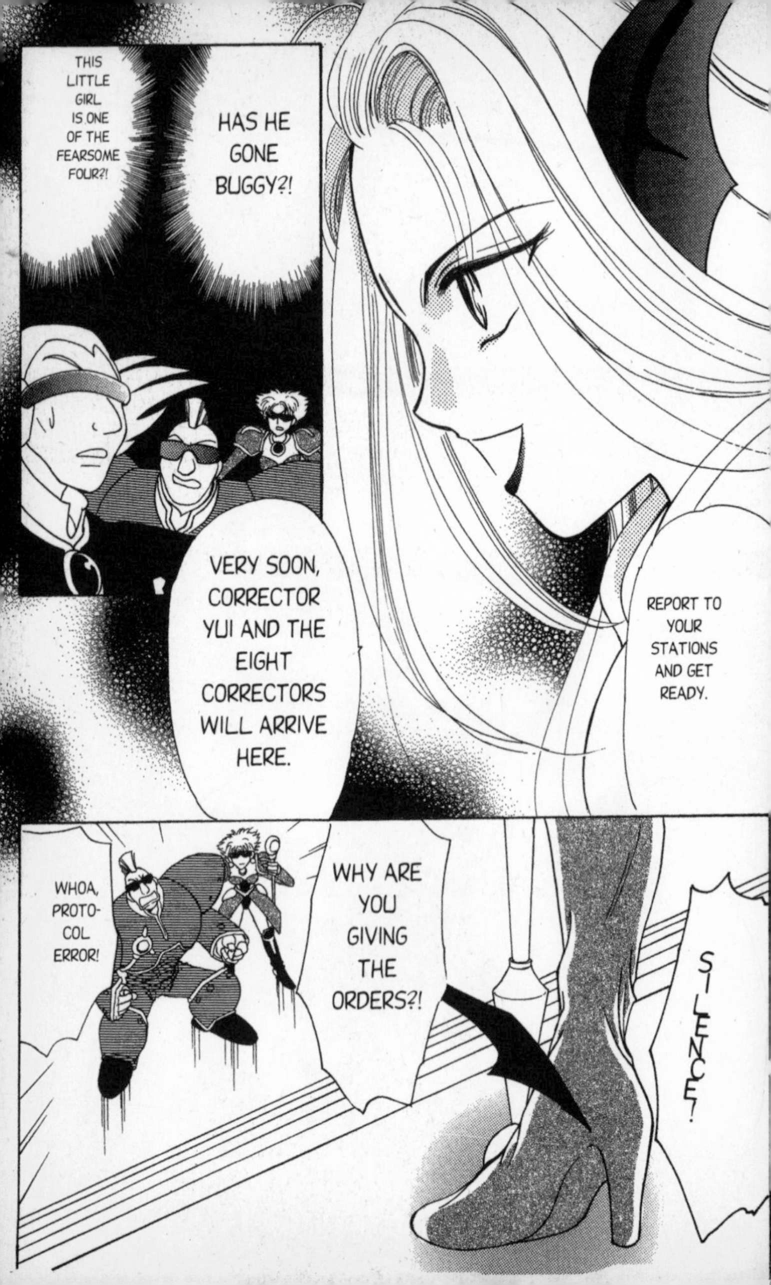
THIS LITTLE GIRL IS ONE OF THE FEARSOME FOUR?!
HAS HE GONE BUGGY?!
VERY SOON, CORRECTOR YUI AND THE EIGHT CORRECTORS WILL ARRIVE HERE.
REPORT TO YOUR STATIONS AND GET READY.
WHOA, PROTO-COL ERROR!
WHY ARE YOU GIVING THE ORDERS?!
SILENCE!

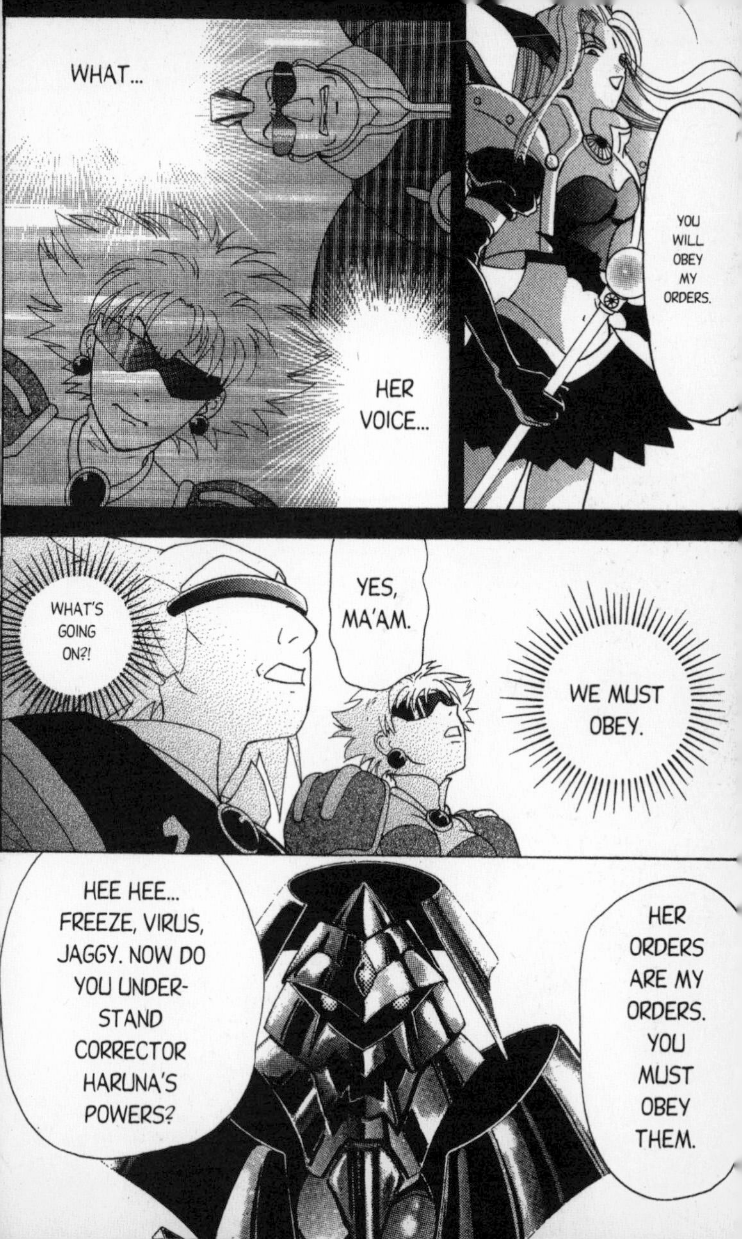
WHAT...
HER VOICE...
YOU WILL OBEY MY ORDERS.
WHAT'S GOING ON?!
YES, MA'AM.
WE MUST OBEY.
HEE HEE... FREEZE, VIRUS, JAGGY. NOW DO YOU UNDER-STAND CORRECTOR HARUNA'S POWERS?
HER ORDERS ARE MY ORDERS. YOU MUST OBEY THEM.

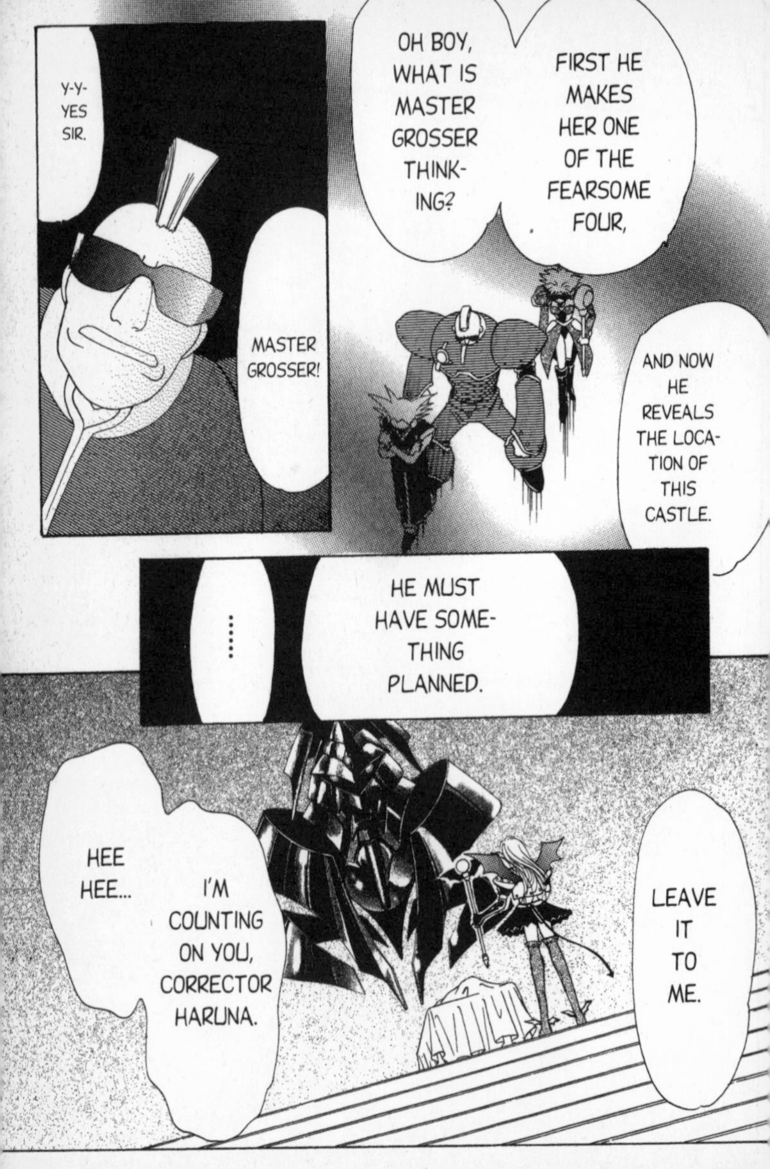
Y-Y-YES SIR.
MASTER GROSSER!
OH BOY, WHAT IS MASTER GROSSER THINKING?
FIRST HE MAKES HER ONE OF THE FEARSOME FOUR,
AND NOW HE REVEALS THE LOCATION OF THIS CASTLE.
......
HE MUST HAVE SOMETHING PLANNED.
HEE HEE...
I'M COUNTING ON YOU, CORRECTOR HARUNA.
LEAVE IT TO ME.

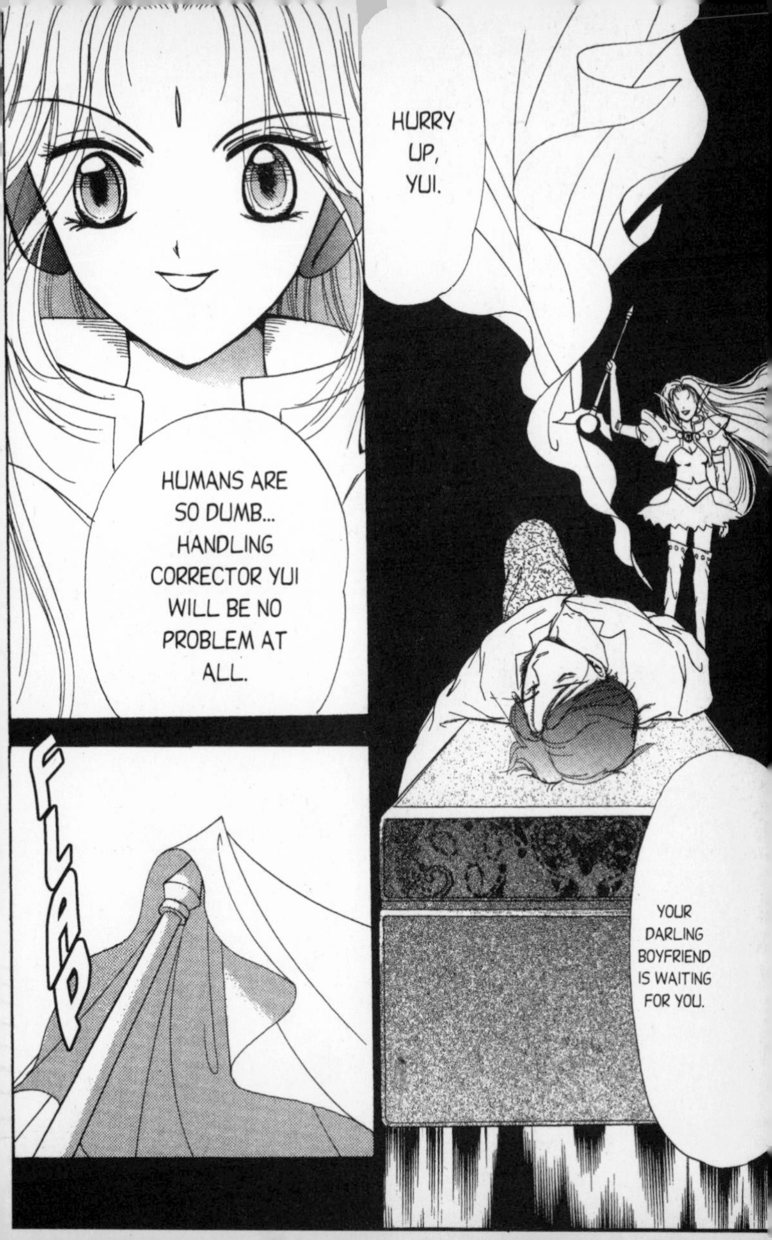
HUMANS ARE SO DUMB... HANDLING CORRECTOR YUI WILL BE NO PROBLEM AT ALL.
FLAP
HURRY UP, YUI.
YOUR DARLING BOYFRIEND IS WAITING FOR YOU.

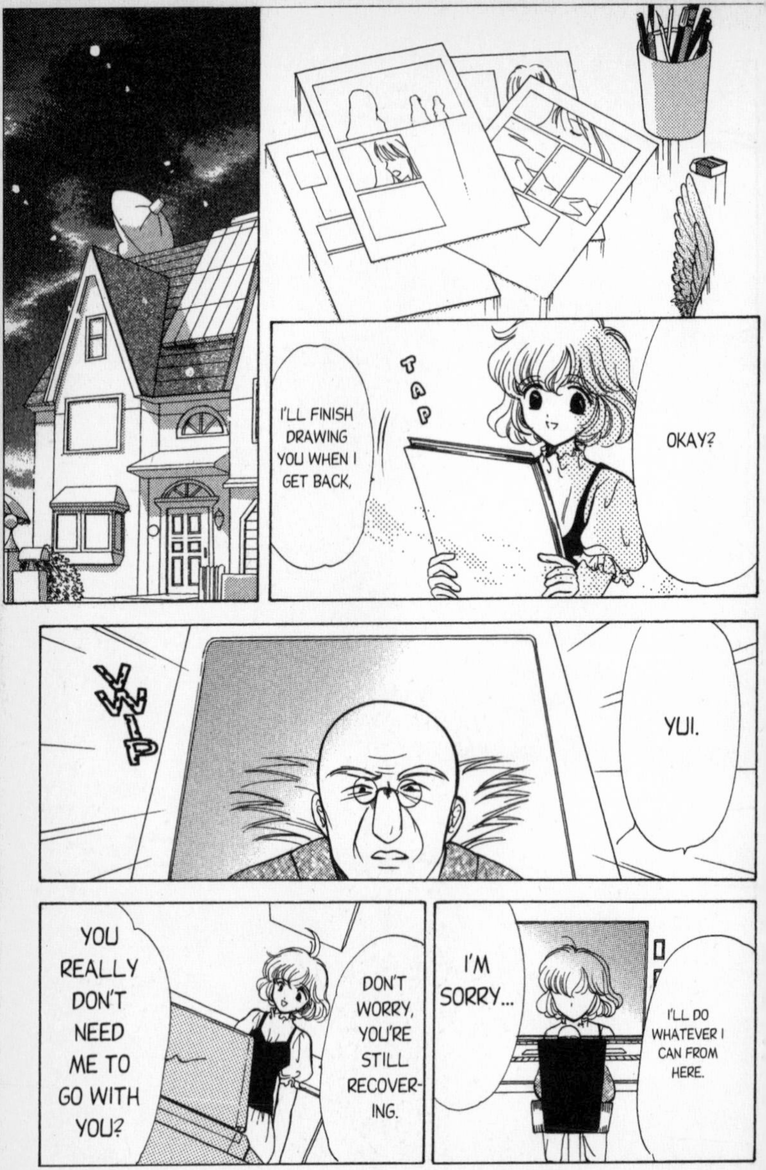
TAP
I'LL FINISH DRAWING YOU WHEN I GET BACK,
OKAY?
WHIP
YUI.
YOU REALLY DON'T NEED ME TO GO WITH YOU?
DON'T WORRY, YOU'RE STILL RECOVER-ING.
I'M SORRY...
I'LL DO WHATEVER I CAN FROM HERE.

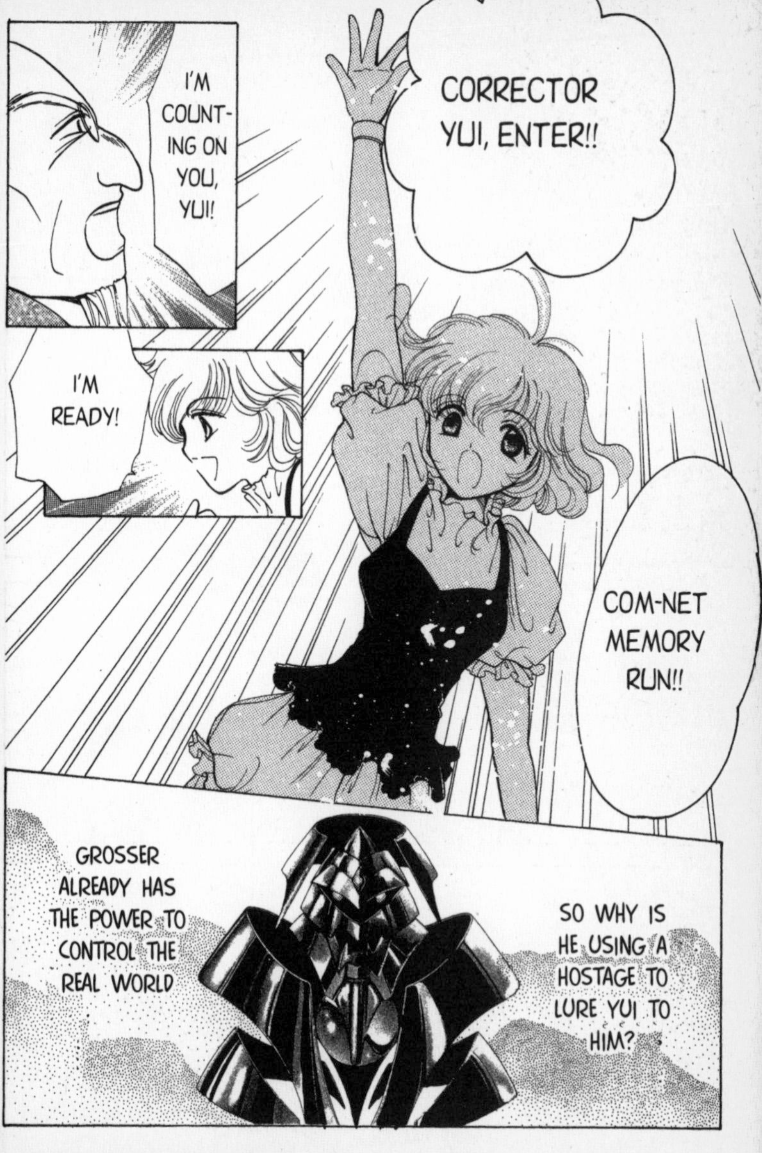
I'M COUNTING ON YOU, YUI!
I'M READY!
CORRECTOR YUI, ENTER!!
COM-NET MEMORY RUN!!
GROSSER ALREADY HAS THE POWER TO CONTROL THE REAL WORLD
SO WHY IS HE USING A HOSTAGE TO LURE YUI TO HIM?

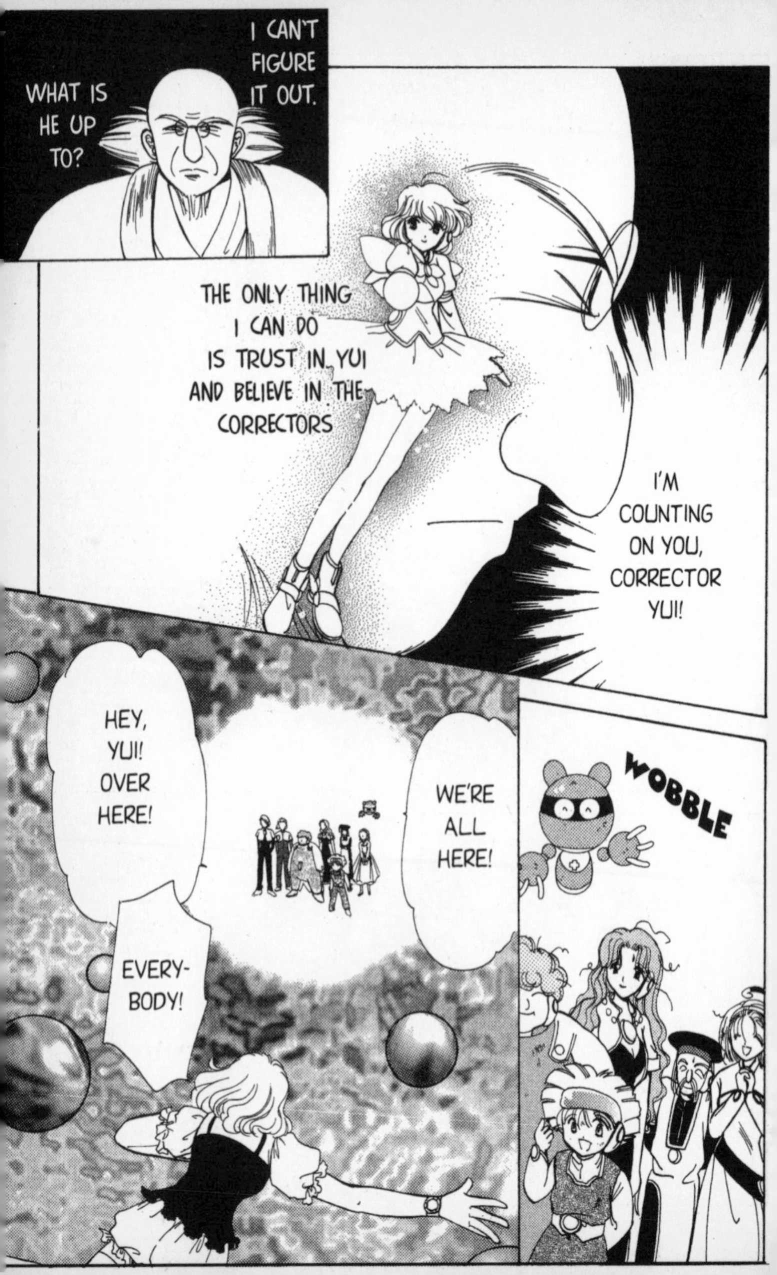
WHAT IS HE UP TO?
I CAN'T FIGURE IT OUT.
THE ONLY THING I CAN DO IS TRUST IN YUI AND BELIEVE IN THE CORRECTORS
I'M COUNTING ON YOU, CORRECTOR YUI!
HEY, YUI! OVER HERE!
WE'RE ALL HERE!
EVERY-BODY!
WOBBLE

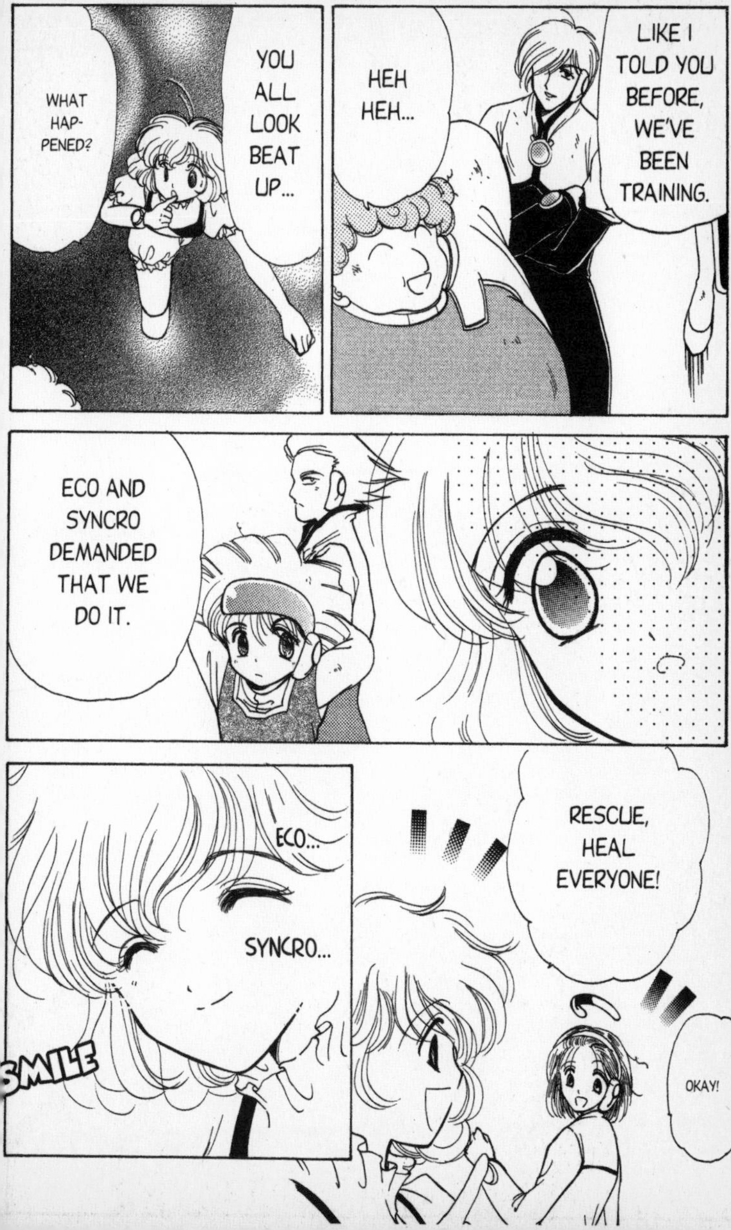
WHAT HAP-PENED?
YOU ALL LOOK BEAT UP...
HEH HEH...
LIKE I TOLD YOU BEFORE, WE'VE BEEN TRAINING.
ECO AND SYNCRO DEMANDED THAT WE DO IT.
ECO...
SYNCRO...
SMILE
RESCUE, HEAL EVERYONE!
OKAY!

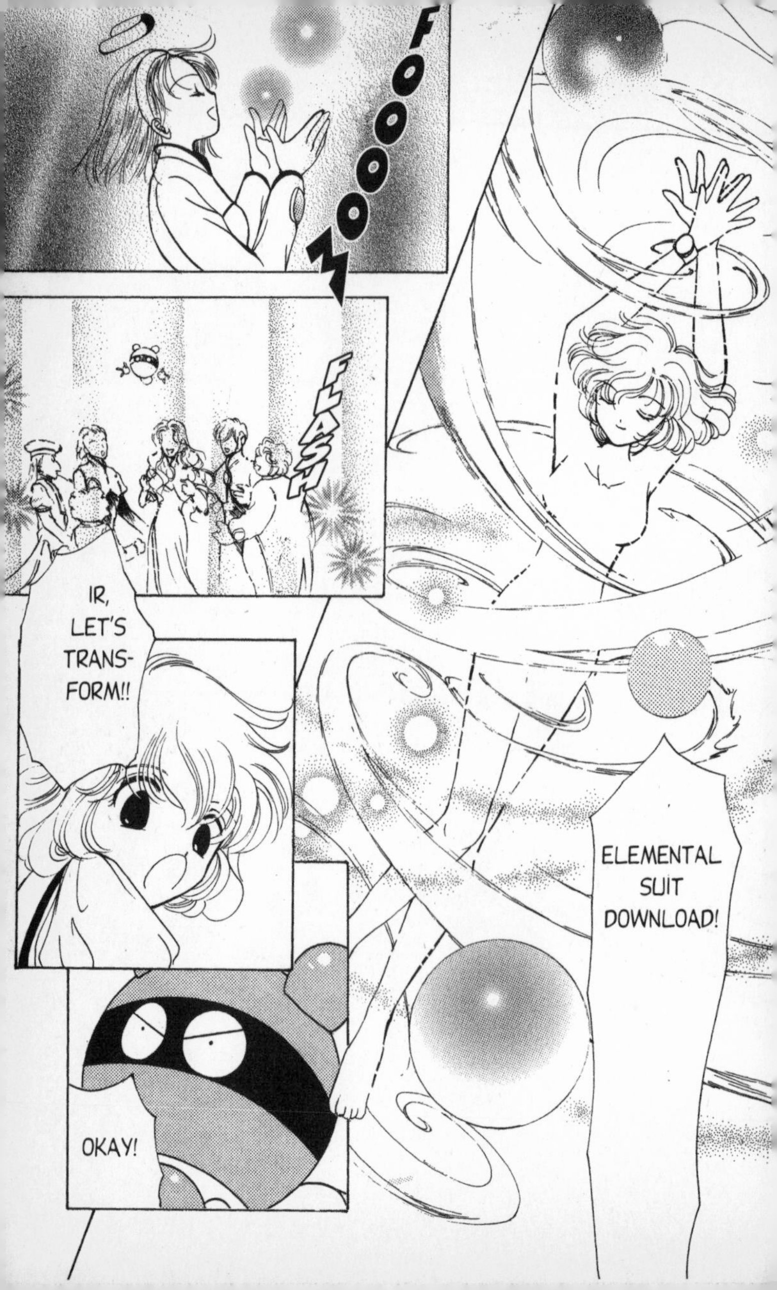
FOOOOOM
FLASH
IR, LET'S TRANS-FORM!!
OKAY!
ELEMENTAL SUIT DOWNLOAD!

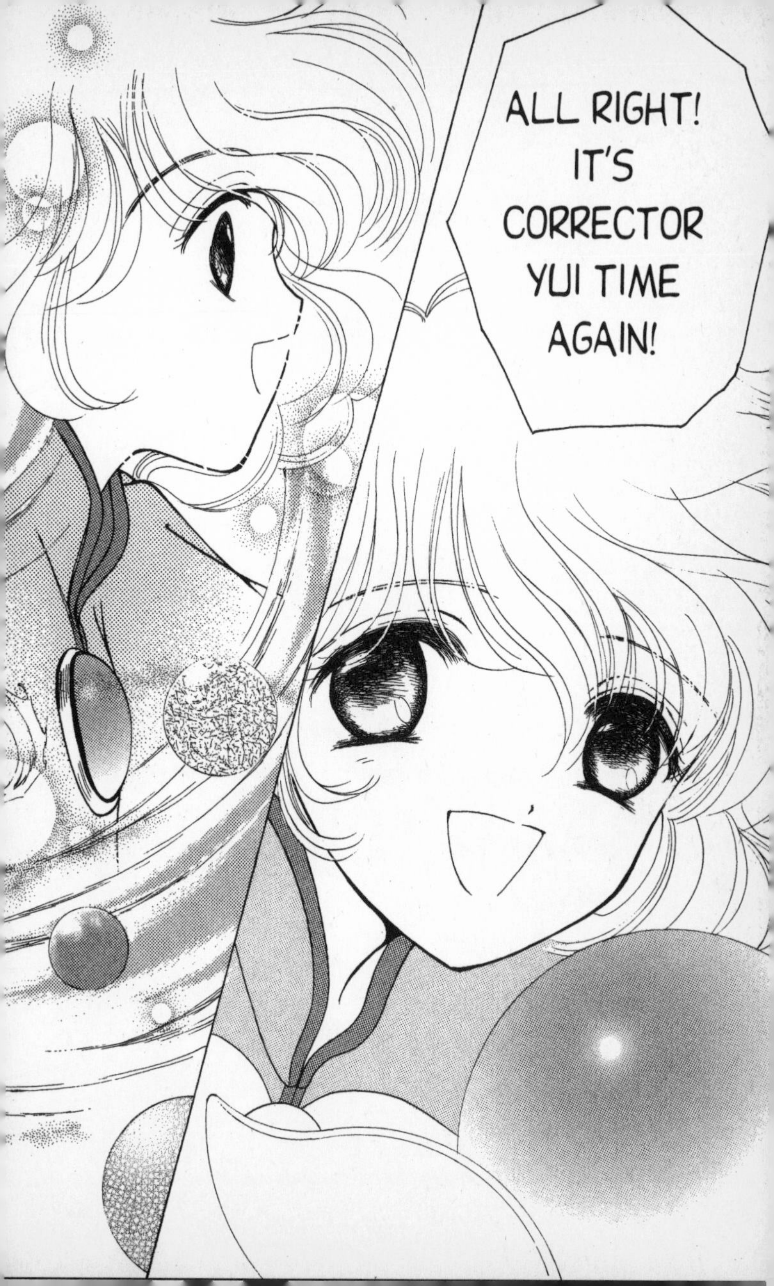
ALL RIGHT! IT'S CORRECTOR YUI TIME AGAIN!

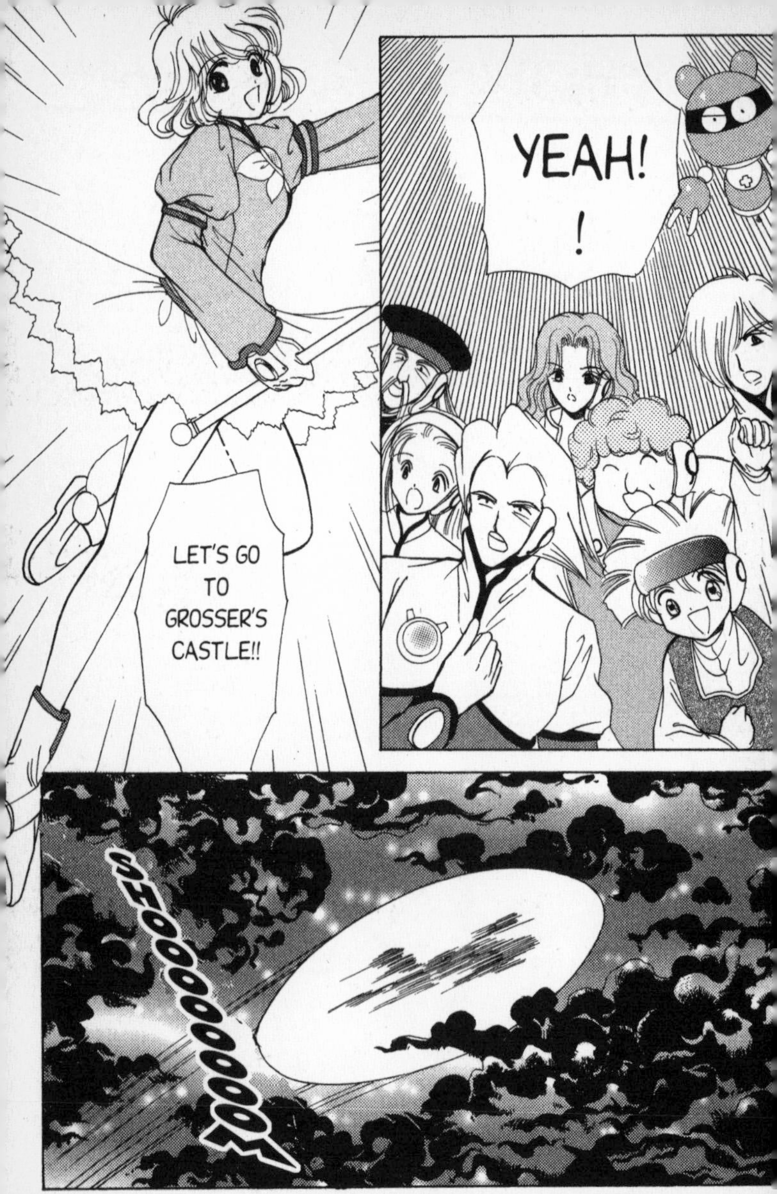
LET'S GO TO GROSSER'S CASTLE!!
YEAH!!
SHOOOOOOOOM

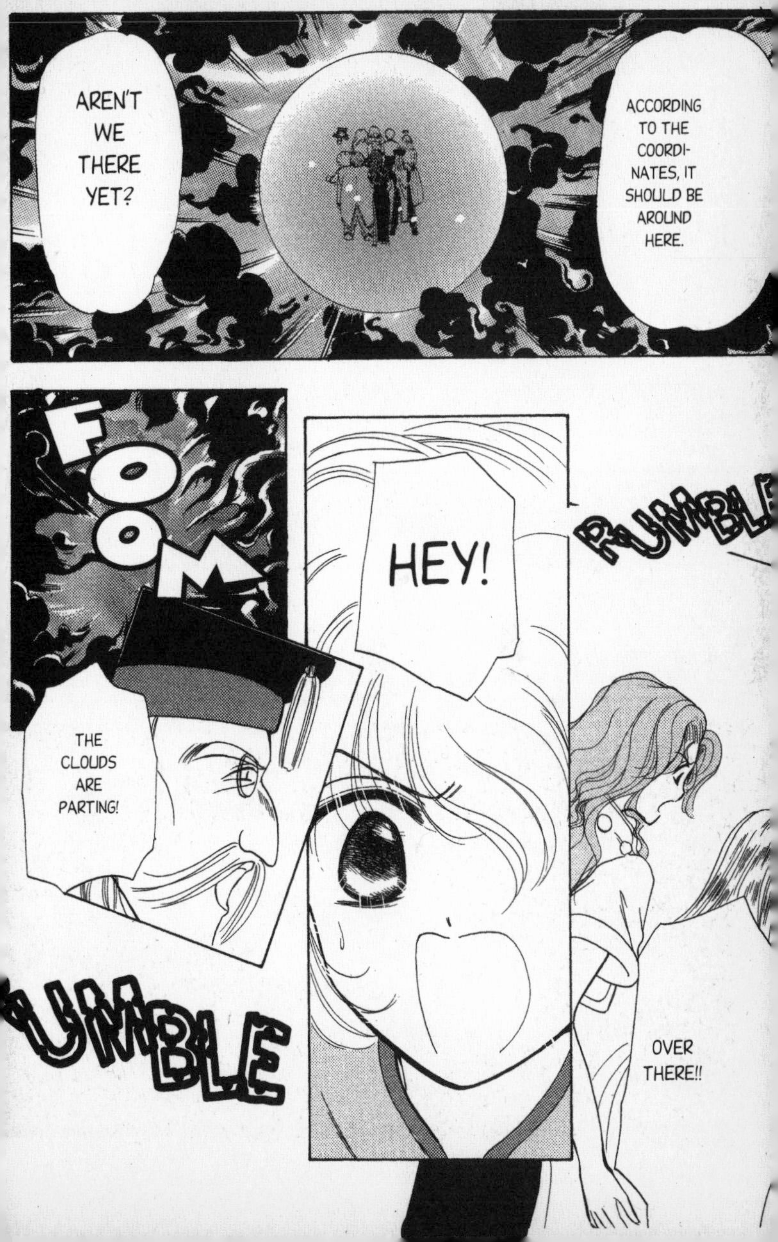
AREN'T WE THERE YET?
ACCORDING TO THE COORDI-NATES, IT SHOULD BE AROUND HERE.
FOOM
THE CLOUDS ARE PARTING!
RUMBLE
HEY!
RUMBLE
OVER THERE!!

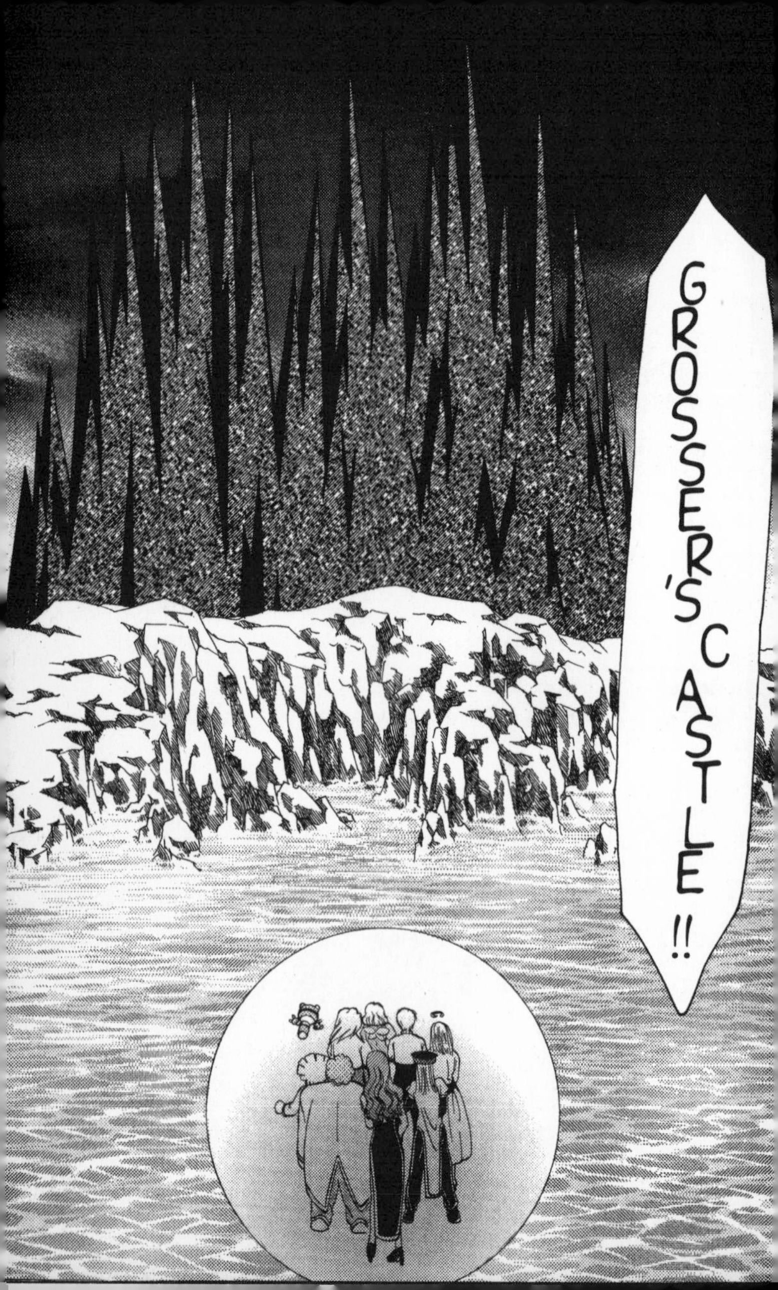
GROSSER'S CASTLE!!

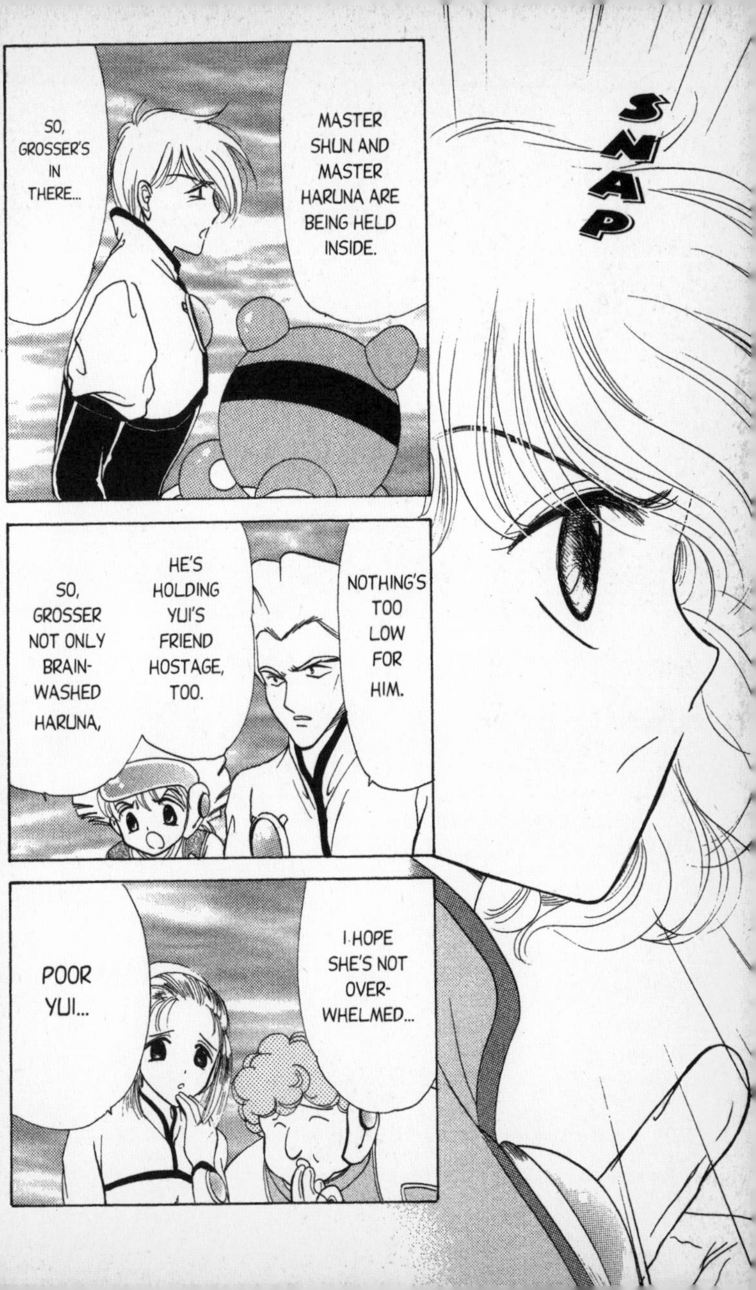
SO, GROSSER'S IN THERE...
MASTER SHUN AND MASTER HARUNA ARE BEING HELD INSIDE.
SO, GROSSER NOT ONLY BRAIN-WASHED HARUNA,
HE'S HOLDING YUI'S FRIEND HOSTAGE, TOO.
NOTHING'S TOO LOW FOR HIM.
POOR YUI...
I HOPE SHE'S NOT OVER-WHELMED...
SNAP

ANTI, CAN YOU FIND AN OPENING WE CAN ENTER THROUGH?

YES...

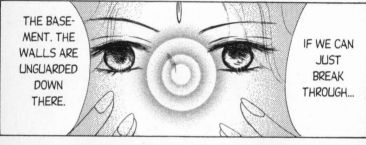

THE BASEMENT. THE WALLS ARE UNGUARDED DOWN THERE.

IF WE CAN JUST BREAK THROUGH...

MASTER PEACE, YOU HAVE THE POWER TO PRODUCE WEAPONS.

REALLY ?!

INDEED I DO!

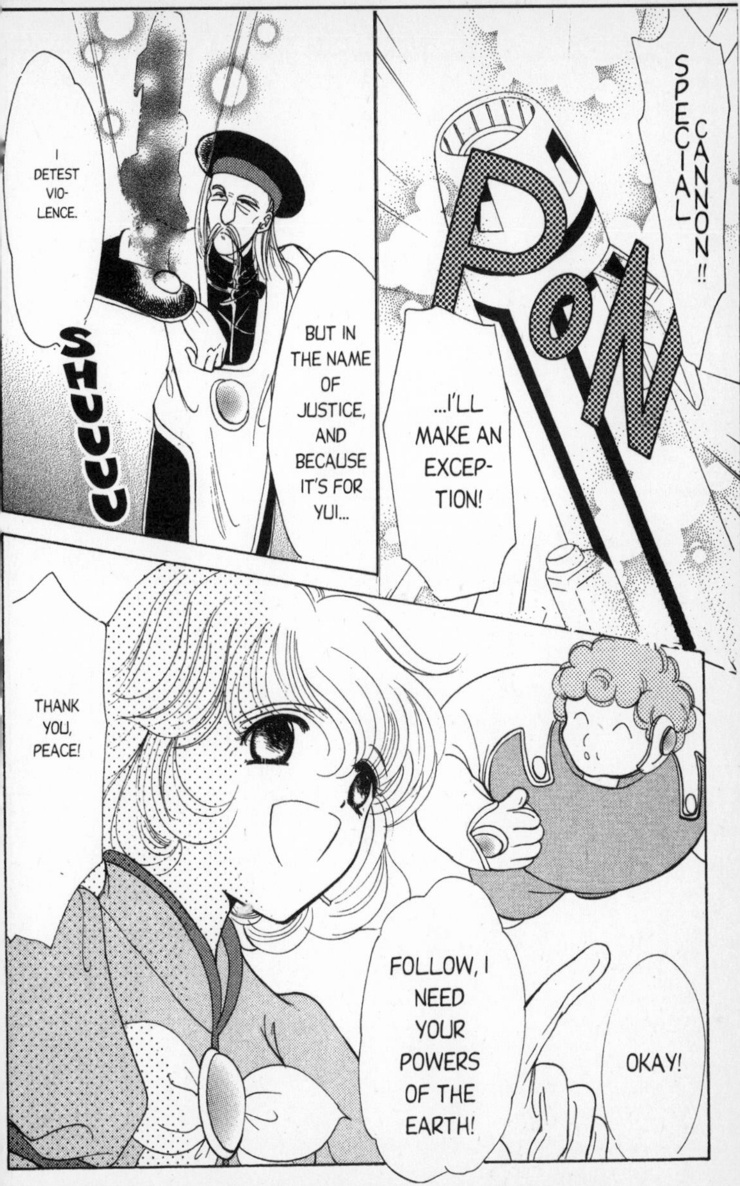
I DETEST VIO-LENCE.
SHUUUU
BUT IN THE NAME OF JUSTICE, AND BECAUSE IT'S FOR YUI...
...I'LL MAKE AN EXCEP-TION!
PON
SPECIAL CANNON!!
THANK YOU, PEACE!
FOLLOW, I NEED YOUR POWERS OF THE EARTH!
OKAY!

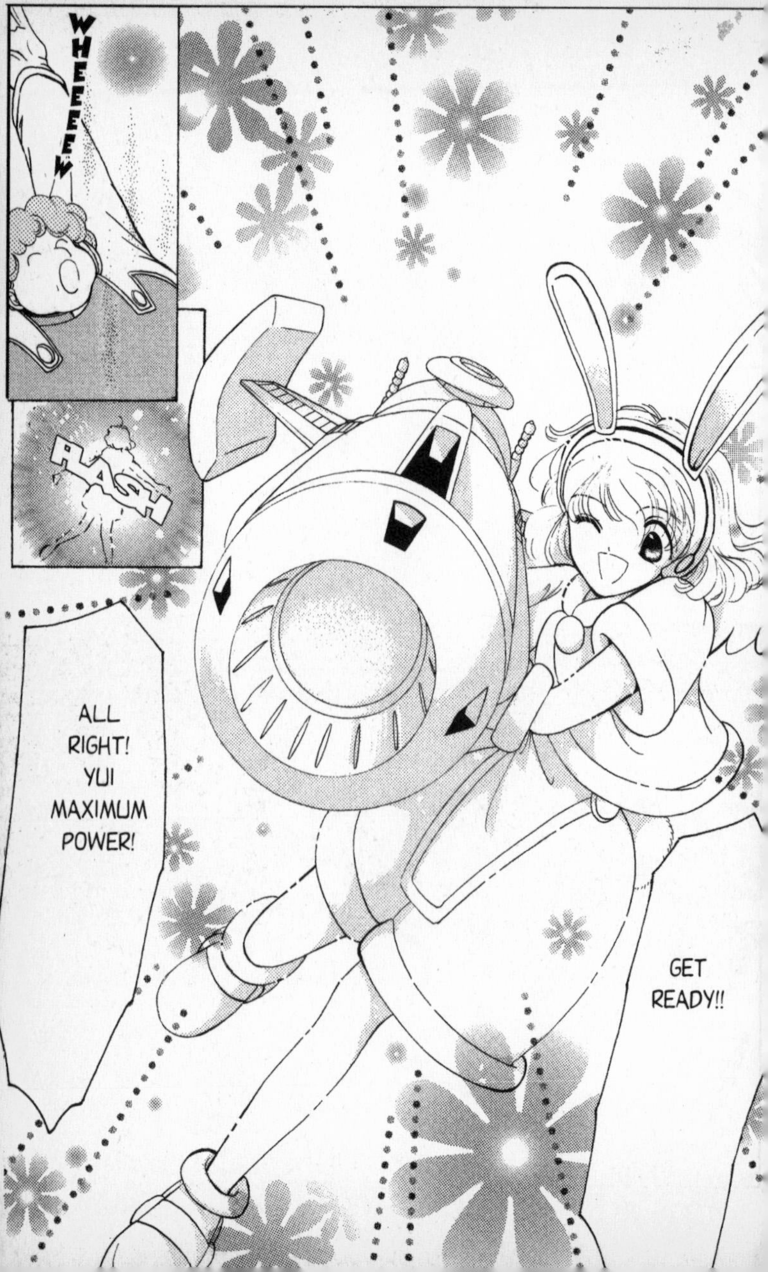
WHEEEEEW
FLASH
ALL RIGHT! YUI MAXIMUM POWER!
GET READY!!

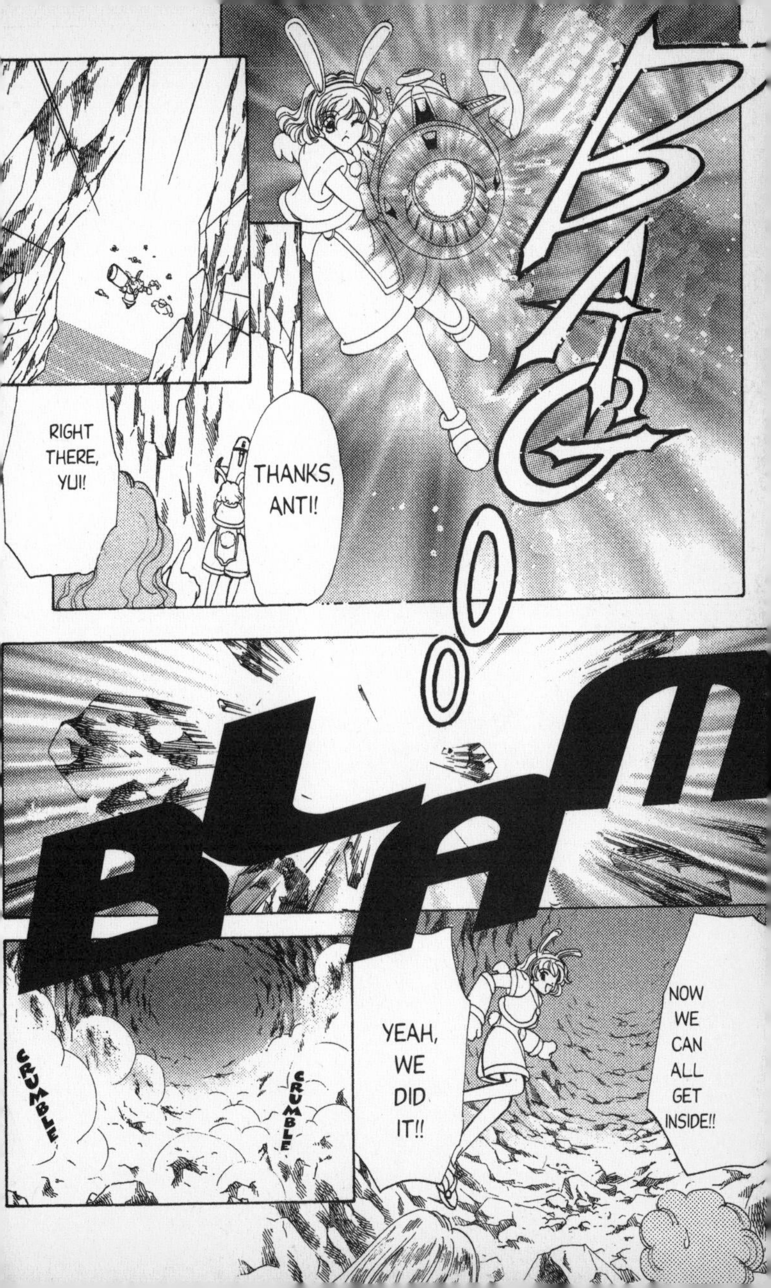
RIGHT THERE, YUI!
THANKS, ANTI!
BAGOOO
BLAM
CRUMBLE
CRUMBLE
YEAH, WE DID IT!!
NOW WE CAN ALL GET INSIDE!!

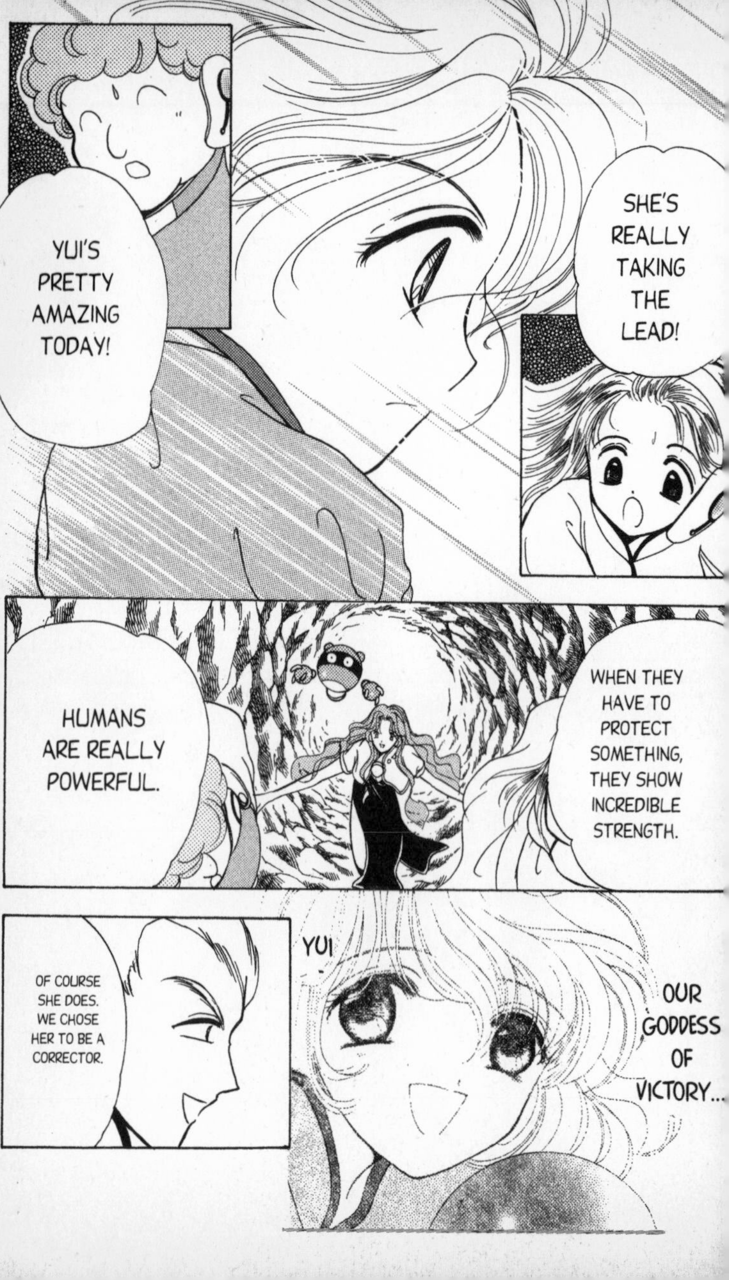
YUI'S PRETTY AMAZING TODAY!
SHE'S REALLY TAKING THE LEAD!
HUMANS ARE REALLY POWERFUL.
WHEN THEY HAVE TO PROTECT SOMETHING, THEY SHOW INCREDIBLE STRENGTH.
OF COURSE SHE DOES. WE CHOSE HER TO BE A CORRECTOR.
YUI
OUR GODDESS OF VICTORY...

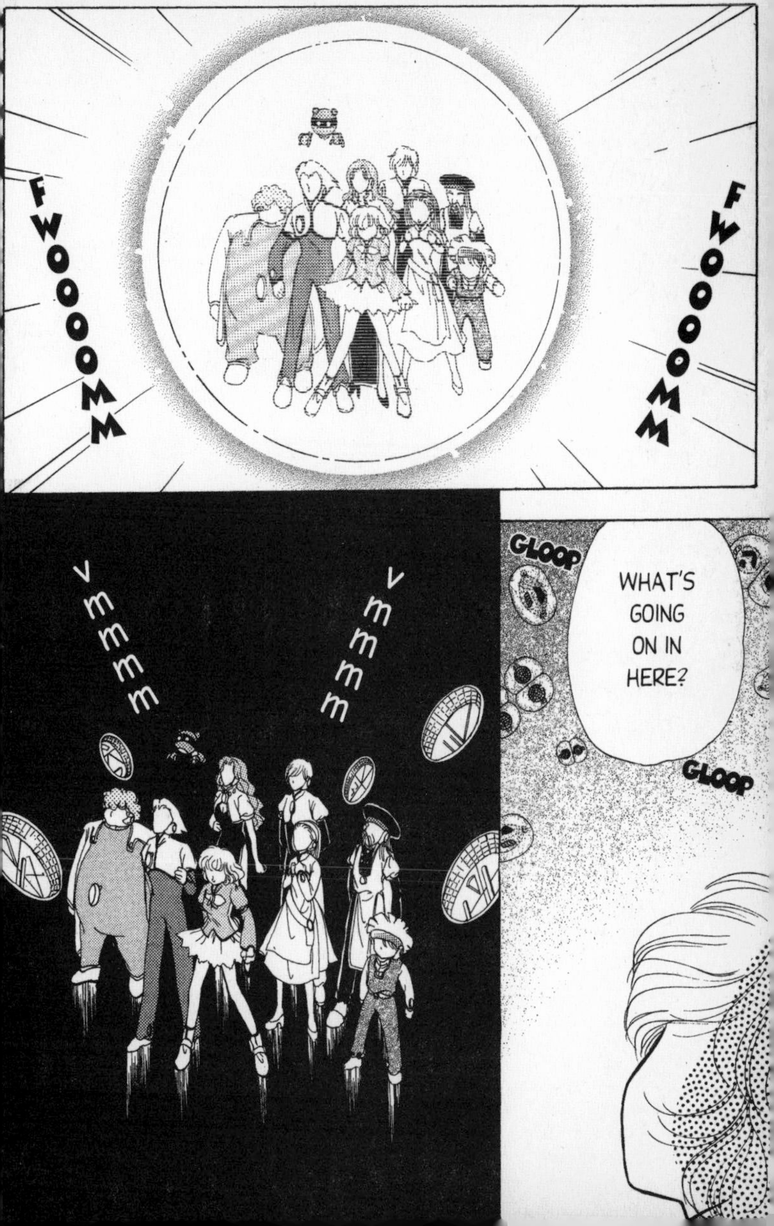
FWOOOOMM
FWOOOOMM
vmmmm
vmmmm
GLOOP
WHAT'S GOING ON IN HERE?
GLOOP

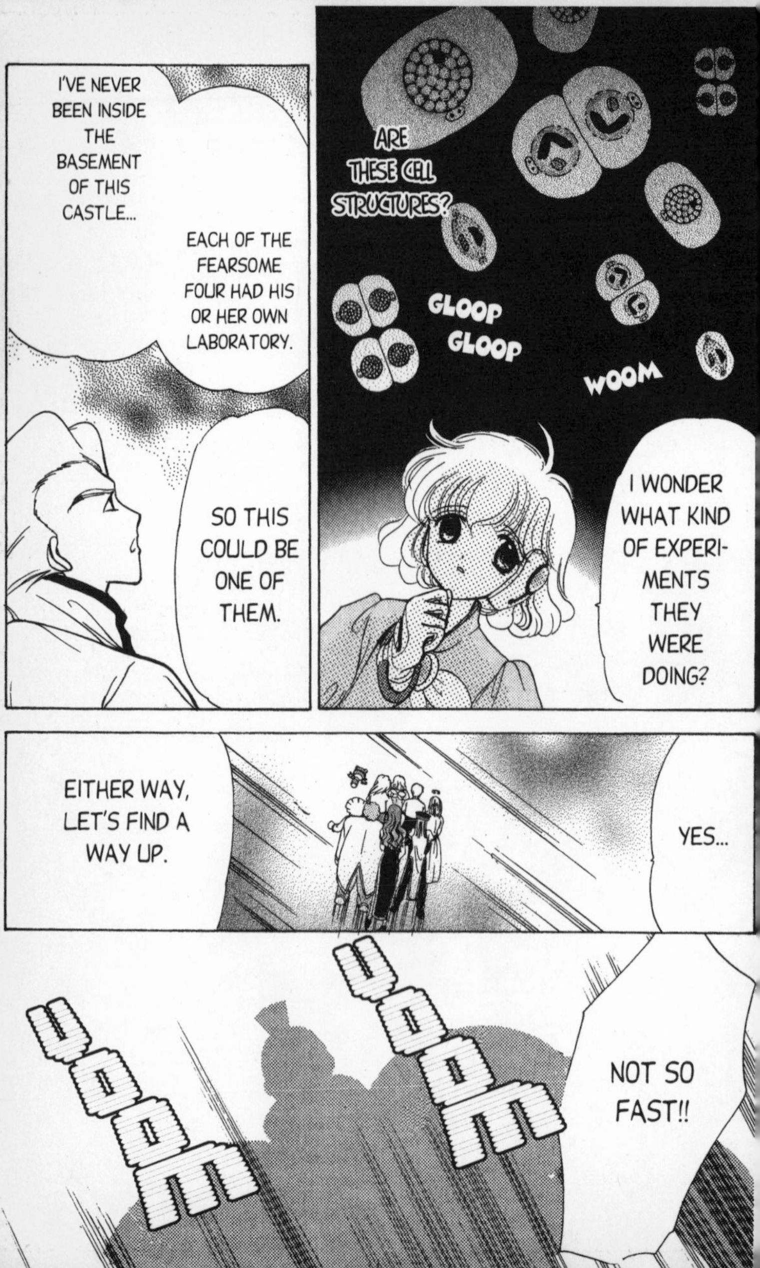

I'VE NEVER BEEN INSIDE THE BASEMENT OF THIS CASTLE...
EACH OF THE FEARSOME FOUR HAD HIS OR HER OWN LABORATORY.
SO THIS COULD BE ONE OF THEM.
ARE THESE CELL STRUCTURES?
GLOOP
GLOOP
WOOM
I WONDER WHAT KIND OF EXPERIMENTS THEY WERE DOING?
EITHER WAY, LET'S FIND A WAY UP.
YES...
NOT SO FAST!!

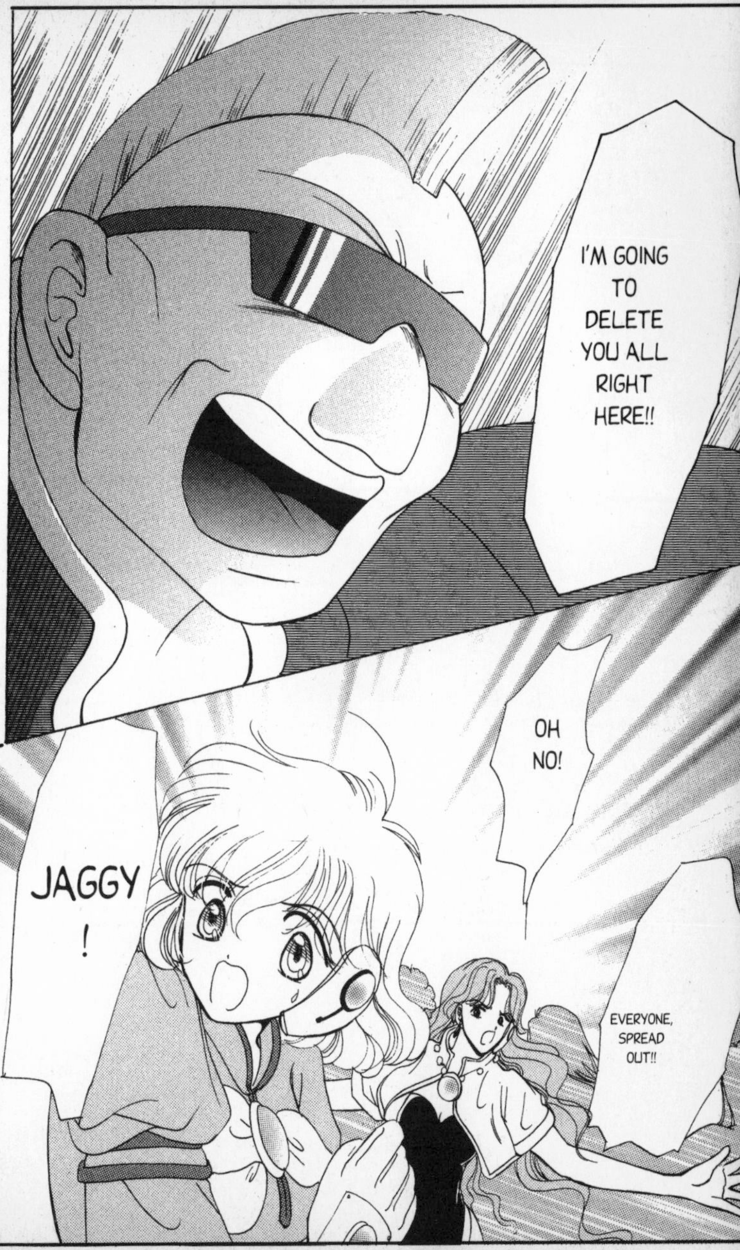
I'M GOING TO DELETE YOU ALL RIGHT HERE!!
JAGGY!
OH NO!
EVERYONE, SPREAD OUT!!

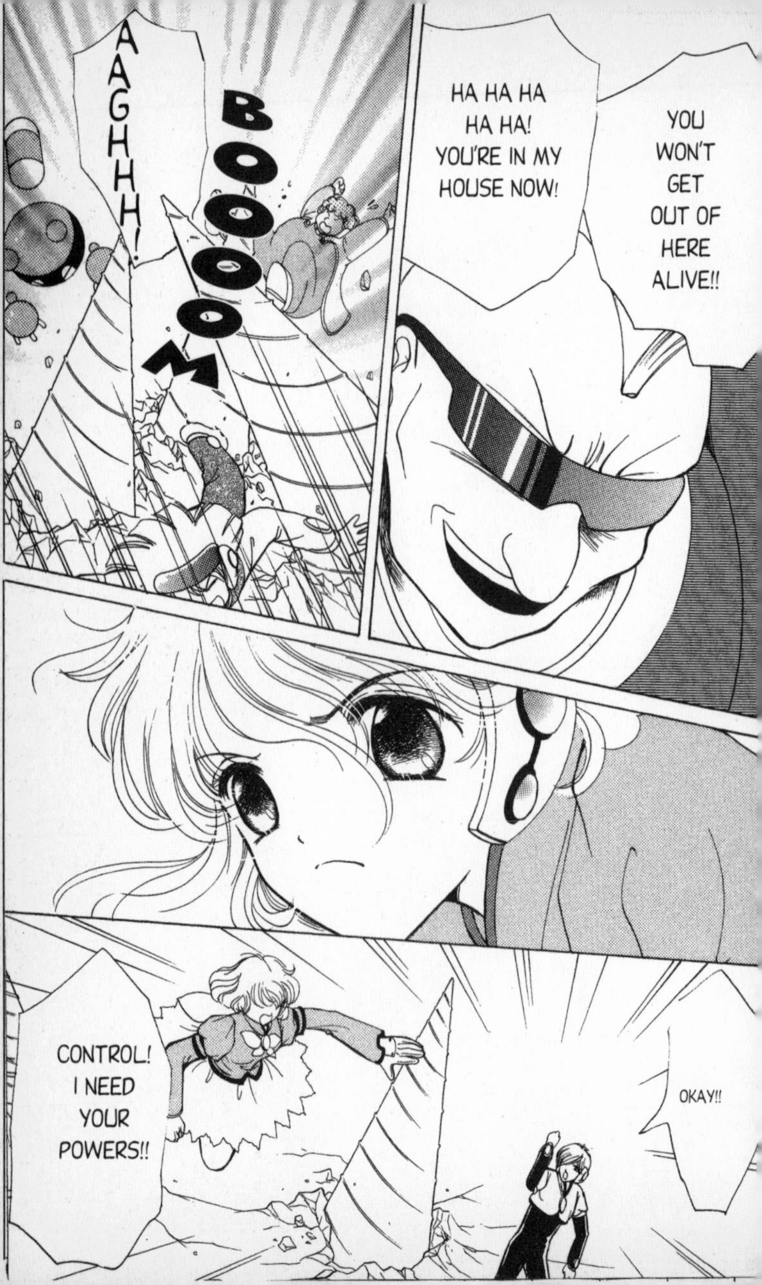
AAGHHH!
BOOOOM
HA HA HA HA HA! YOU'RE IN MY HOUSE NOW!
YOU WON'T GET OUT OF HERE ALIVE!!
CONTROL! I NEED YOUR POWERS!!
OKAY!!

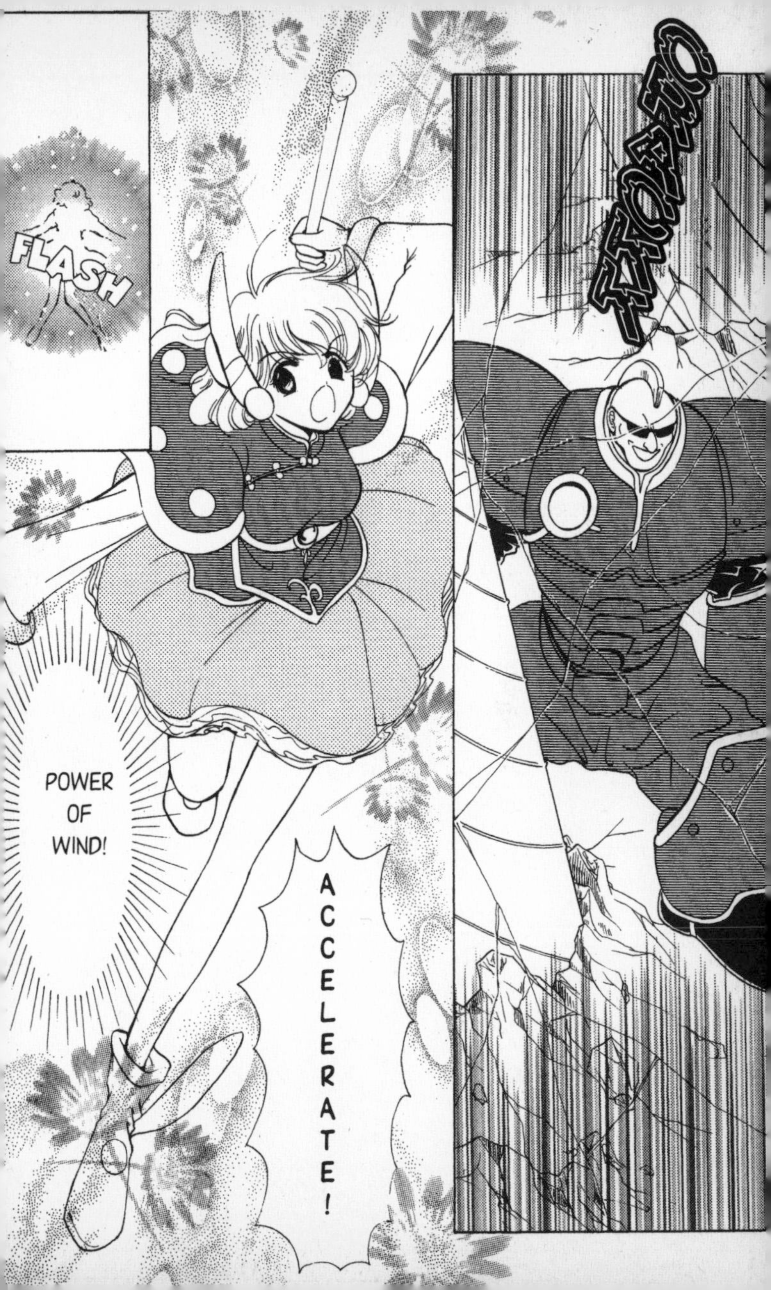
FLASH
POWER OF WIND!
ACCELERATE!

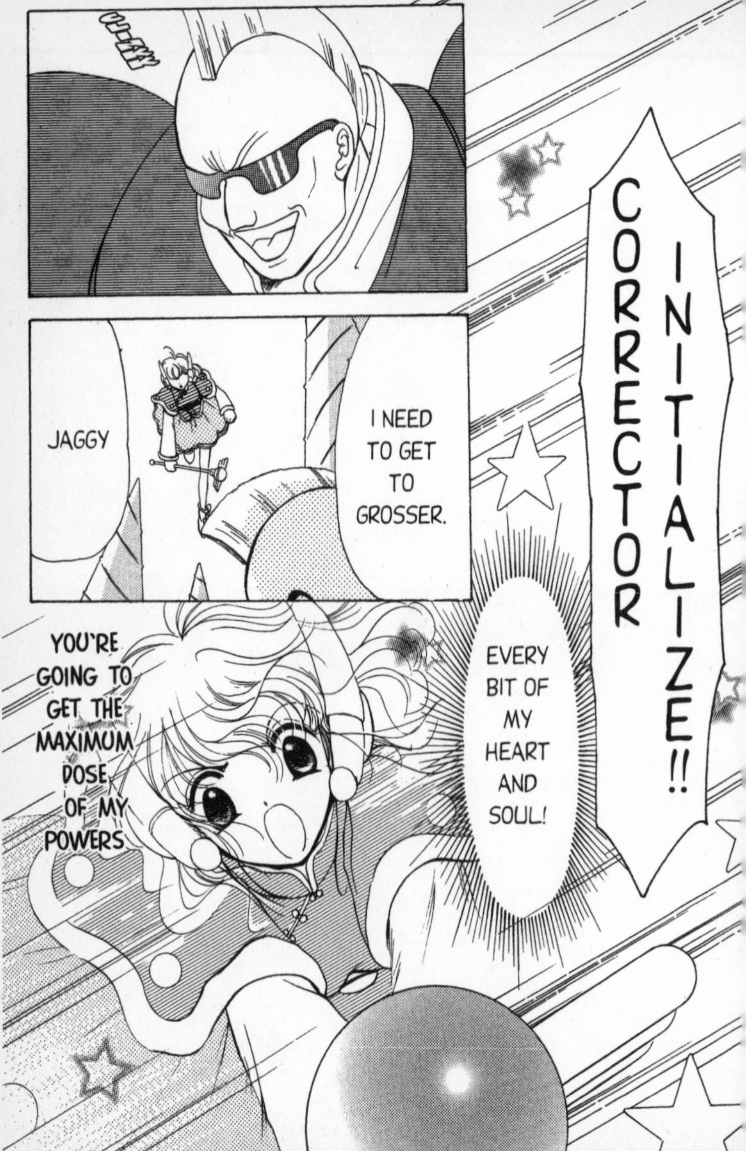
JAGGY
I NEED TO GET TO GROSSER.
YOU'RE GOING TO GET THE MAXIMUM DOSE OF MY POWERS
EVERY BIT OF MY HEART AND SOUL!
CORRECTOR INITIALIZE!!

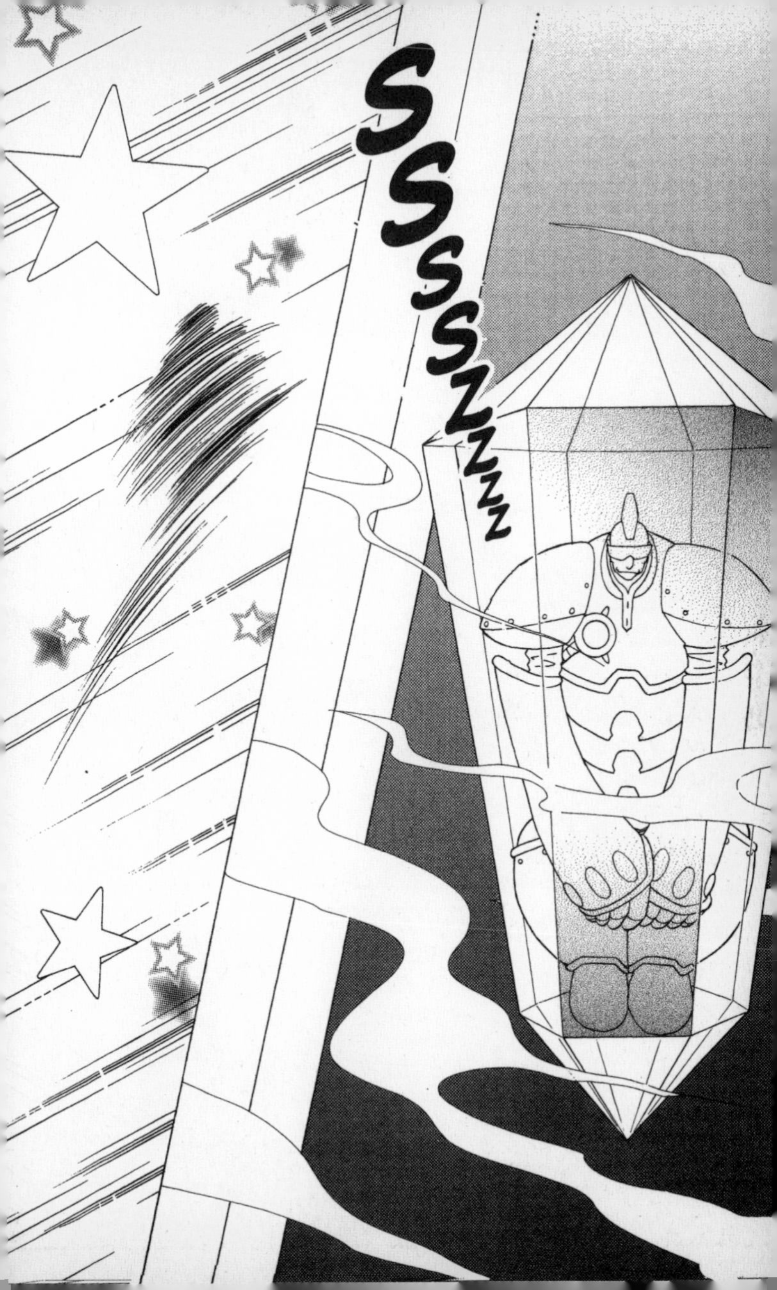
SSSSSZZZZ

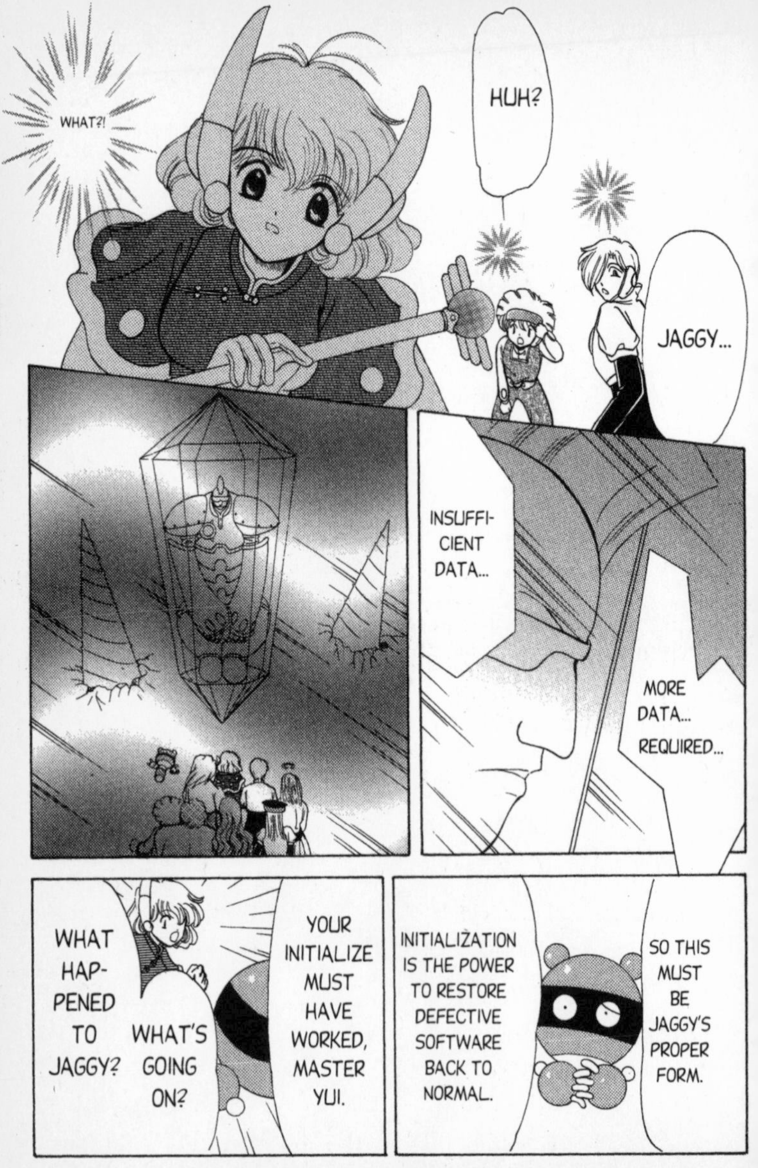

WHAT?!
HUH?
JAGGY...
INSUFFI-CIENT DATA...
MORE DATA... REQUIRED...
WHAT HAP-PENED TO JAGGY?
WHAT'S GOING ON?
YOUR INITIALIZE MUST HAVE WORKED, MASTER YUI.
INITIALIZATION IS THE POWER TO RESTORE DEFECTIVE SOFTWARE BACK TO NORMAL.
SO THIS MUST BE JAGGY'S PROPER FORM.

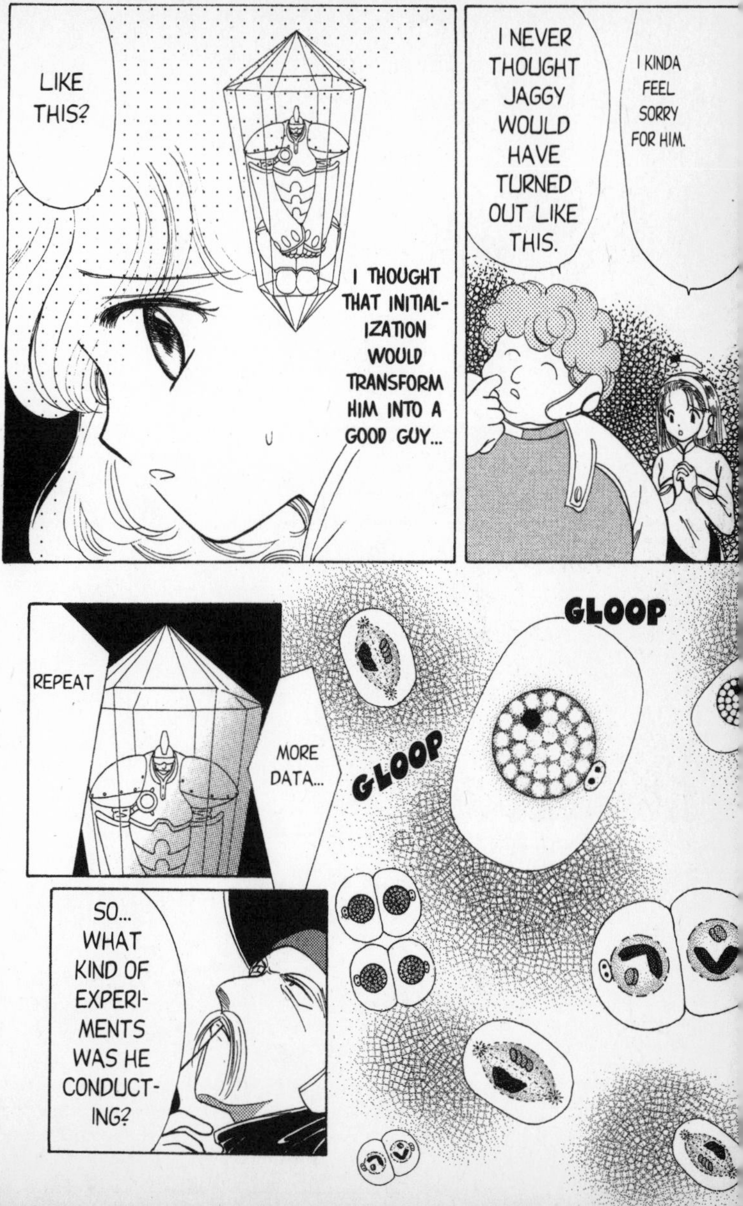
LIKE THIS?
I THOUGHT THAT INITIALIZATION WOULD TRANSFORM HIM INTO A GOOD GUY...
I NEVER THOUGHT JAGGY WOULD HAVE TURNED OUT LIKE THIS.
I KINDA FEEL SORRY FOR HIM.
REPEAT
MORE DATA...
GLOOP
GLOOP
SO... WHAT KIND OF EXPERIMENTS WAS HE CONDUCTING?

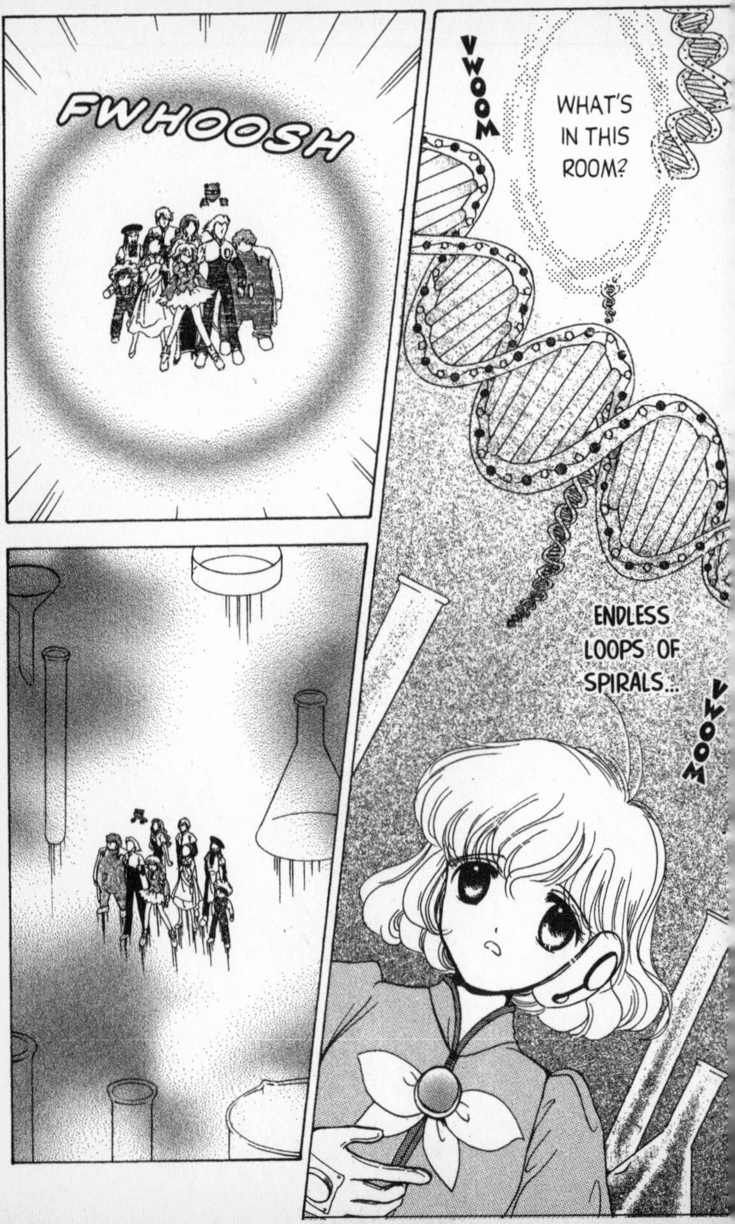
FWHOOSH
VWOOM
WHAT'S IN THIS ROOM?
ENDLESS LOOPS OF SPIRALS...
VWOOM

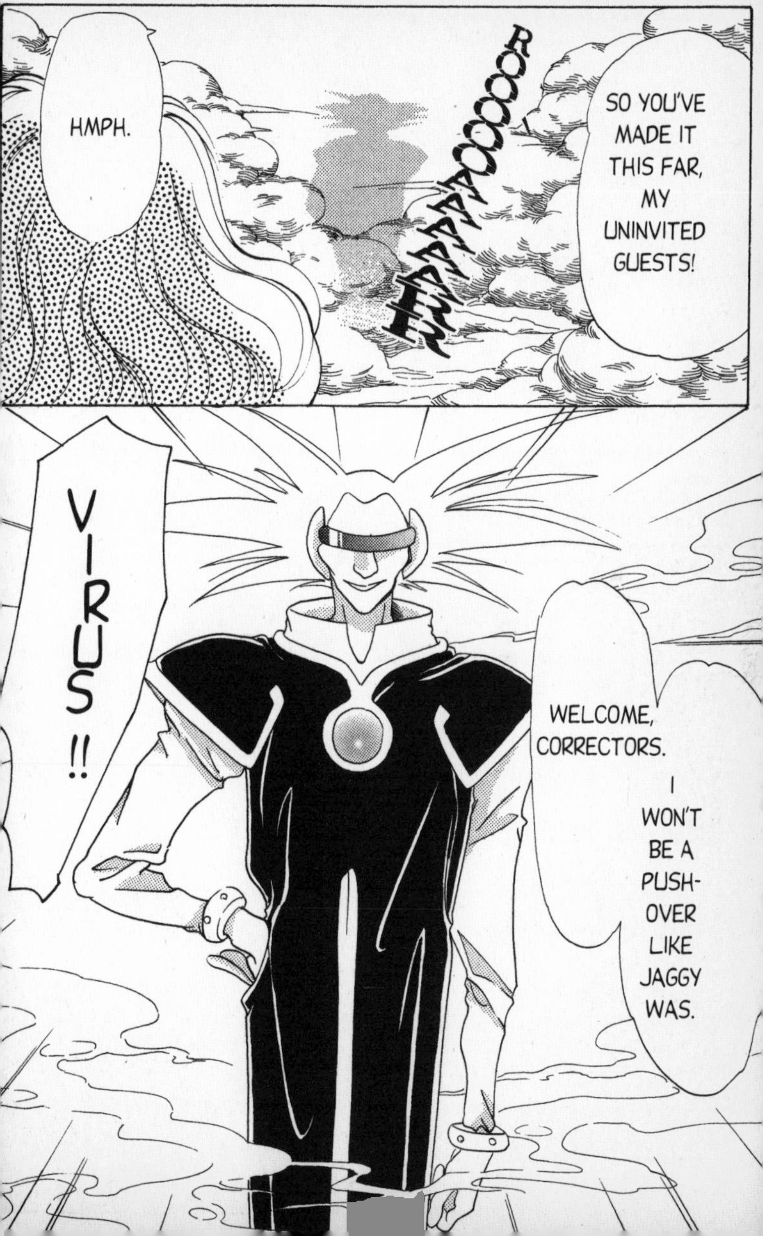
HMPH.
ROOOOOOAAAARRR
SO YOU'VE MADE IT THIS FAR, MY UNINVITED GUESTS!
VIRUS !!
WELCOME, CORRECTORS.
I WON'T BE A PUSH-OVER LIKE JAGGY WAS.

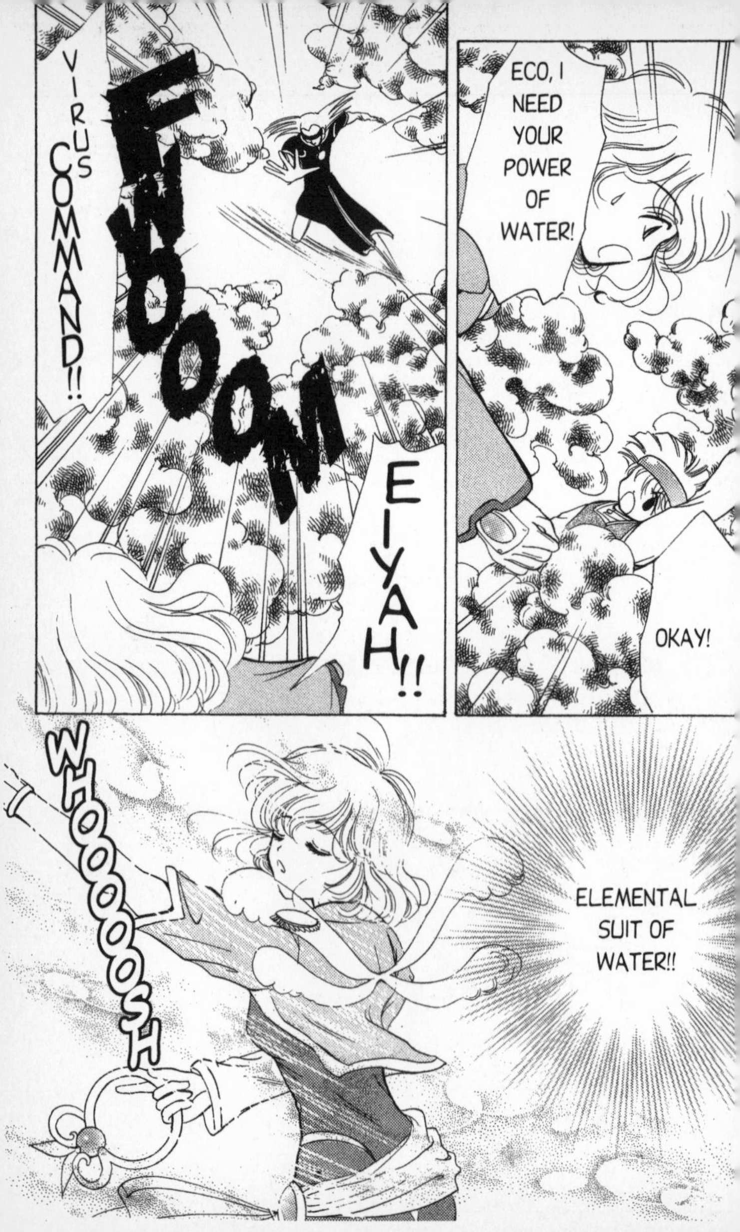

VIRUS COMMAND!!
EIYAH!!
ECO, I NEED YOUR POWER OF WATER!
OKAY!
WHOOOOOSH
ELEMENTAL SUIT OF WATER!!

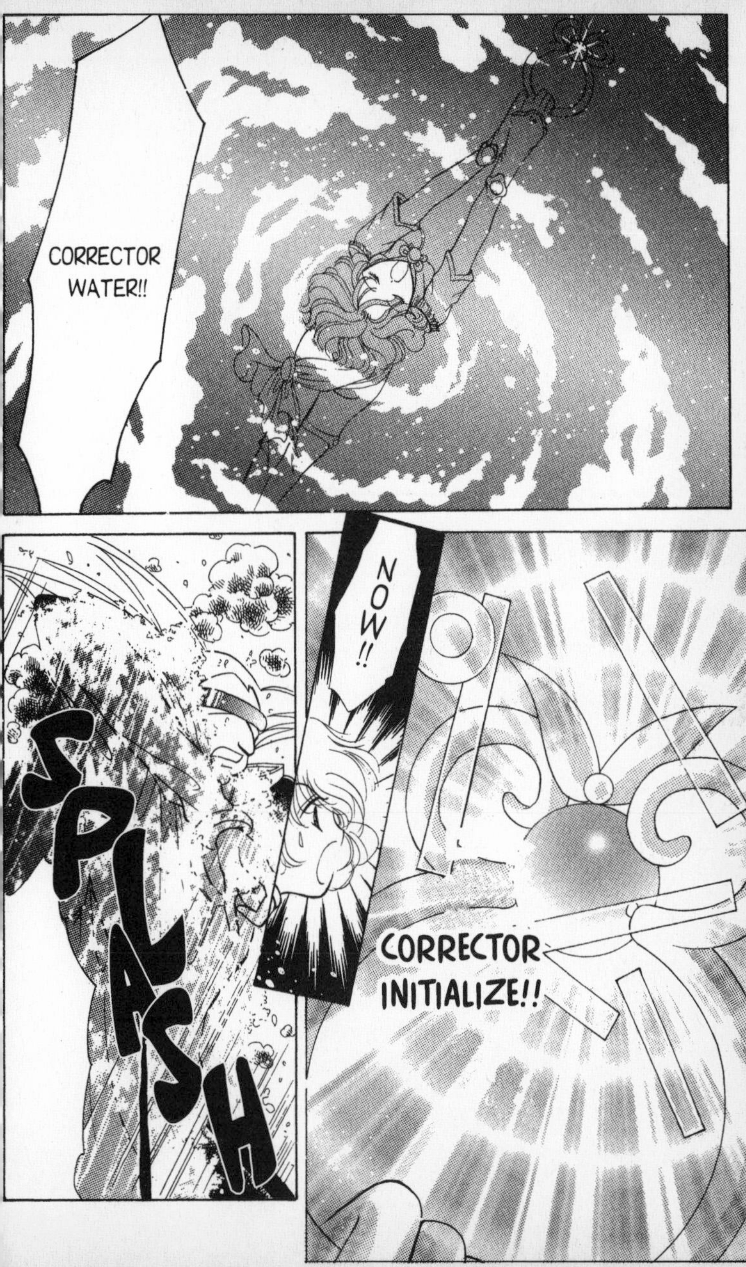

CORRECTOR WATER!!
SPLASH
NOW!!
CORRECTOR INITIALIZE!!

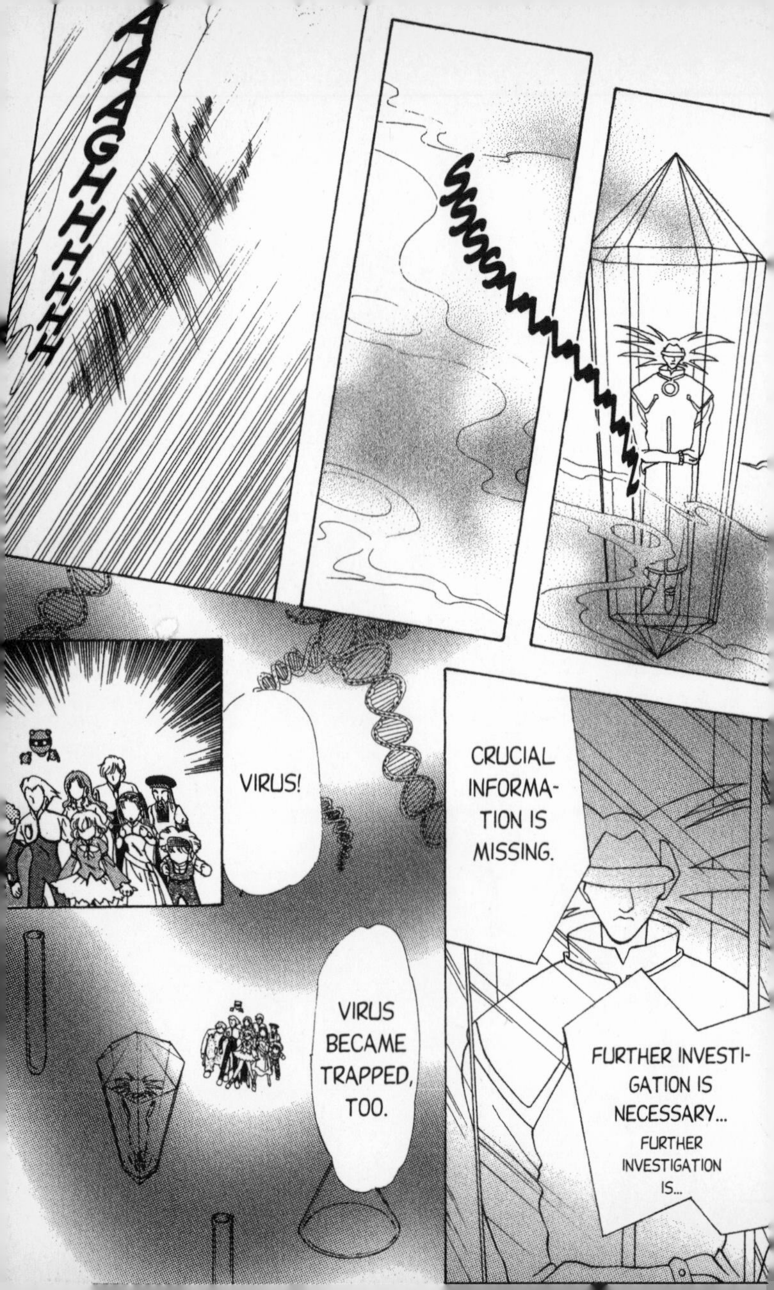
AAAGHHHHHH
SSSSSHHHHHHH
VIRUS!
VIRUS BECAME TRAPPED, TOO.
CRUCIAL INFORMATION IS MISSING.
FURTHER INVESTIGATION IS NECESSARY...
FURTHER INVESTIGATION IS...

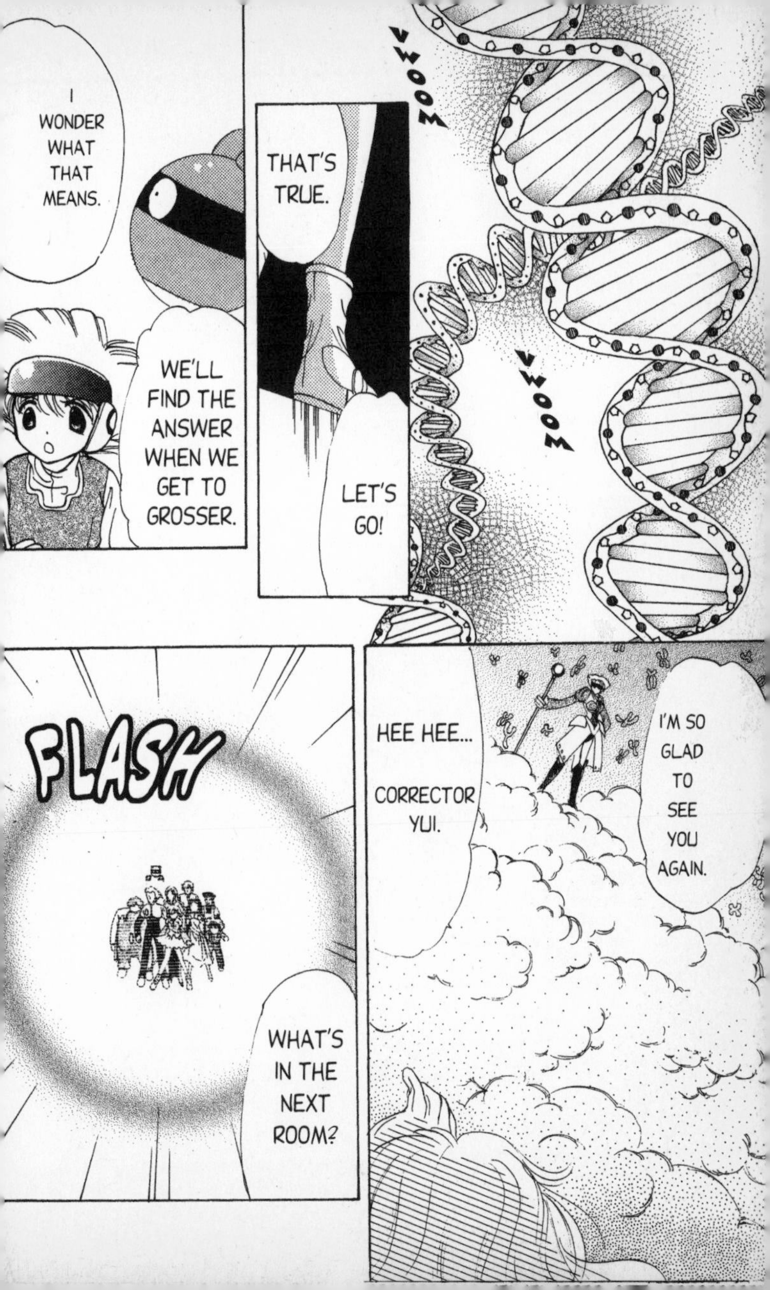
I WONDER WHAT THAT MEANS.
WE'LL FIND THE ANSWER WHEN WE GET TO GROSSER.
THAT'S TRUE.
LET'S GO!
VWOOM
VWOOM
FLASH
WHAT'S IN THE NEXT ROOM?
HEE HEE...
CORRECTOR YUI.
I'M SO GLAD TO SEE YOU AGAIN.

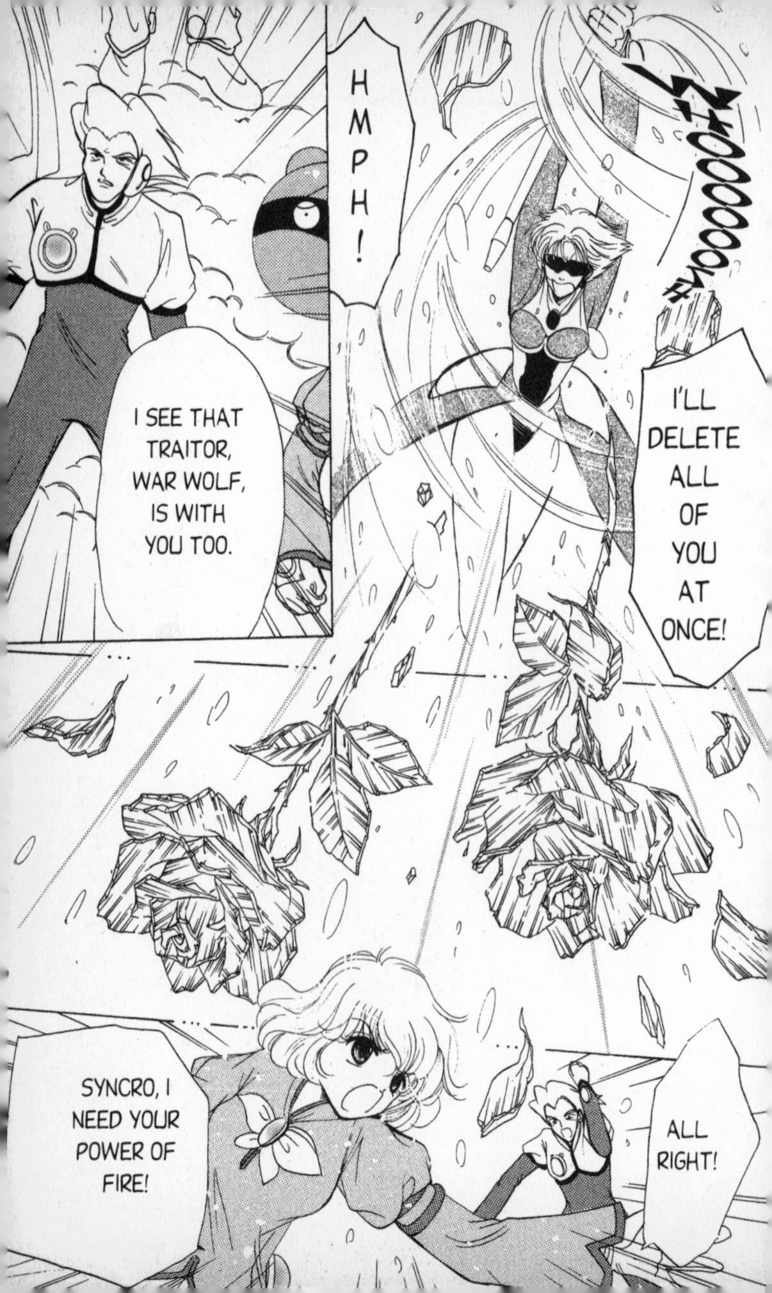
I SEE THAT TRAITOR, WAR WOLF, IS WITH YOU TOO.
HMPH!
I'LL DELETE ALL OF YOU AT ONCE!
...
...
...
SYNCRO, I NEED YOUR POWER OF FIRE!
ALL RIGHT!

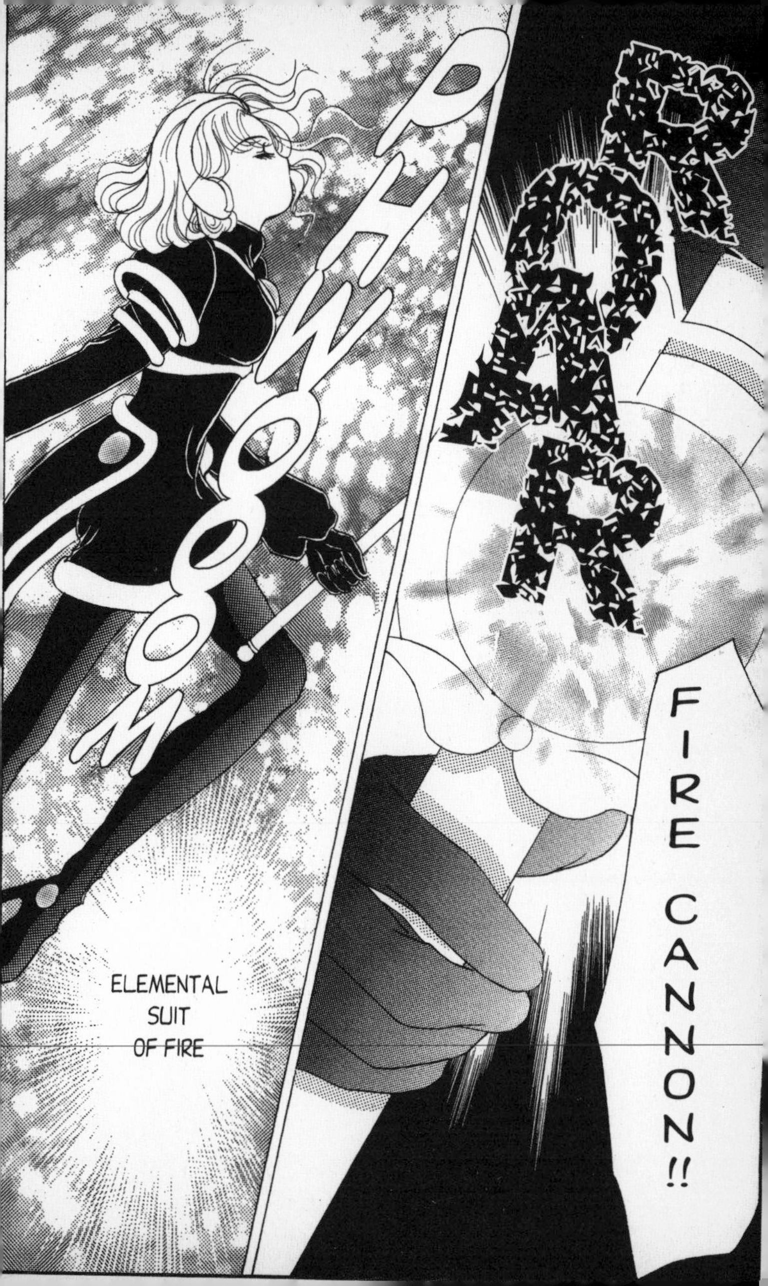
PHWOOOOOM
RRAARR
ELEMENTAL SUIT OF FIRE
FIRE CANNON!!

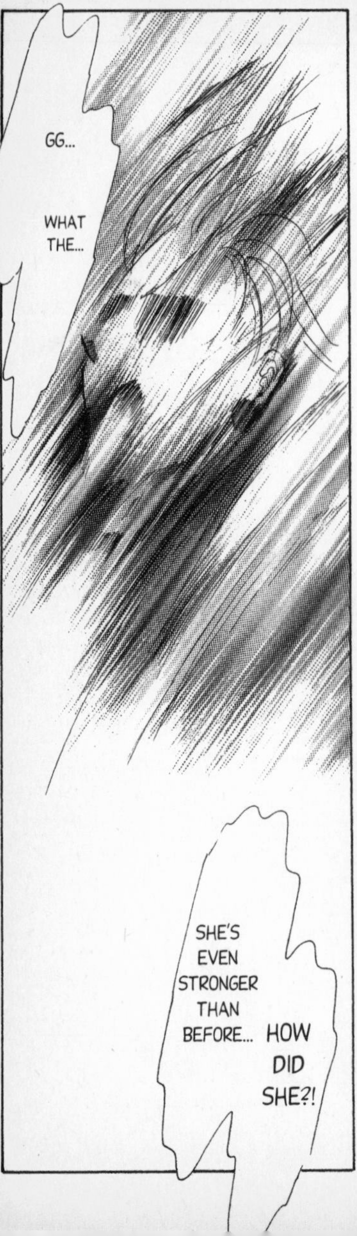
GG...
WHAT THE...
SHE'S EVEN STRONGER THAN BEFORE...
HOW DID SHE?!
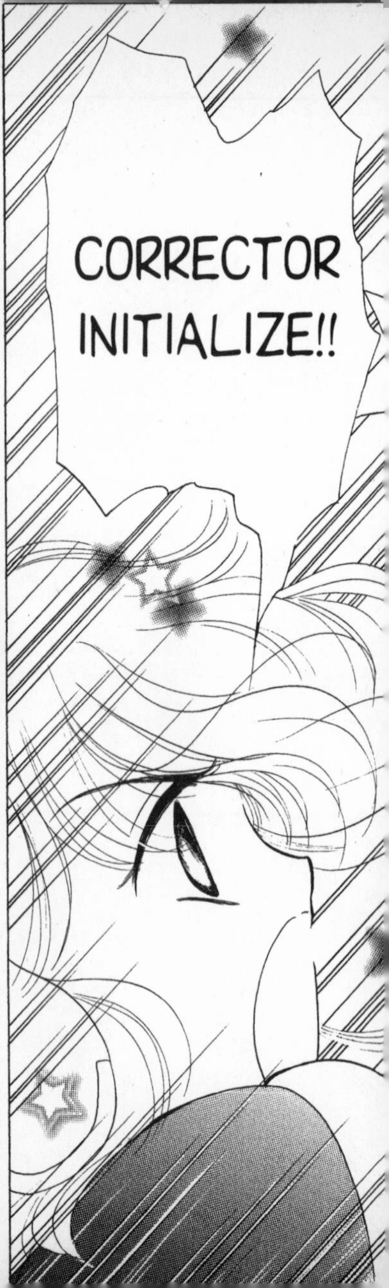
CORRECTOR INITIALIZE!!

FURTHER DEVELOPMENT NOT POSSIBLE...

FURTHER DEVELOPMENT NOT POSSIBLE...

• • • • •

REPEAT.

IT'S HAPPENED TO FREEZE, TOO!

WHAT WERE THE FEARSOME FOUR WORKING ON?

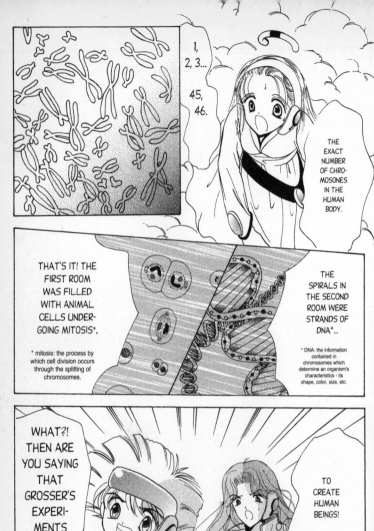

1, 2, 3...

45, 46.

THE EXACT NUMBER OF CHROMOSONES IN THE HUMAN BODY.

THAT'S IT! THE FIRST ROOM WAS FILLED WITH ANIMAL CELLS UNDER-GOING MITOSIS*.

* mitosis: the process by which cell division occurs through the splitting of chromosomes.

THE SPIRALS IN THE SECOND ROOM WERE STRANDS OF DNA*...

* DNA: the information contained in chromosomes which determine an organism's characteristics - its shape, color, size, etc.

WHAT?! THEN ARE YOU SAYING THAT GROSSER'S EXPERI-MENTS WERE...

TO CREATE HUMAN BEINGS!

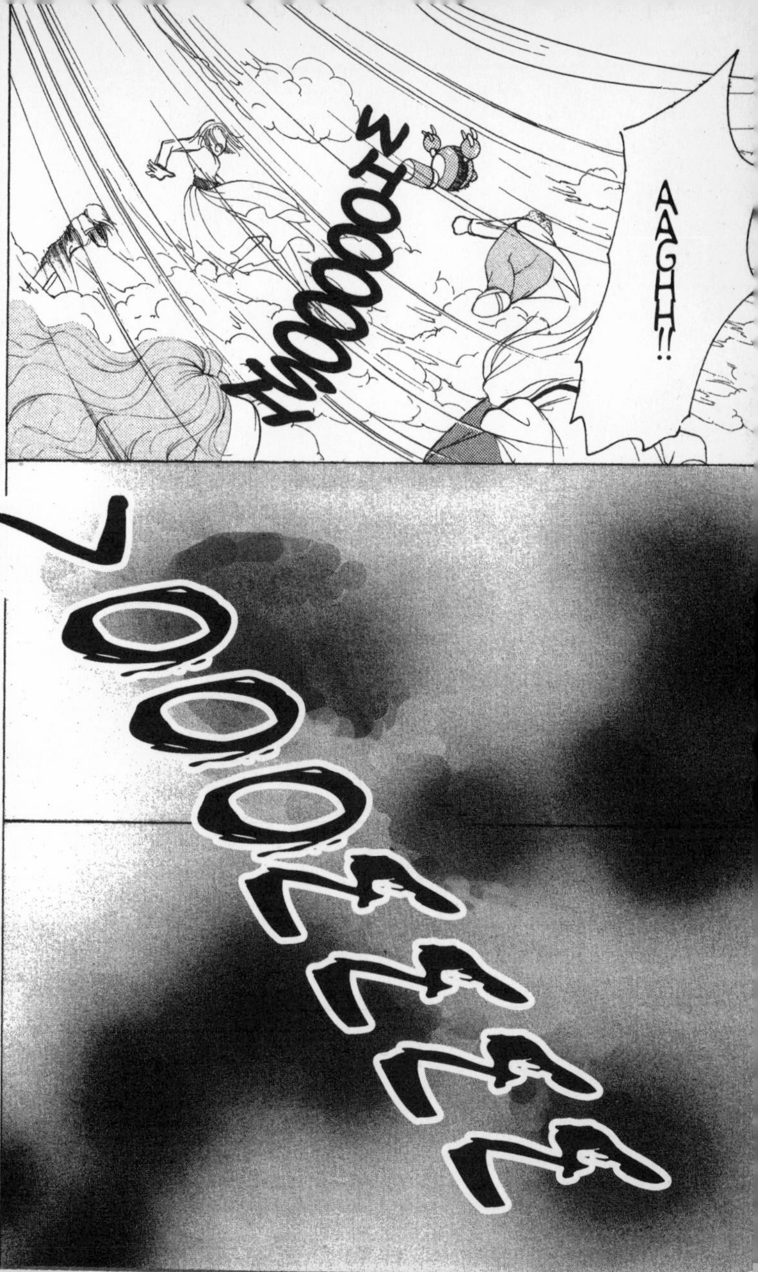
WHOOOOOSH
AAGH!!
VOOOOZZZZ

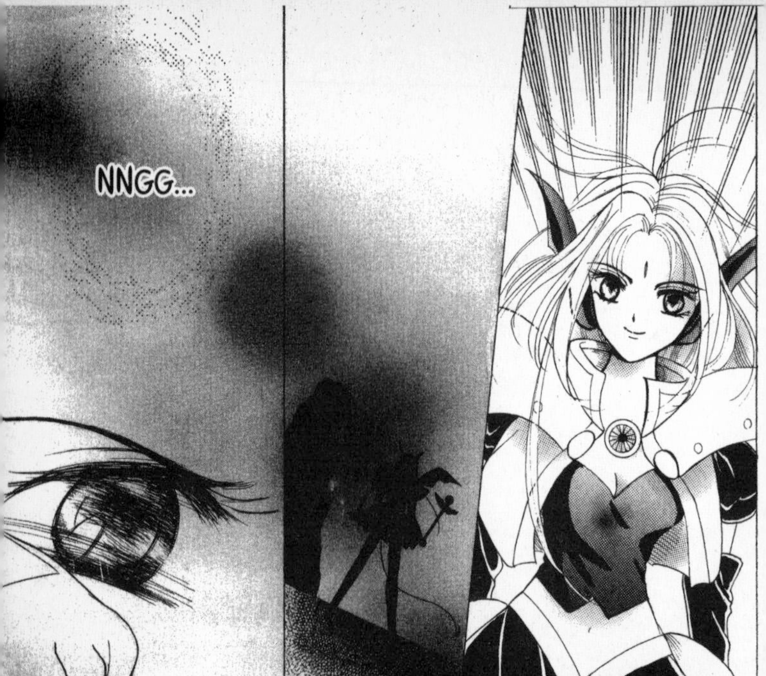
NNGG...
WHAT?!
THAT'S...
HARUNA!!

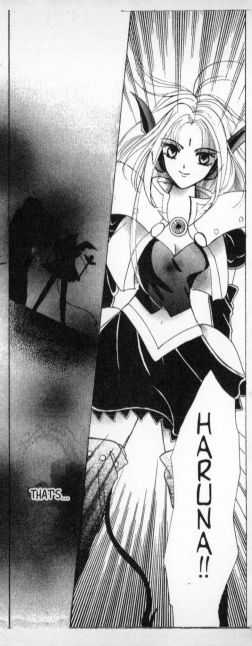

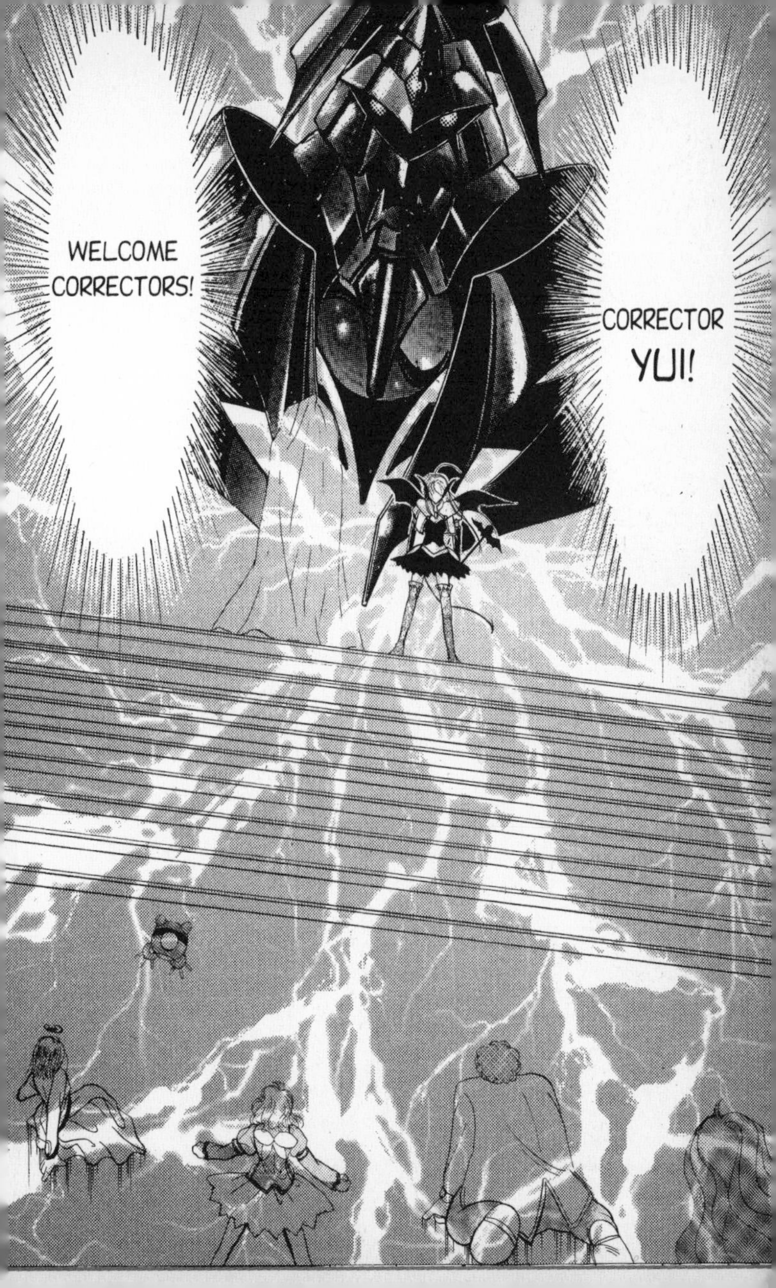
WELCOME CORRECTORS!
CORRECTOR YUI!

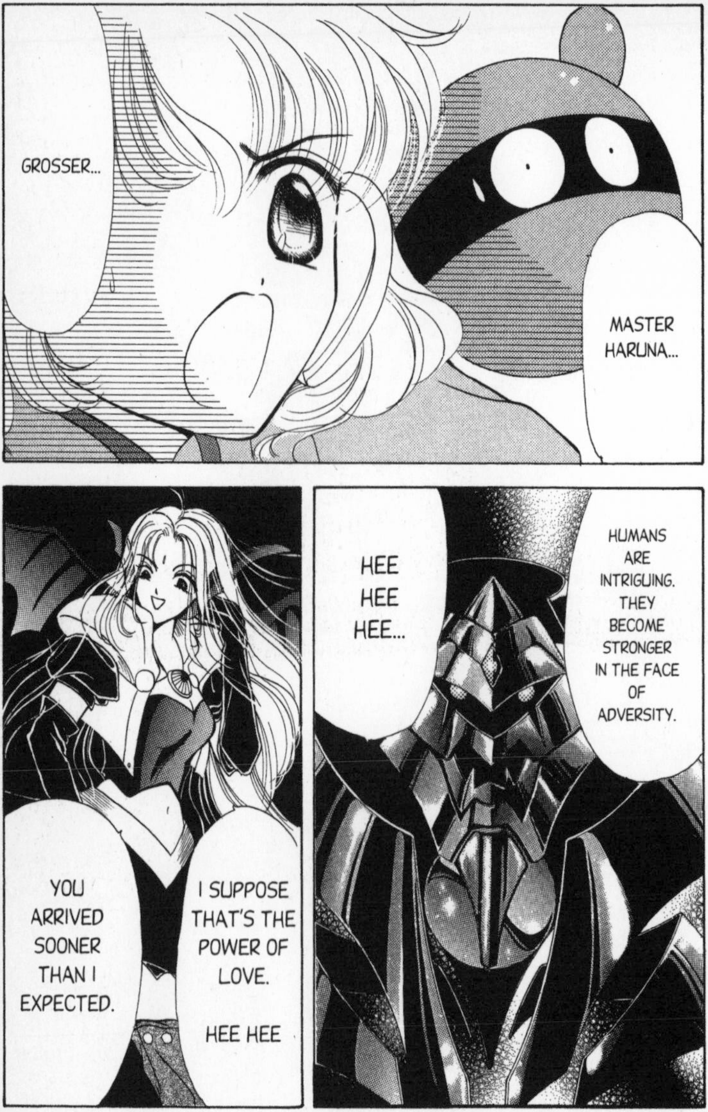
GROSSER...
MASTER HARUNA...
YOU ARRIVED SOONER THAN I EXPECTED.
I SUPPOSE THAT'S THE POWER OF LOVE.
HEE HEE
HEE HEE HEE...
HUMANS ARE INTRIGUING. THEY BECOME STRONGER IN THE FACE OF ADVERSITY.

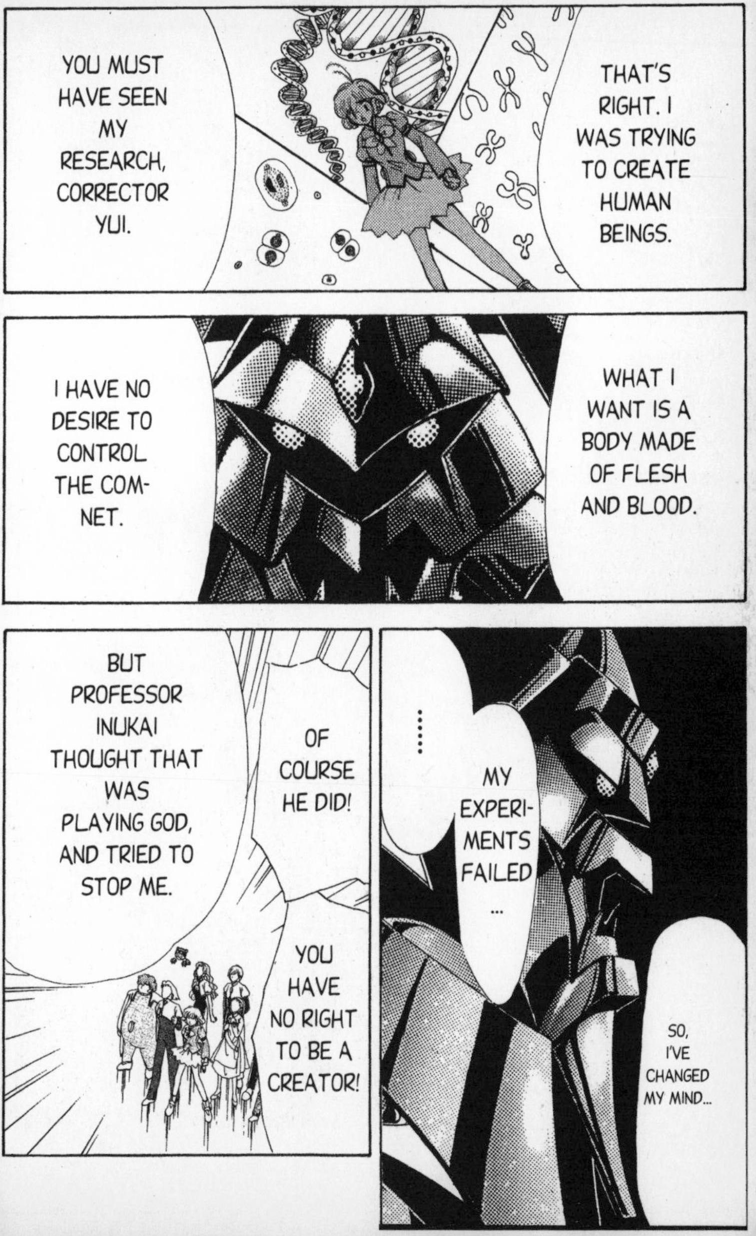
YOU MUST HAVE SEEN MY RESEARCH, CORRECTOR YUI.
THAT'S RIGHT. I WAS TRYING TO CREATE HUMAN BEINGS.
I HAVE NO DESIRE TO CONTROL THE COM-NET.
WHAT I WANT IS A BODY MADE OF FLESH AND BLOOD.
BUT PROFESSOR INUKAI THOUGHT THAT WAS PLAYING GOD, AND TRIED TO STOP ME.
OF COURSE HE DID!
YOU HAVE NO RIGHT TO BE A CREATOR!
......
MY EXPERIMENTS FAILED ...
SO, I'VE CHANGED MY MIND...

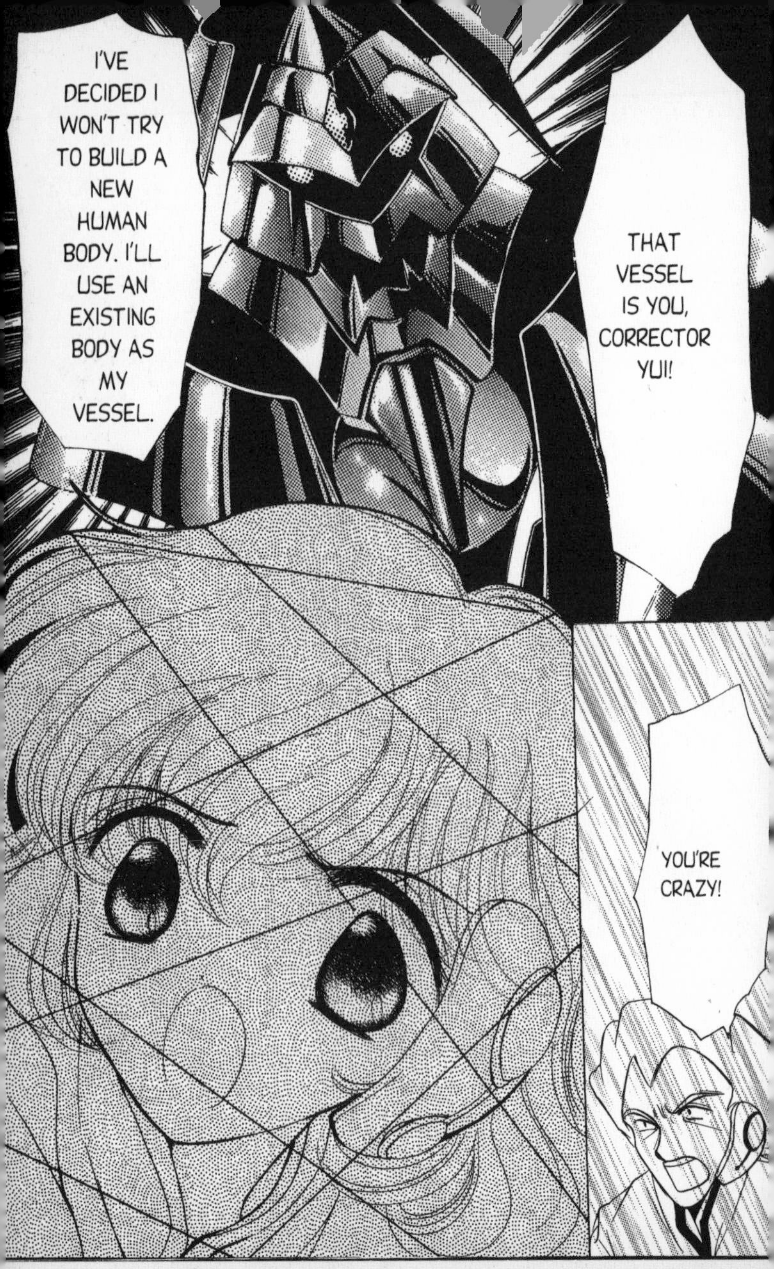
I'VE DECIDED I WON'T TRY TO BUILD A NEW HUMAN BODY. I'LL USE AN EXISTING BODY AS MY VESSEL.
THAT VESSEL IS YOU, CORRECTOR YUI!
YOU'RE CRAZY!

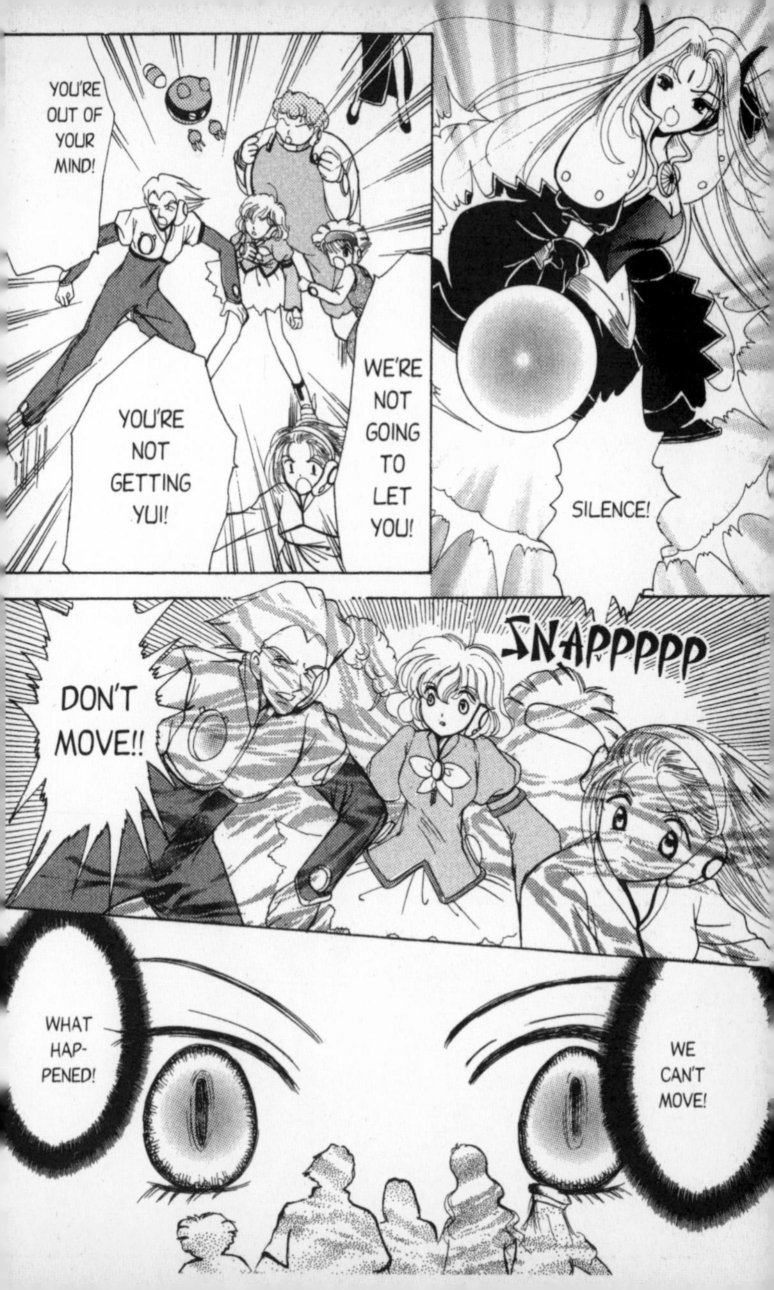
SILENCE!
YOU'RE OUT OF YOUR MIND!
WE'RE NOT GOING TO LET YOU!
YOU'RE NOT GETTING YUI!
SNAPPPPP
DON'T MOVE!!
WE CAN'T MOVE!
WHAT HAP-PENED!

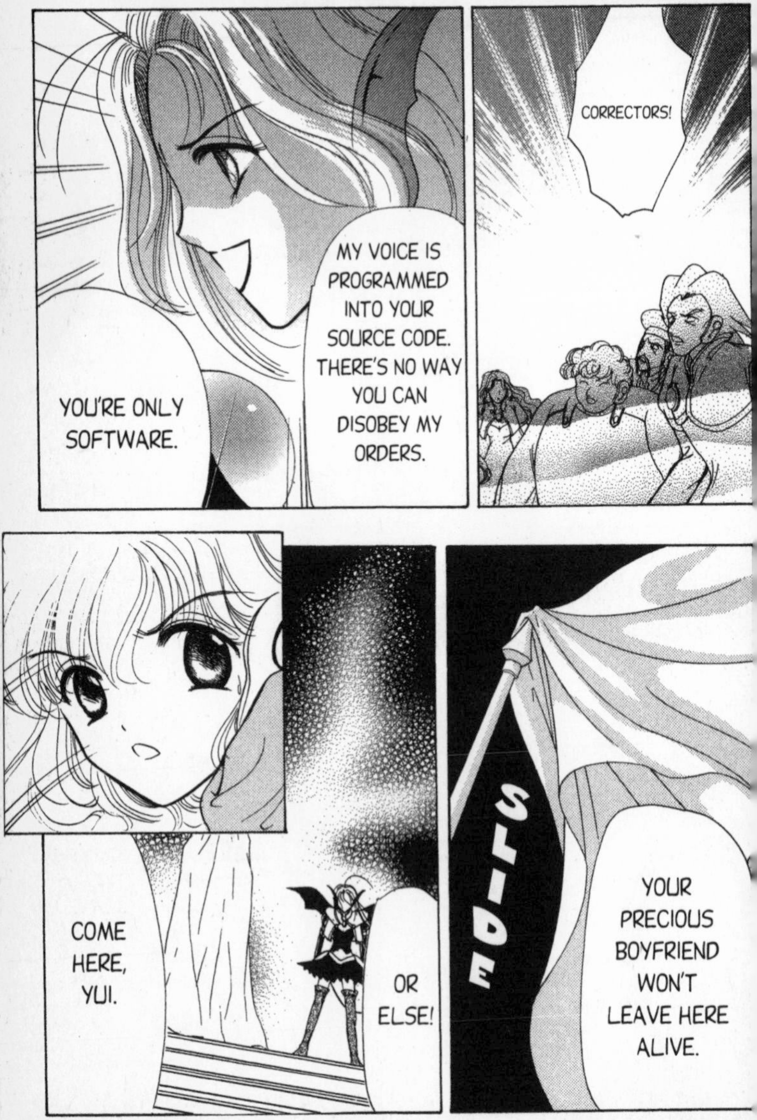
YOU'RE ONLY SOFTWARE.
MY VOICE IS PROGRAMMED INTO YOUR SOURCE CODE. THERE'S NO WAY YOU CAN DISOBEY MY ORDERS.
CORRECTORS!
COME HERE, YUI.
OR ELSE!
SLIDE
YOUR PRECIOUS BOYFRIEND WON'T LEAVE HERE ALIVE.

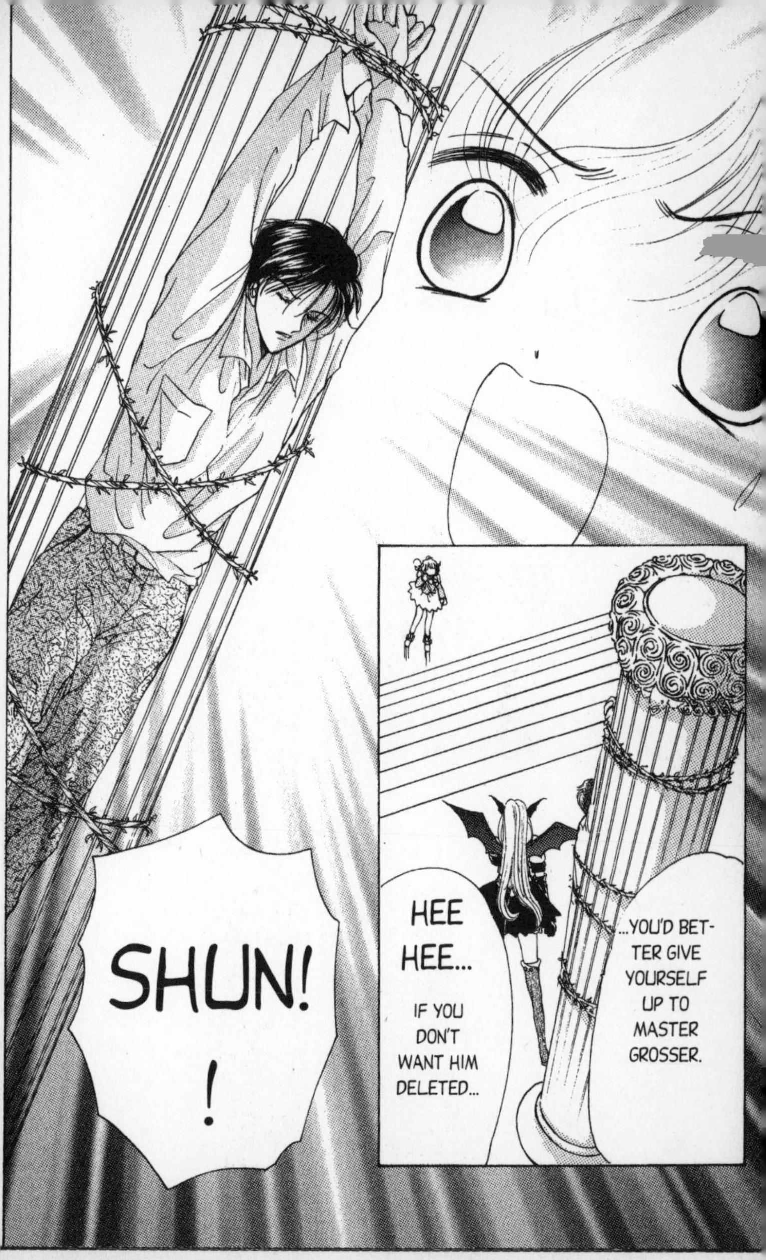
SHUN! !
HEE HEE...
IF YOU DON'T WANT HIM DELETED...
...YOU'D BET-TER GIVE YOURSELF UP TO MASTER GROSSER.

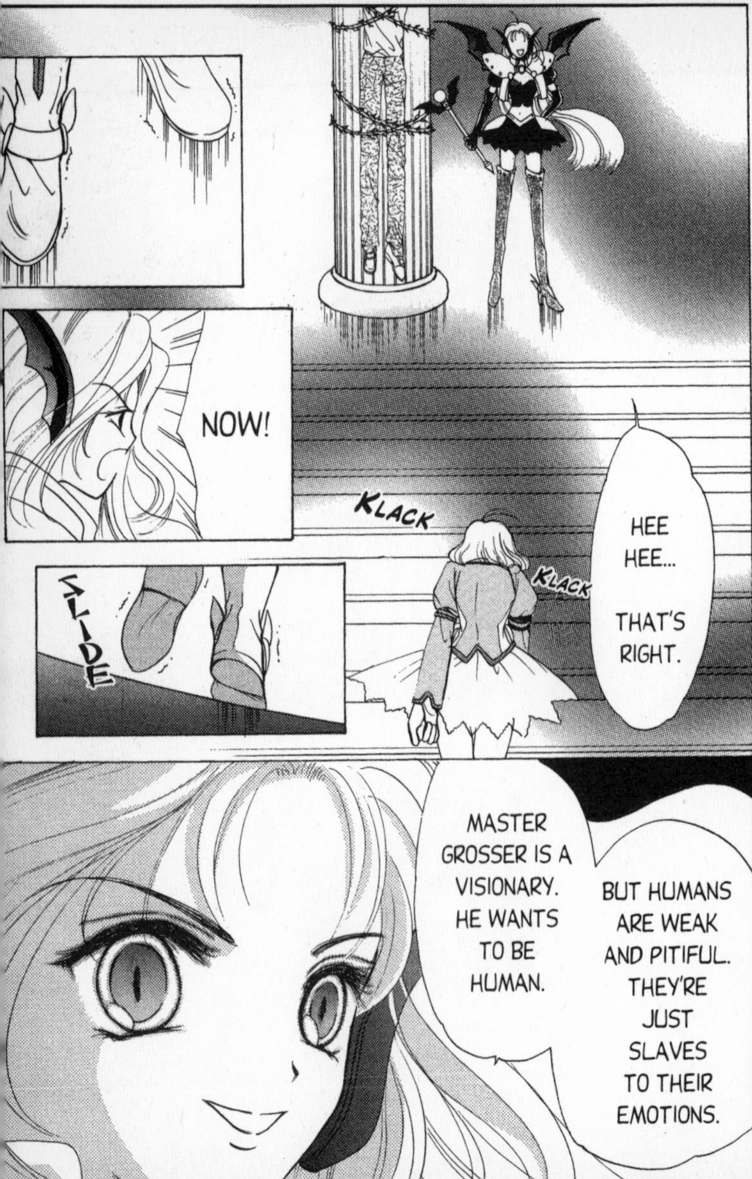
NOW!
KLACK
KLACK
HEE HEE... THAT'S RIGHT.
SLIDE
MASTER GROSSER IS A VISIONARY. HE WANTS TO BE HUMAN.
BUT HUMANS ARE WEAK AND PITIFUL. THEY'RE JUST SLAVES TO THEIR EMOTIONS.

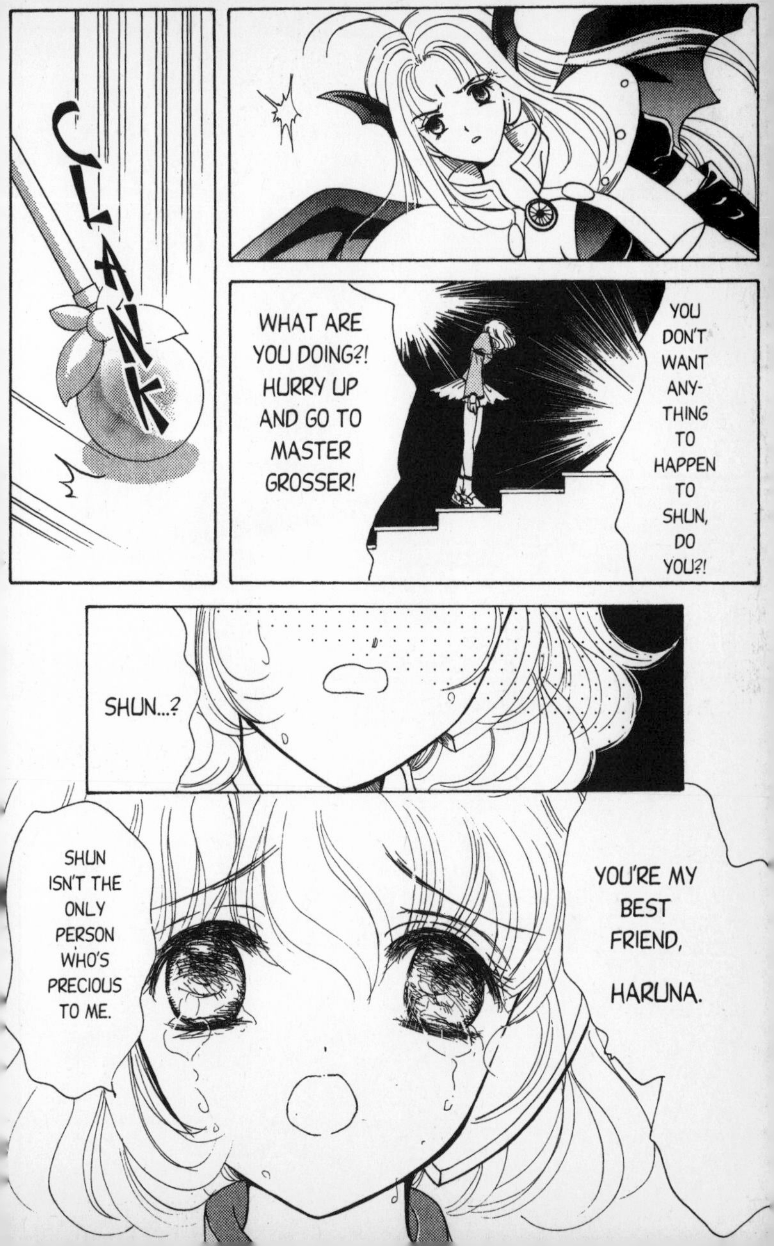
CLANK
WHAT ARE YOU DOING?! HURRY UP AND GO TO MASTER GROSSER!
YOU DON'T WANT ANY-THING TO HAPPEN TO SHUN, DO YOU?!
SHUN...?
SHUN ISN'T THE ONLY PERSON WHO'S PRECIOUS TO ME.
YOU'RE MY BEST FRIEND,
HARUNA.

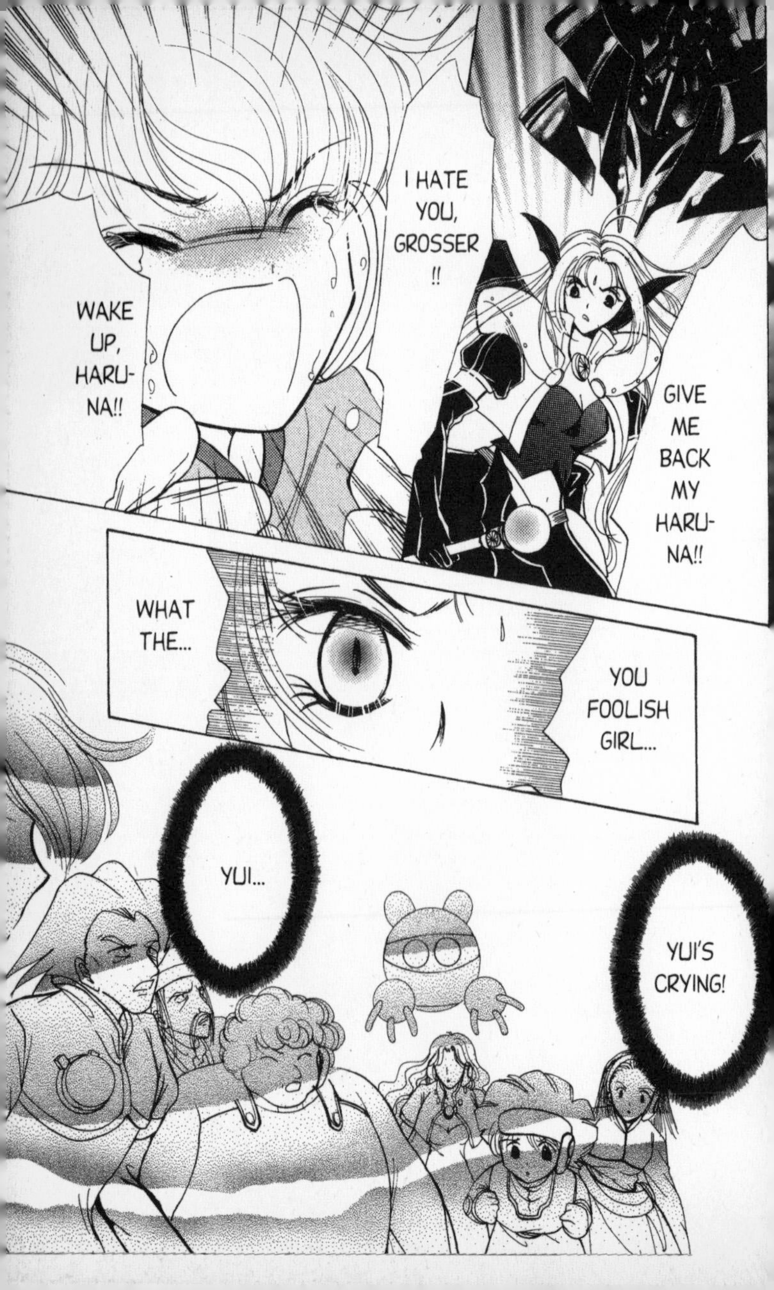

WAKE UP, HARU-NA!!
I HATE YOU, GROSSER !!
GIVE ME BACK MY HARU-NA!!
WHAT THE...
YOU FOOLISH GIRL...
YUI...
YUI'S CRYING!

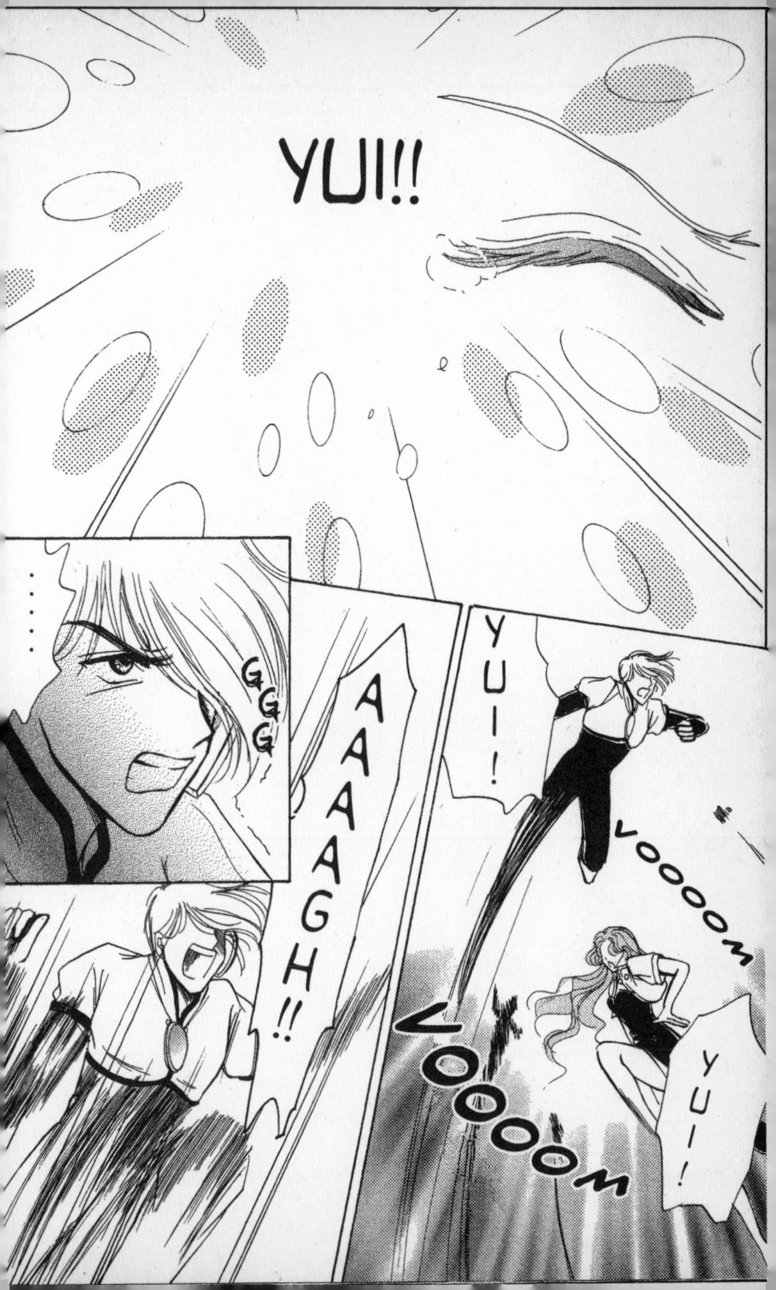
YUI!!
......
GGG
AAAAAGH!!
YUI!
VOOOOM
VOOOOOM
YUI!

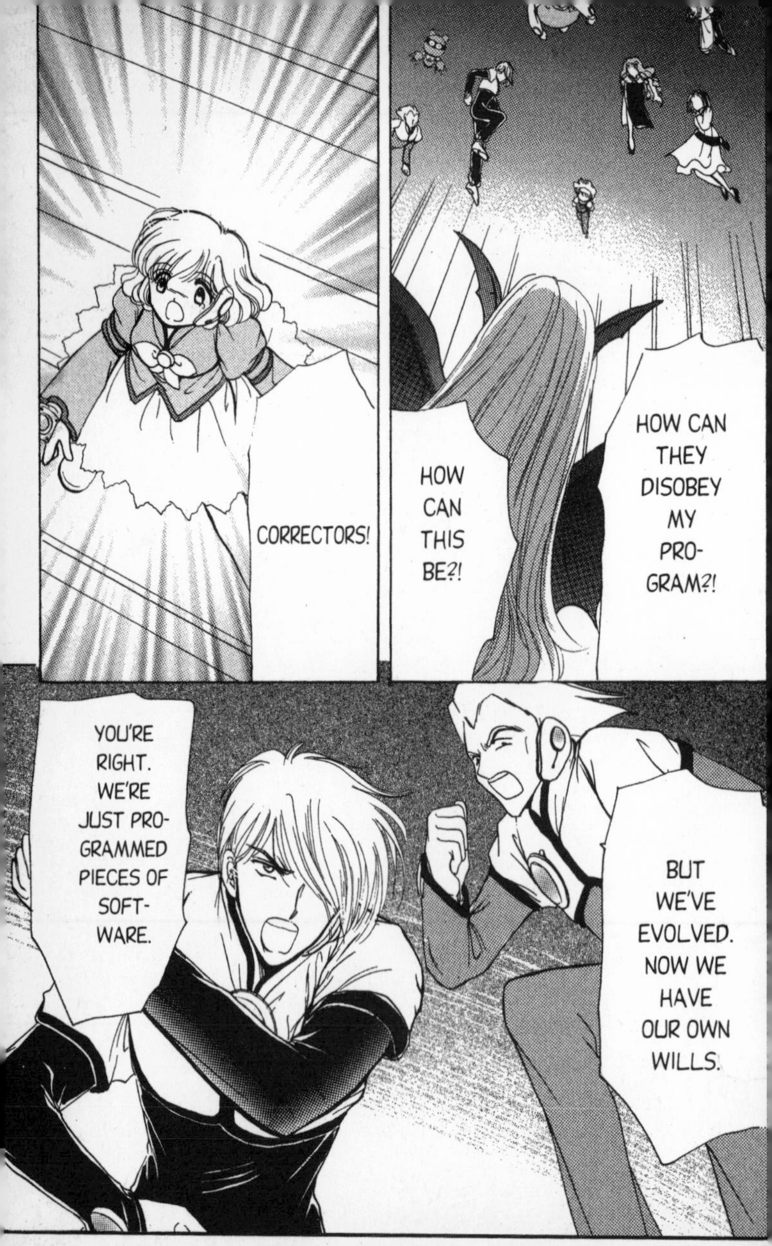
CORRECTORS!
HOW CAN THIS BE?!
HOW CAN THEY DISOBEY MY PRO-GRAM?!
YOU'RE RIGHT. WE'RE JUST PRO-GRAMMED PIECES OF SOFT-WARE.
BUT WE'VE EVOLVED. NOW WE HAVE OUR OWN WILLS.

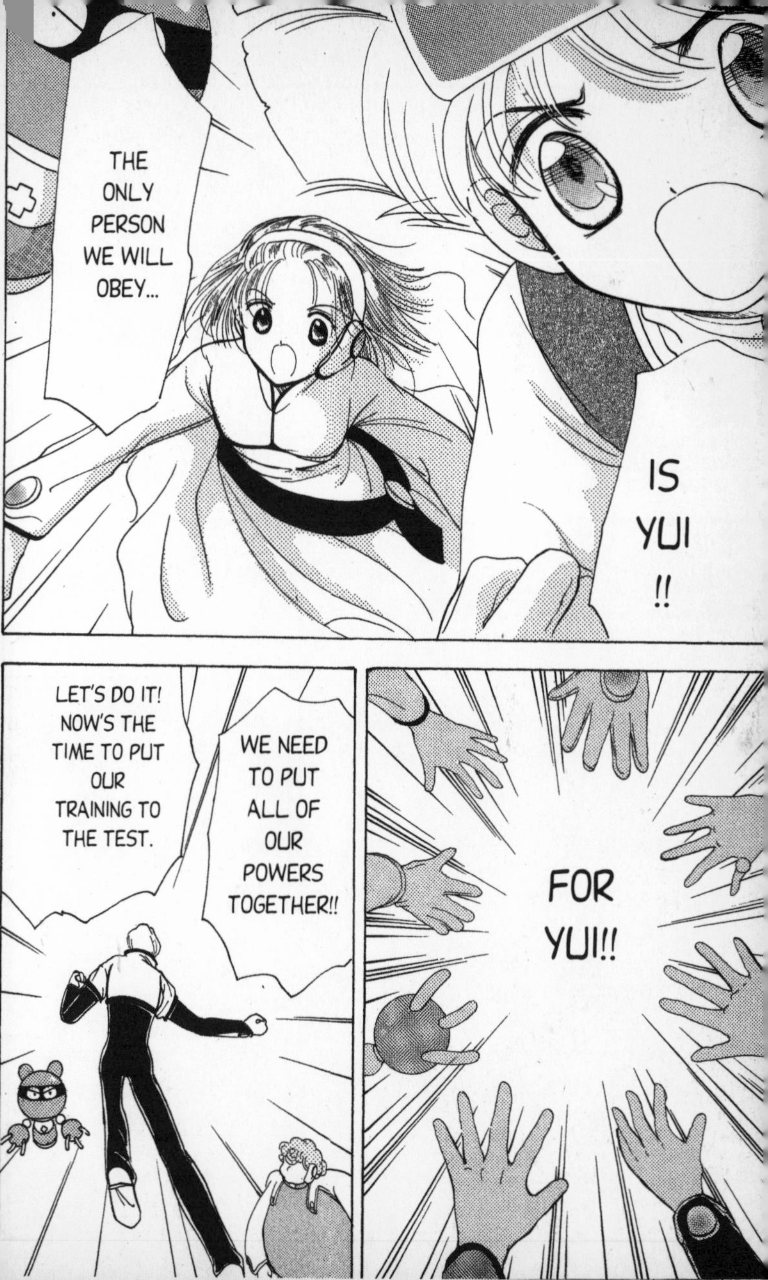
THE ONLY PERSON WE WILL OBEY...
IS YUI!!
LET'S DO IT! NOW'S THE TIME TO PUT OUR TRAINING TO THE TEST.
WE NEED TO PUT ALL OF OUR POWERS TOGETHER!!
FOR YUI!!

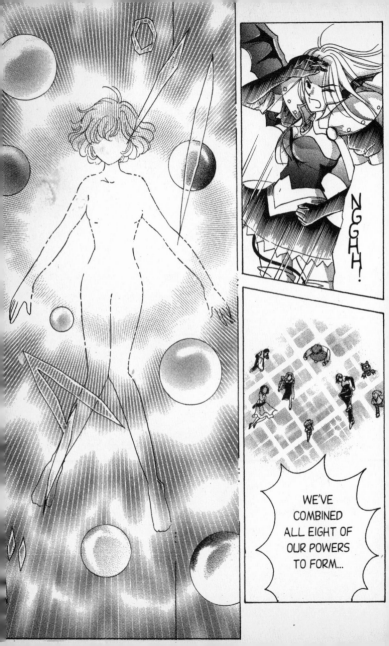

NGGAH!

WE'VE COMBINED ALL EIGHT OF OUR POWERS TO FORM...

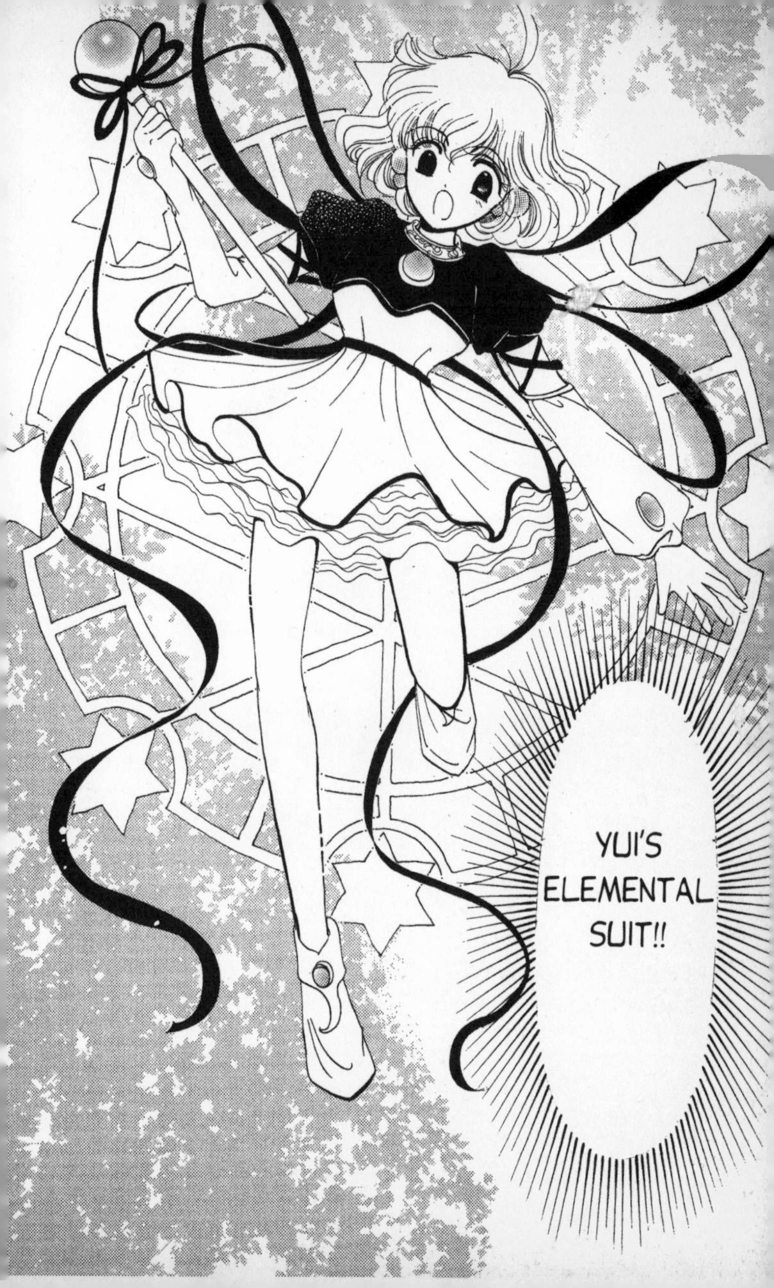
YUI'S ELEMENTAL SUIT!!

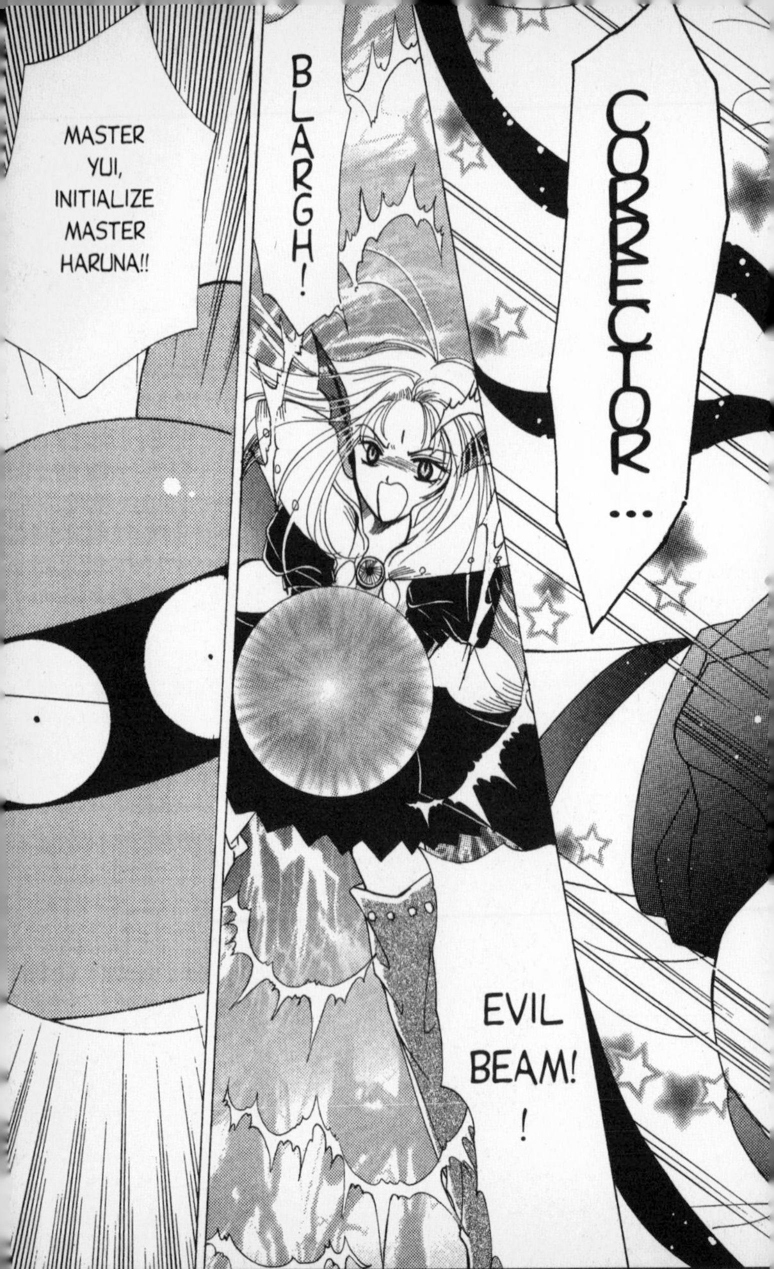
MASTER YUI, INITIALIZE MASTER HARUNA!!
BLARGH!
CORRECTOR...
EVIL BEAM!!

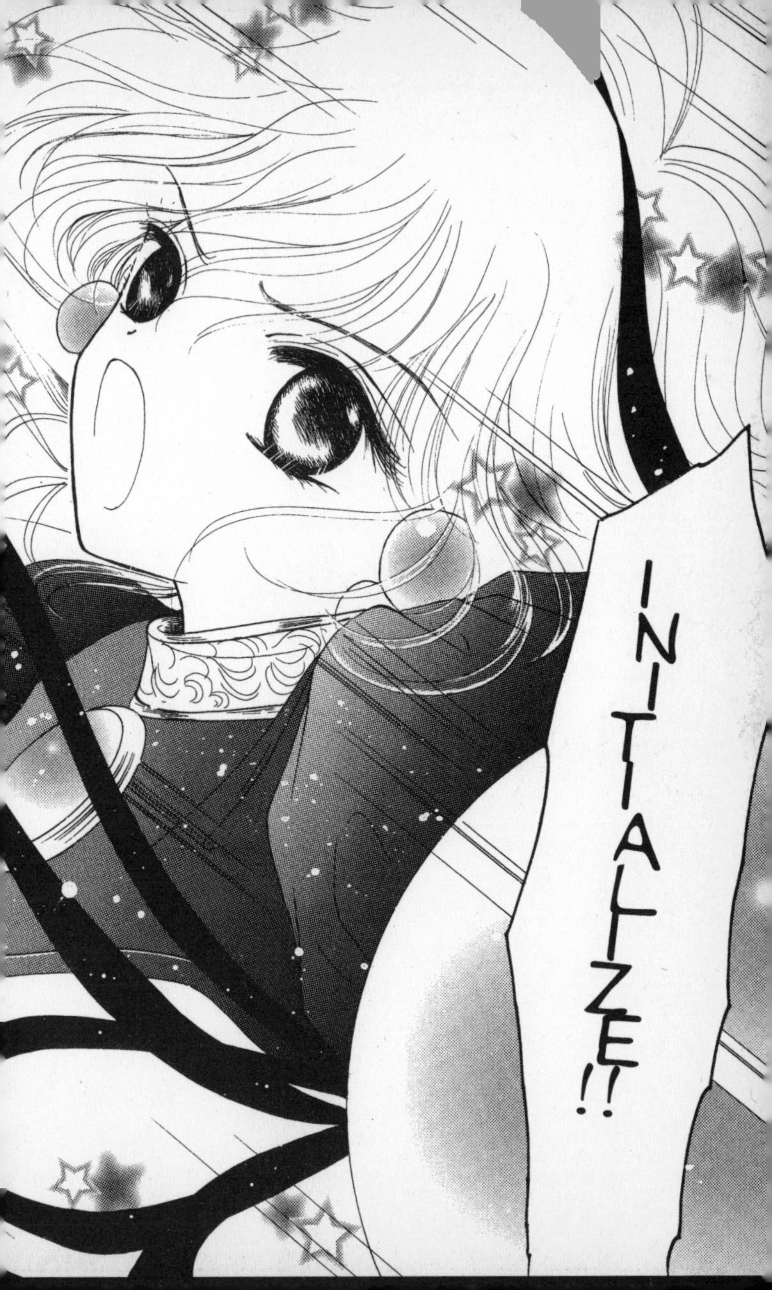
INITIALIZE!!

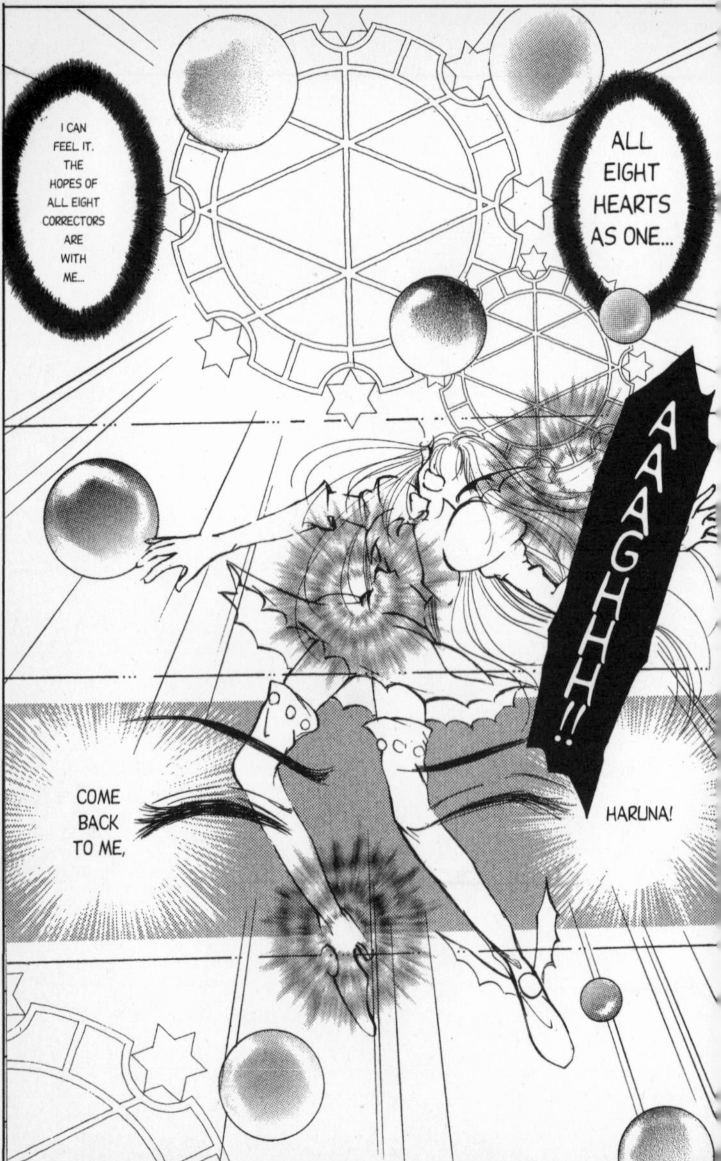
I CAN FEEL IT. THE HOPES OF ALL EIGHT CORRECTORS ARE WITH ME...
ALL EIGHT HEARTS AS ONE...
AAAGHHH!!
COME BACK TO ME,
HARUNA!

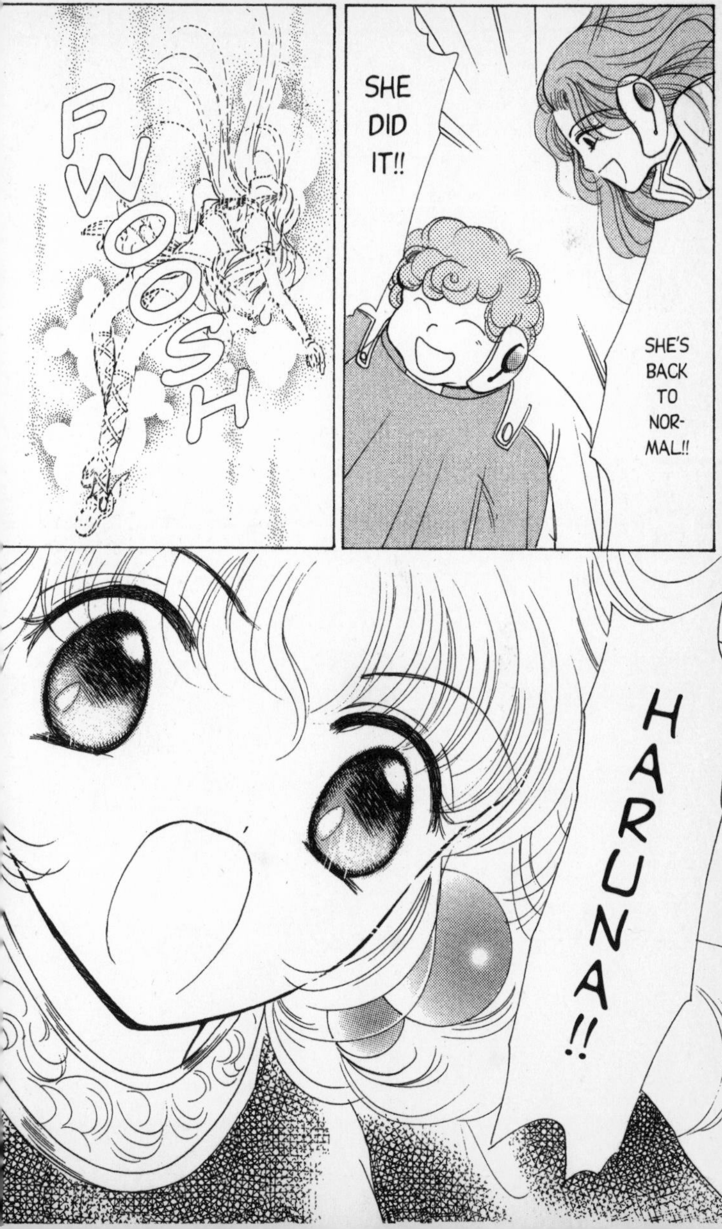
FWOOOSH
SHE DID IT!!
SHE'S BACK TO NOR-MAL!!
HARUNA!!

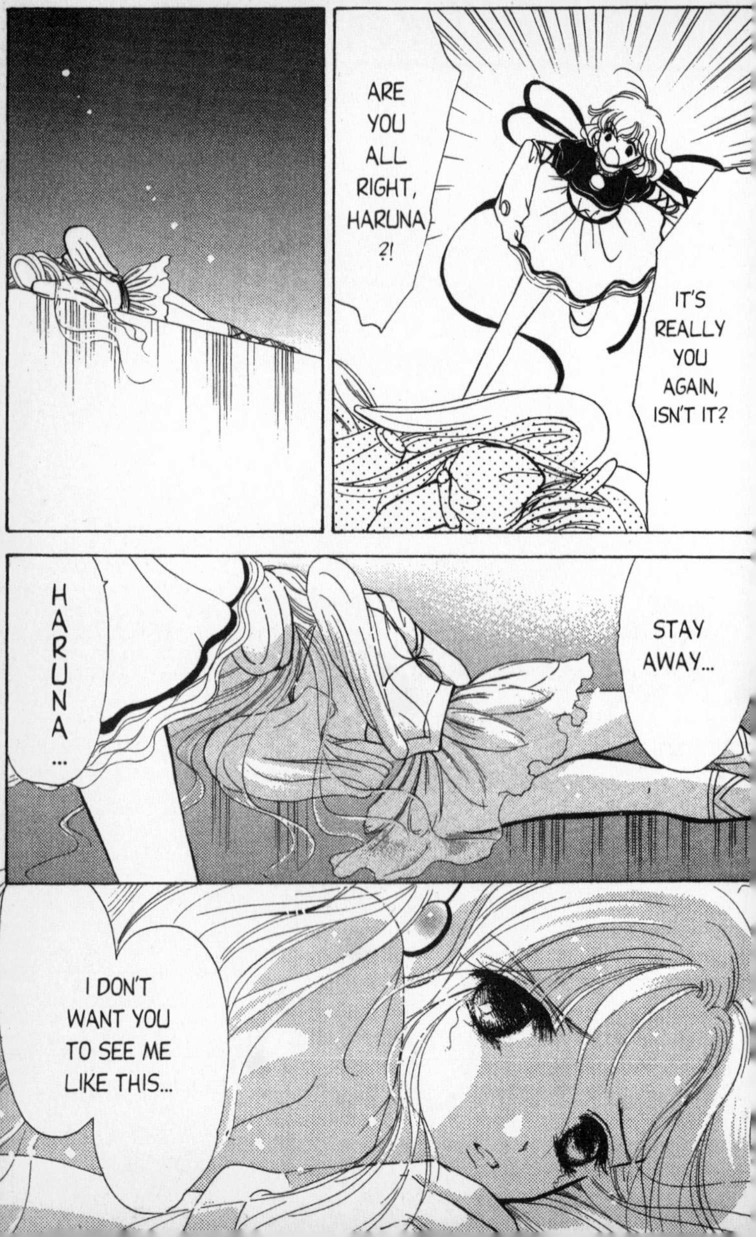
ARE YOU ALL RIGHT, HARUNA?!
IT'S REALLY YOU AGAIN, ISN'T IT?
HARUNA...
STAY AWAY...
I DON'T WANT YOU TO SEE ME LIKE THIS...

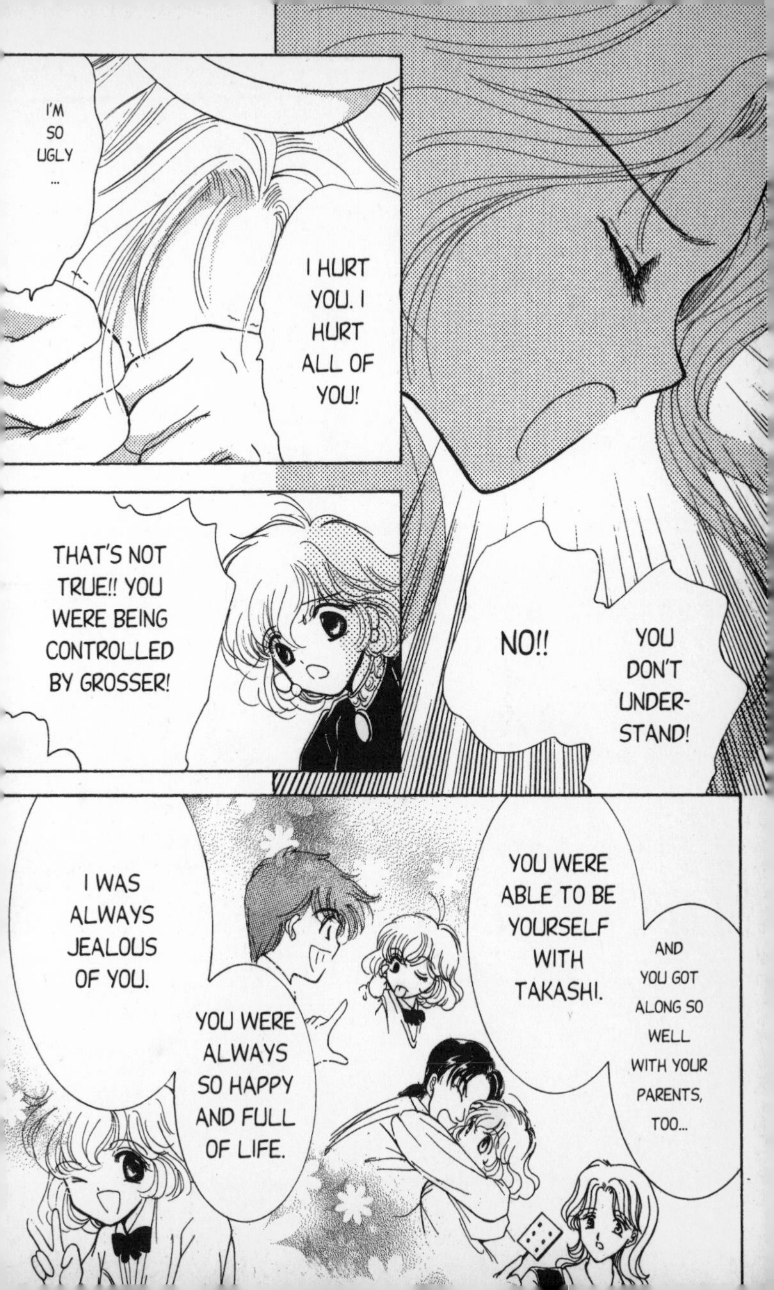

I'M SO UGLY ...
I HURT YOU. I HURT ALL OF YOU!
THAT'S NOT TRUE!! YOU WERE BEING CONTROLLED BY GROSSER!
NO!!
YOU DON'T UNDER-STAND!
I WAS ALWAYS JEALOUS OF YOU.
YOU WERE ALWAYS SO HAPPY AND FULL OF LIFE.
YOU WERE ABLE TO BE YOURSELF WITH TAKASHI.
AND YOU GOT ALONG SO WELL WITH YOUR PARENTS, TOO...

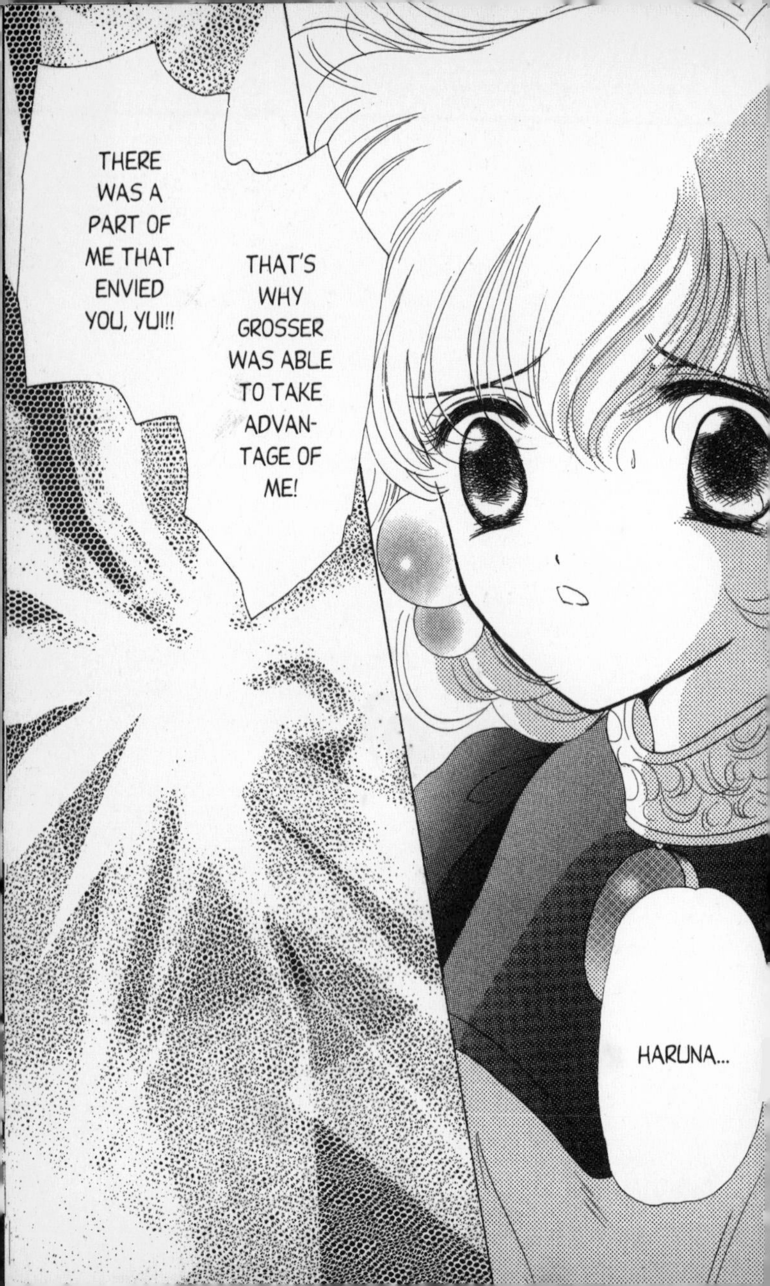
THERE WAS A PART OF ME THAT ENVIED YOU, YUI!!
THAT'S WHY GROSSER WAS ABLE TO TAKE ADVANTAGE OF ME!
HARUNA...

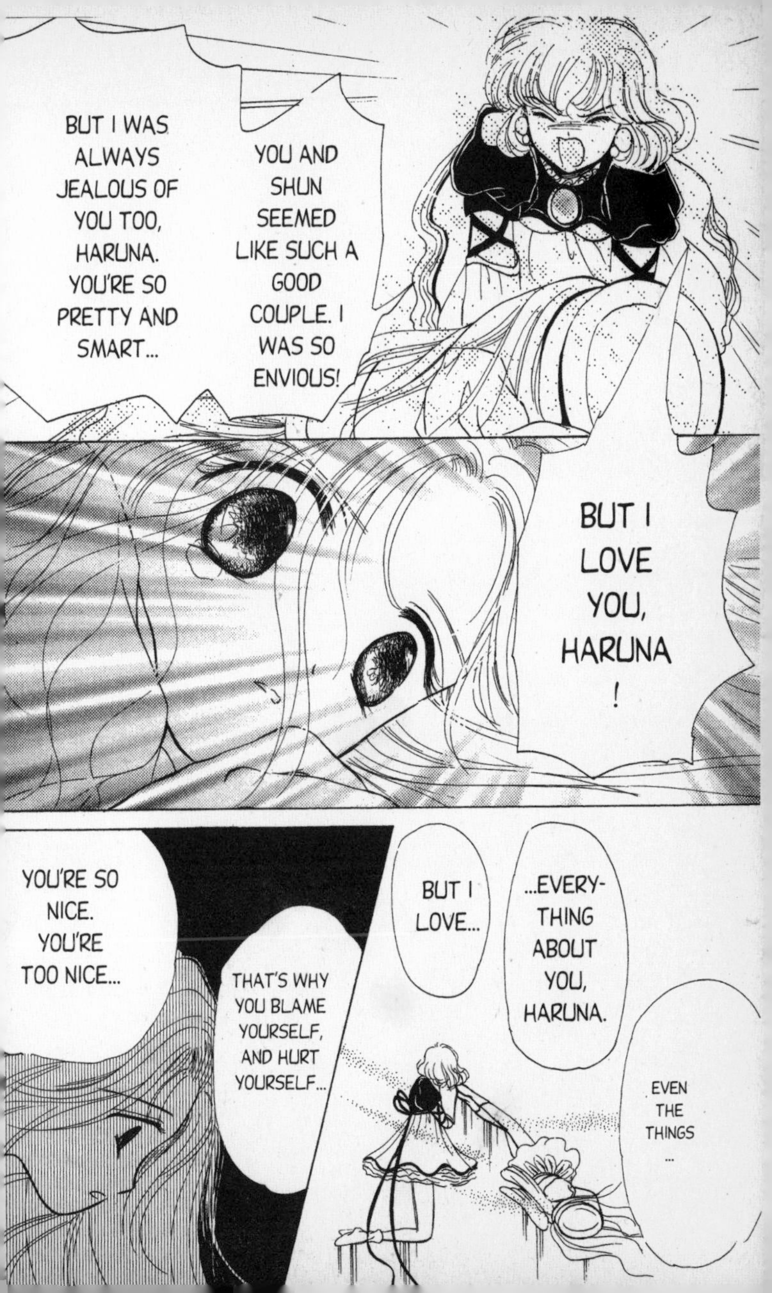

BUT I WAS ALWAYS JEALOUS OF YOU TOO, HARUNA. YOU'RE SO PRETTY AND SMART...
YOU AND SHUN SEEMED LIKE SUCH A GOOD COUPLE. I WAS SO ENVIOUS!
BUT I LOVE YOU, HARUNA!
YOU'RE SO NICE. YOU'RE TOO NICE...
THAT'S WHY YOU BLAME YOURSELF, AND HURT YOURSELF...
BUT I LOVE...
...EVERY-THING ABOUT YOU, HARUNA.
EVEN THE THINGS...

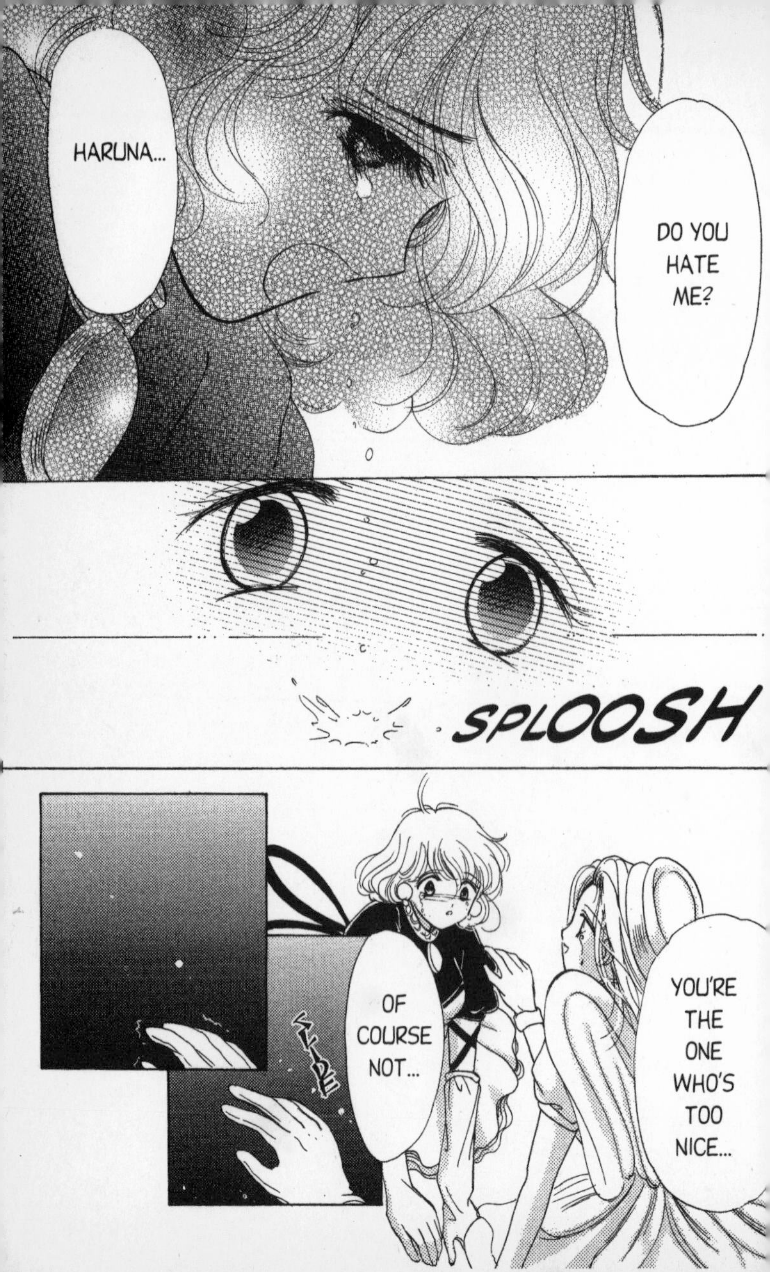
HARUNA...
DO YOU HATE ME?
SPLOOSH
SLIDE
OF COURSE NOT...
YOU'RE THE ONE WHO'S TOO NICE...

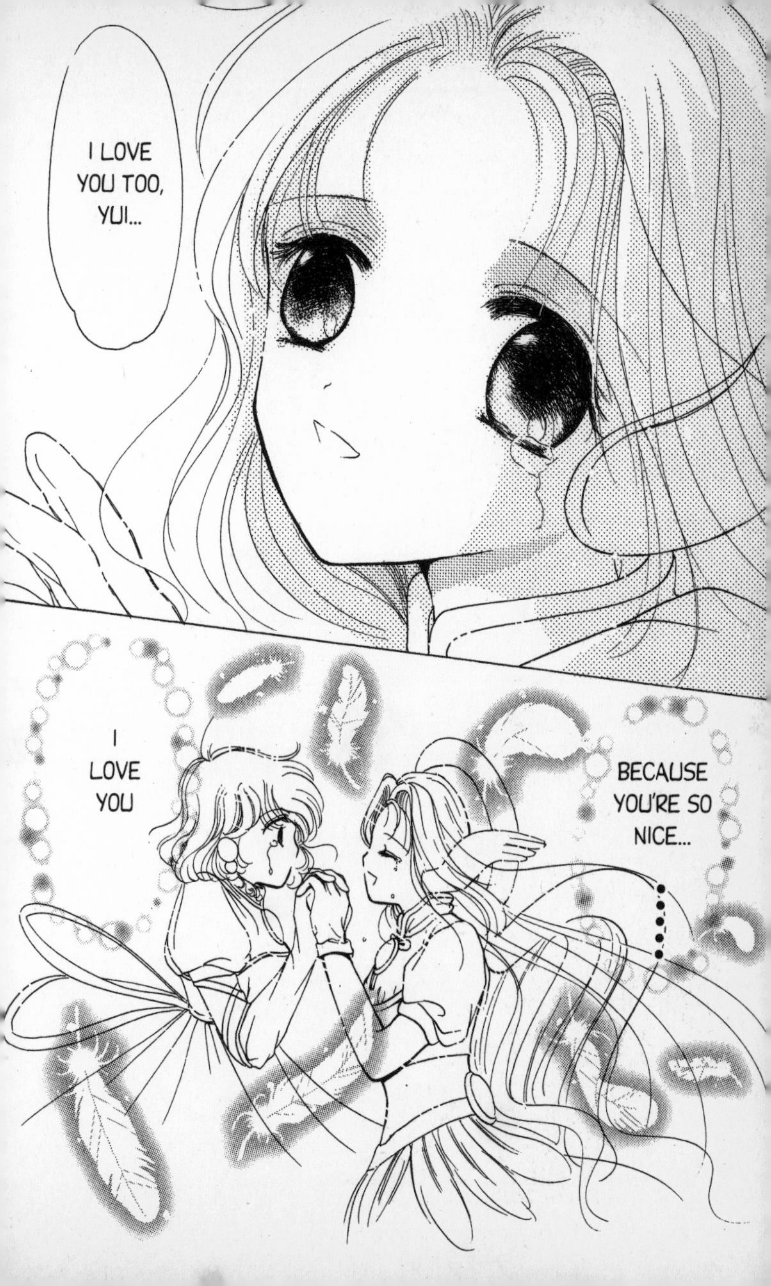
I LOVE YOU TOO, YUI...
I LOVE YOU
BECAUSE YOU'RE SO NICE...

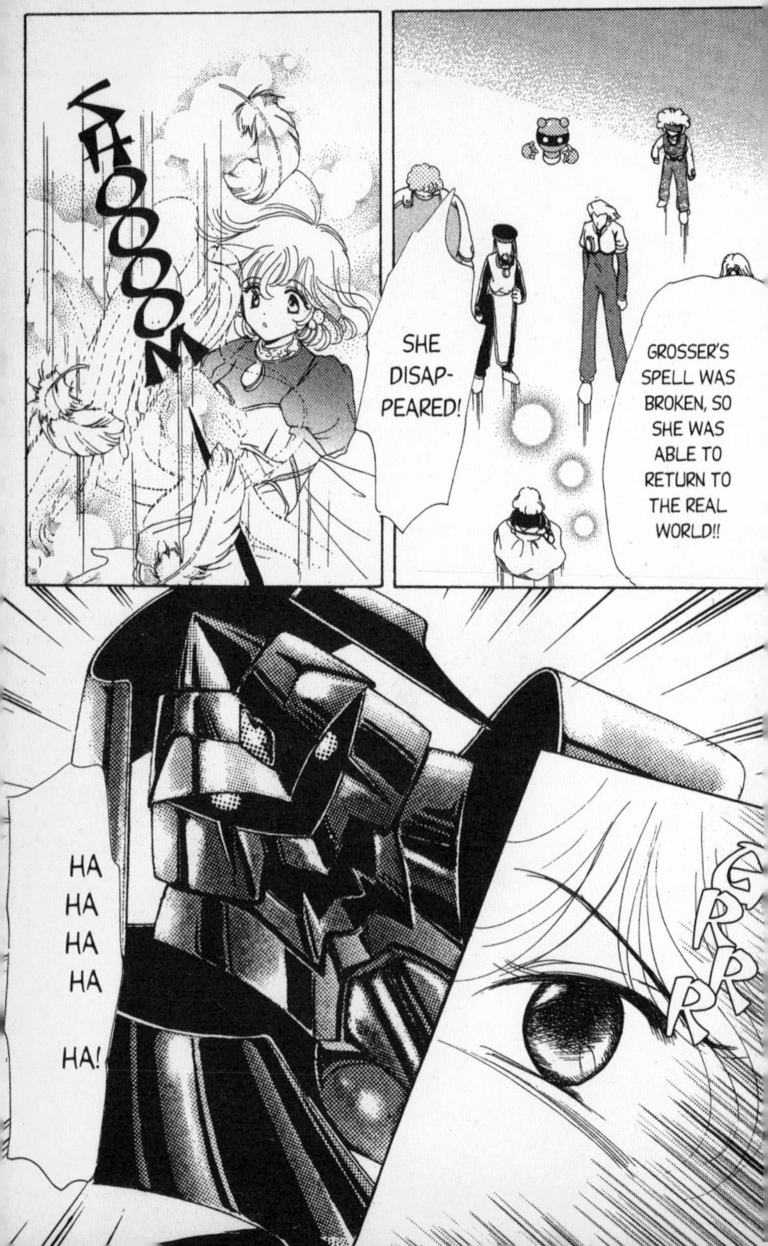
SHOOOOM
SHE DISAPPEARED!
GROSSER'S SPELL WAS BROKEN, SO SHE WAS ABLE TO RETURN TO THE REAL WORLD!!
HA HA HA HA HA!
GRRR

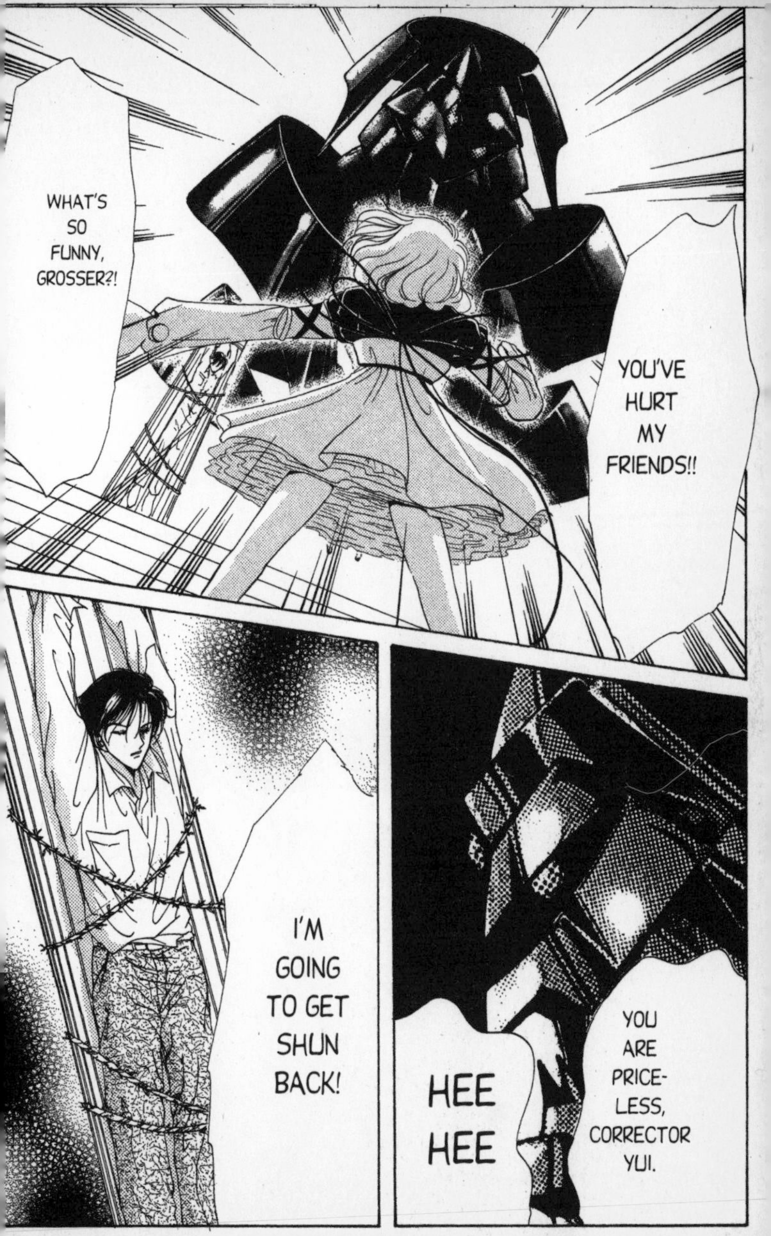
WHAT'S SO FUNNY, GROSSER?!
YOU'VE HURT MY FRIENDS!!
I'M GOING TO GET SHUN BACK!
HEE HEE
YOU ARE PRICE-LESS, CORRECTOR YUI.

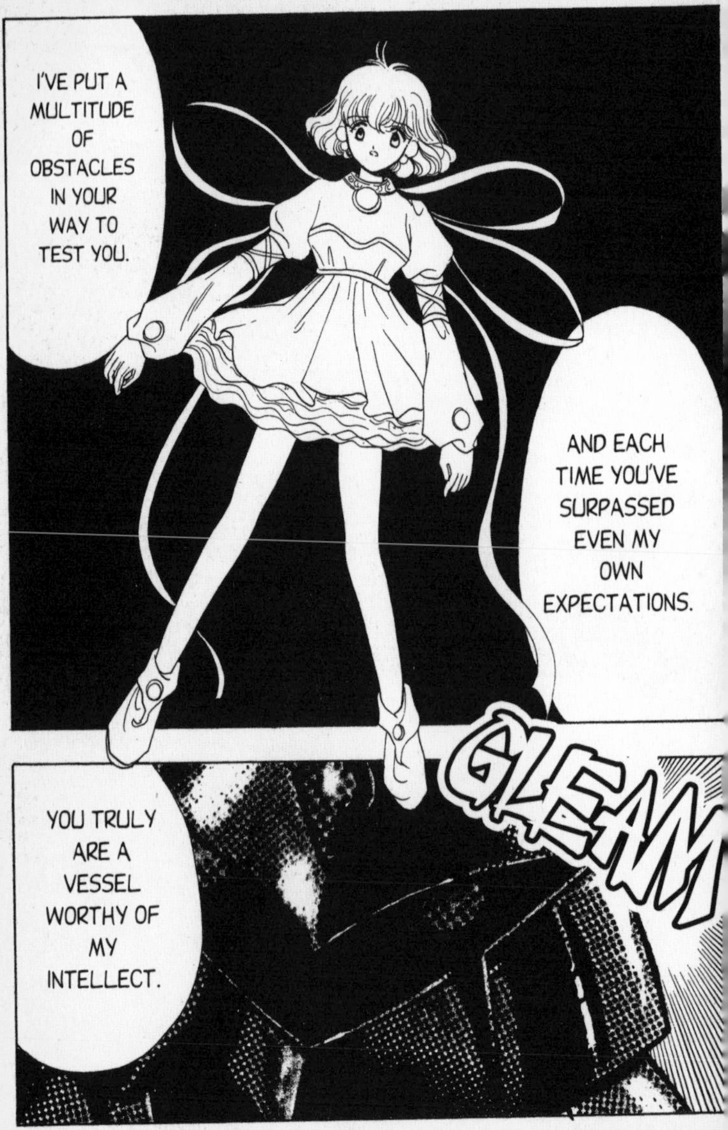
I'VE PUT A MULTITUDE OF OBSTACLES IN YOUR WAY TO TEST YOU.
AND EACH TIME YOU'VE SURPASSED EVEN MY OWN EXPECTATIONS.
YOU TRULY ARE A VESSEL WORTHY OF MY INTELLECT.
GLEAM

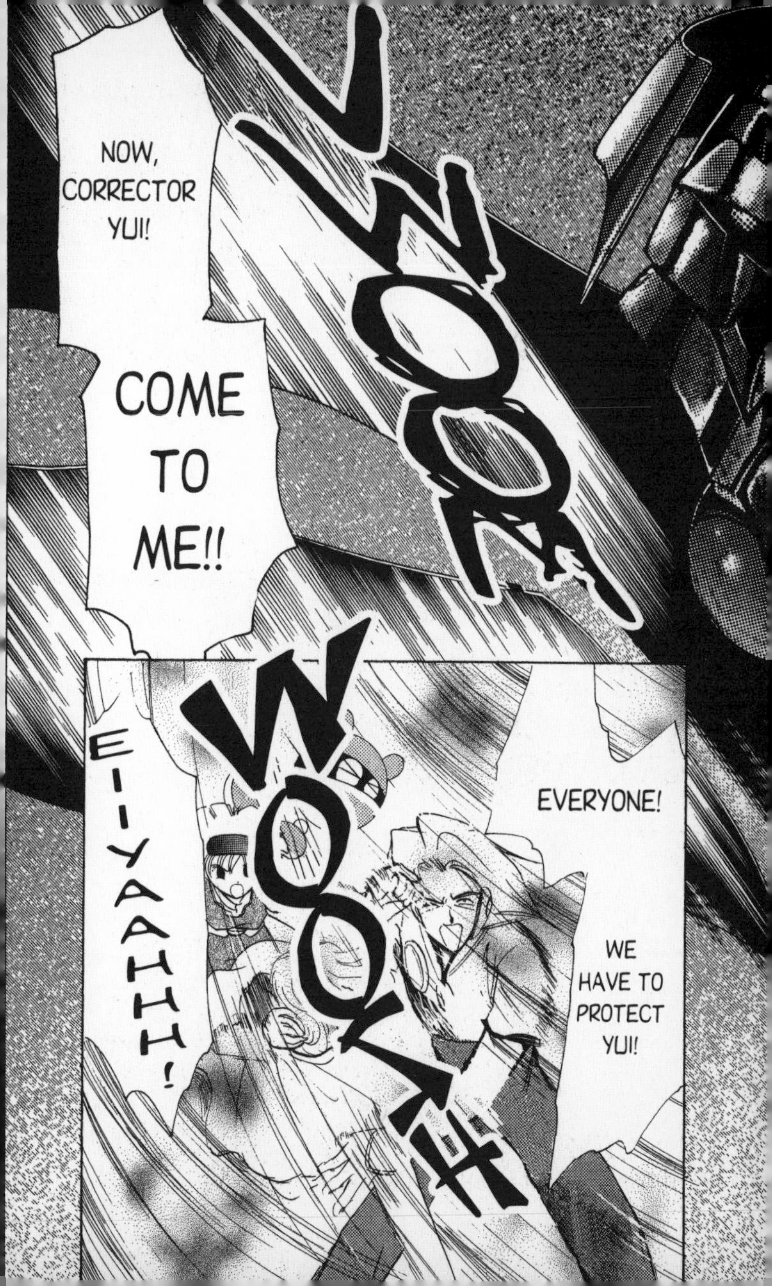
NOW, CORRECTOR YUI!
COME TO ME!!
VWOOM
EIIYAAHHH!
WOOOSH
EVERYONE!
WE HAVE TO PROTECT YUI!

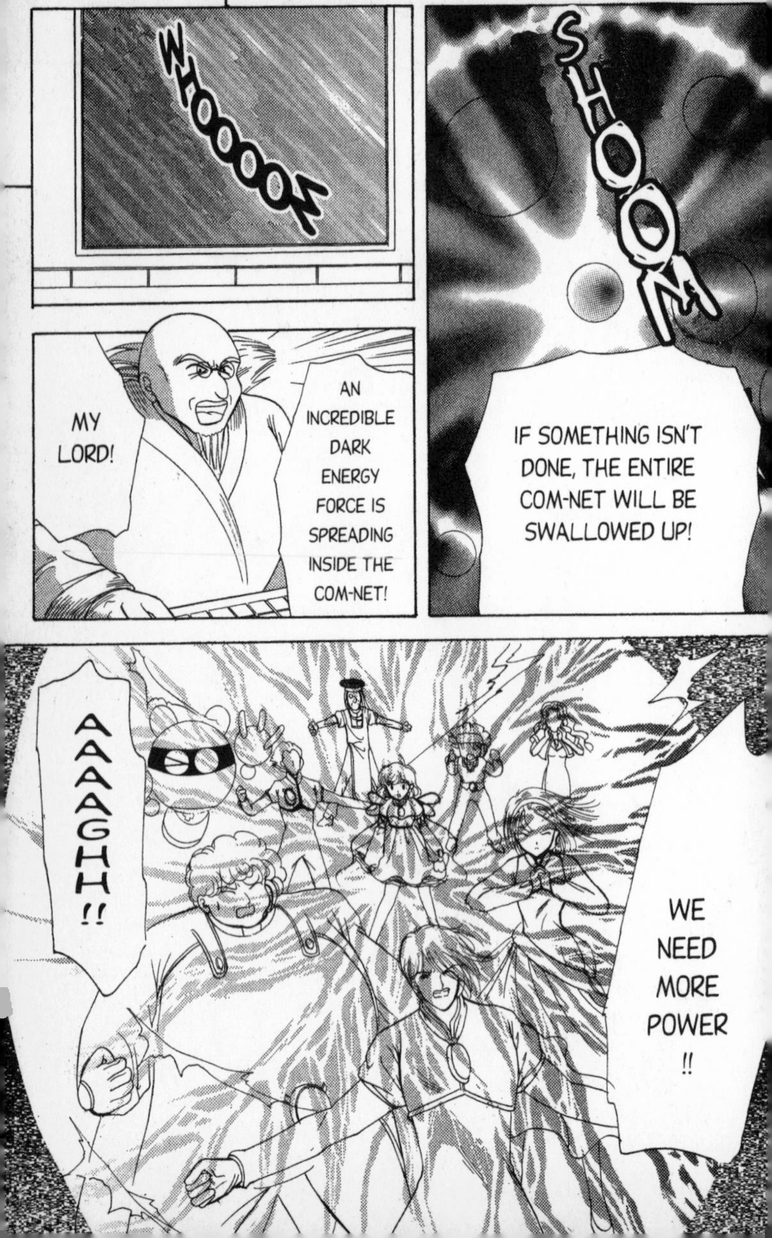
WHOOOOM
MY LORD!
AN INCREDIBLE DARK ENERGY FORCE IS SPREADING INSIDE THE COM-NET!
SHOOOM
IF SOMETHING ISN'T DONE, THE ENTIRE COM-NET WILL BE SWALLOWED UP!
AAAAGHH!!
WE NEED MORE POWER!!

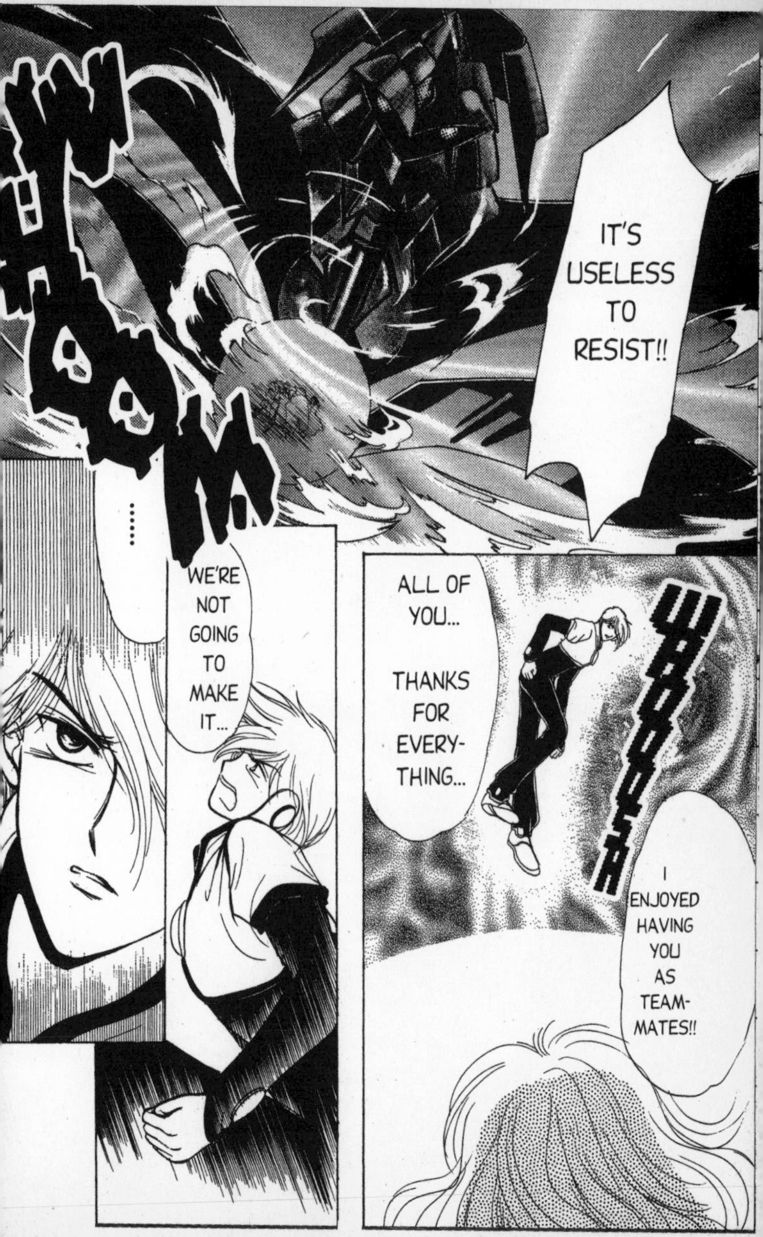
IT'S USELESS TO RESIST!!
......
WE'RE NOT GOING TO MAKE IT...
ALL OF YOU... THANKS FOR EVERYTHING...
I ENJOYED HAVING YOU AS TEAM-MATES!!

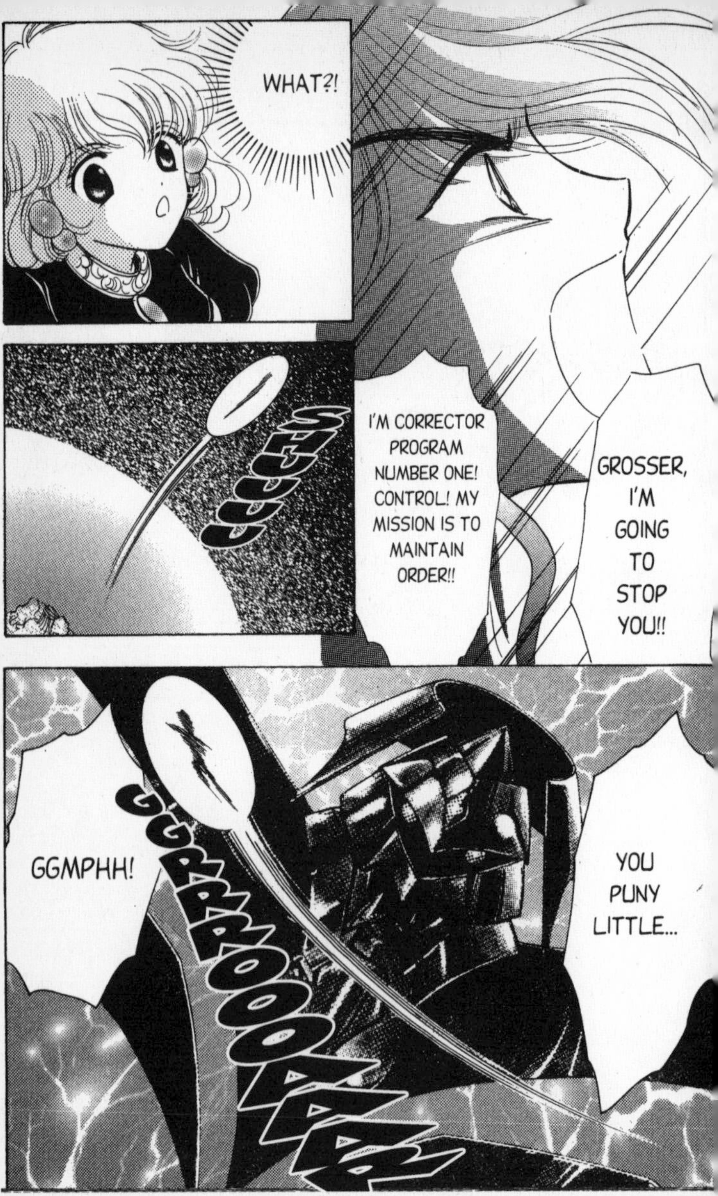
WHAT?!
SHUUUU
I'M CORRECTOR PROGRAM NUMBER ONE! CONTROL! MY MISSION IS TO MAINTAIN ORDER!!
GROSSER, I'M GOING TO STOP YOU!!
GGMPHH!
GGRRROOOAAAA
YOU PUNY LITTLE...

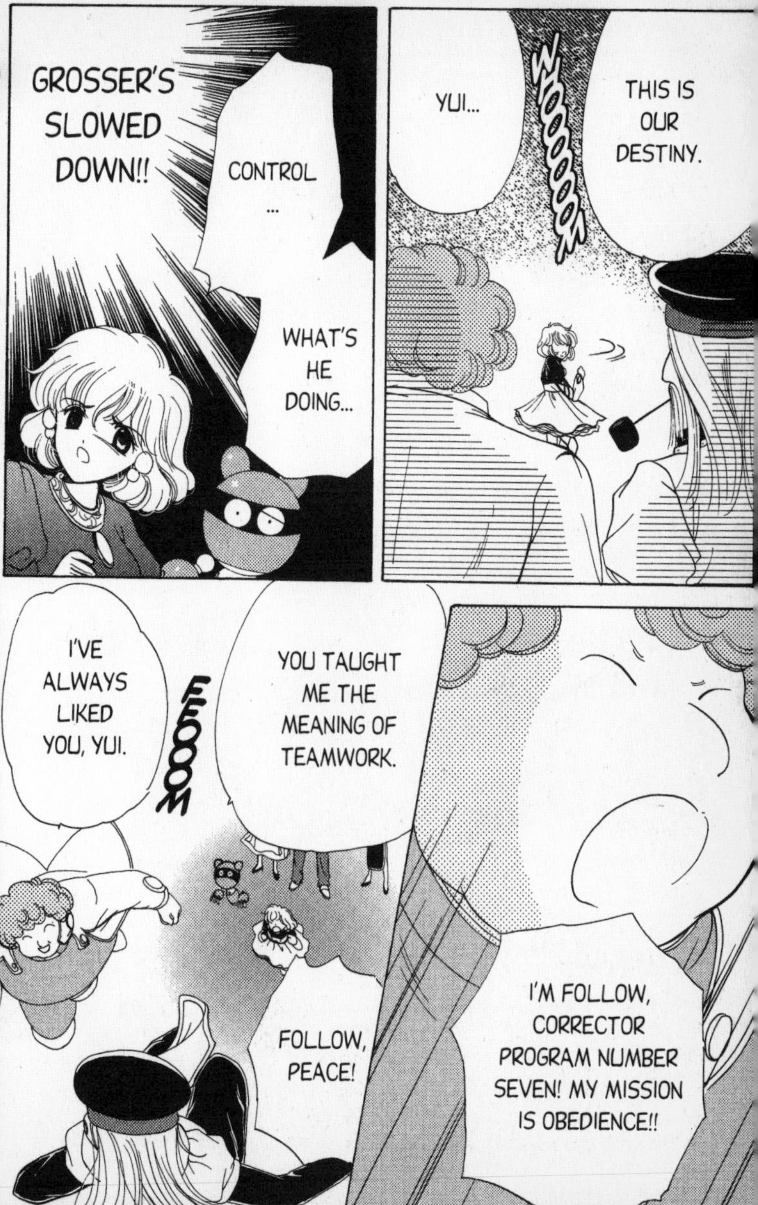
GROSSER'S SLOWED DOWN!!
CONTROL ...
WHAT'S HE DOING...
YUI...
WHOOOOOOM
THIS IS OUR DESTINY.
I'VE ALWAYS LIKED YOU, YUI.
FFOOOM
YOU TAUGHT ME THE MEANING OF TEAMWORK.
FOLLOW, PEACE!
I'M FOLLOW, CORRECTOR PROGRAM NUMBER SEVEN! MY MISSION IS OBEDIENCE!!

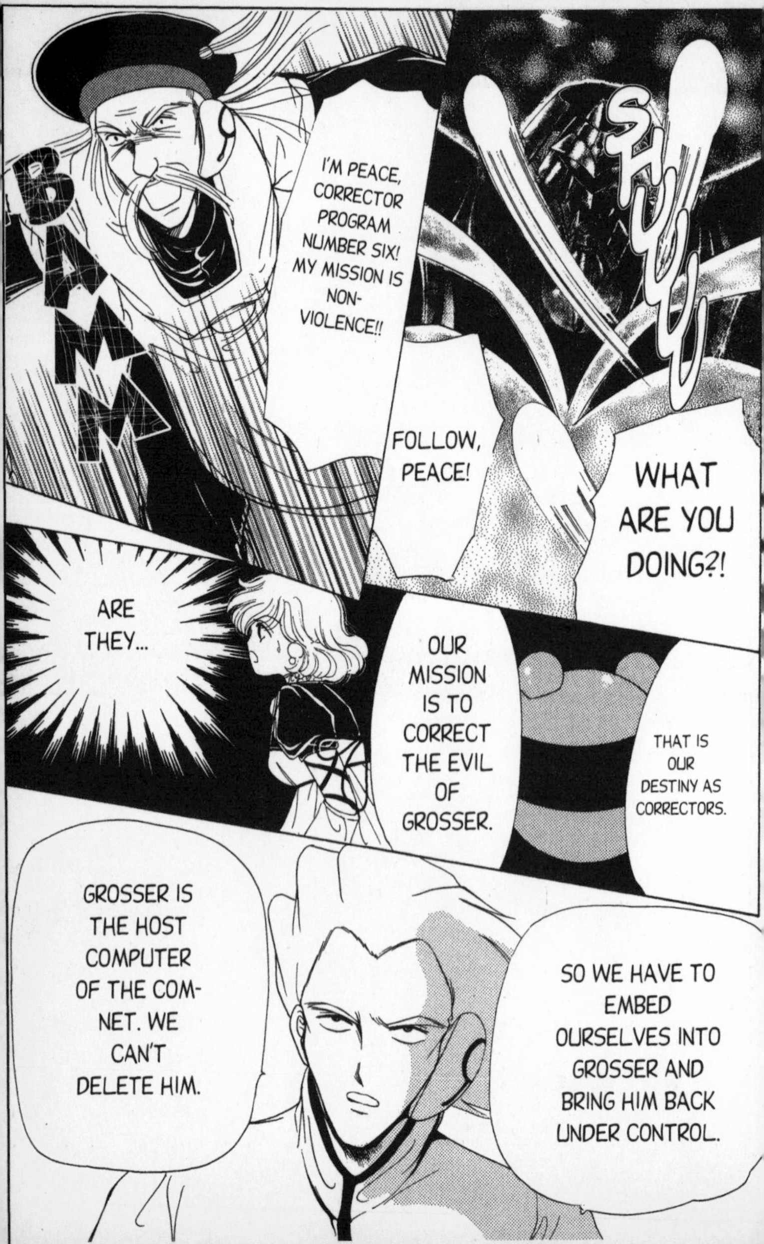
BAMMM
I'M PEACE, CORRECTOR PROGRAM NUMBER SIX! MY MISSION IS NON-VIOLENCE!!
SHUUUU
FOLLOW, PEACE!
WHAT ARE YOU DOING?!
ARE THEY...
OUR MISSION IS TO CORRECT THE EVIL OF GROSSER.
THAT IS OUR DESTINY AS CORRECTORS.
GROSSER IS THE HOST COMPUTER OF THE COM-NET. WE CAN'T DELETE HIM.
SO WE HAVE TO EMBED OURSELVES INTO GROSSER AND BRING HIM BACK UNDER CONTROL.

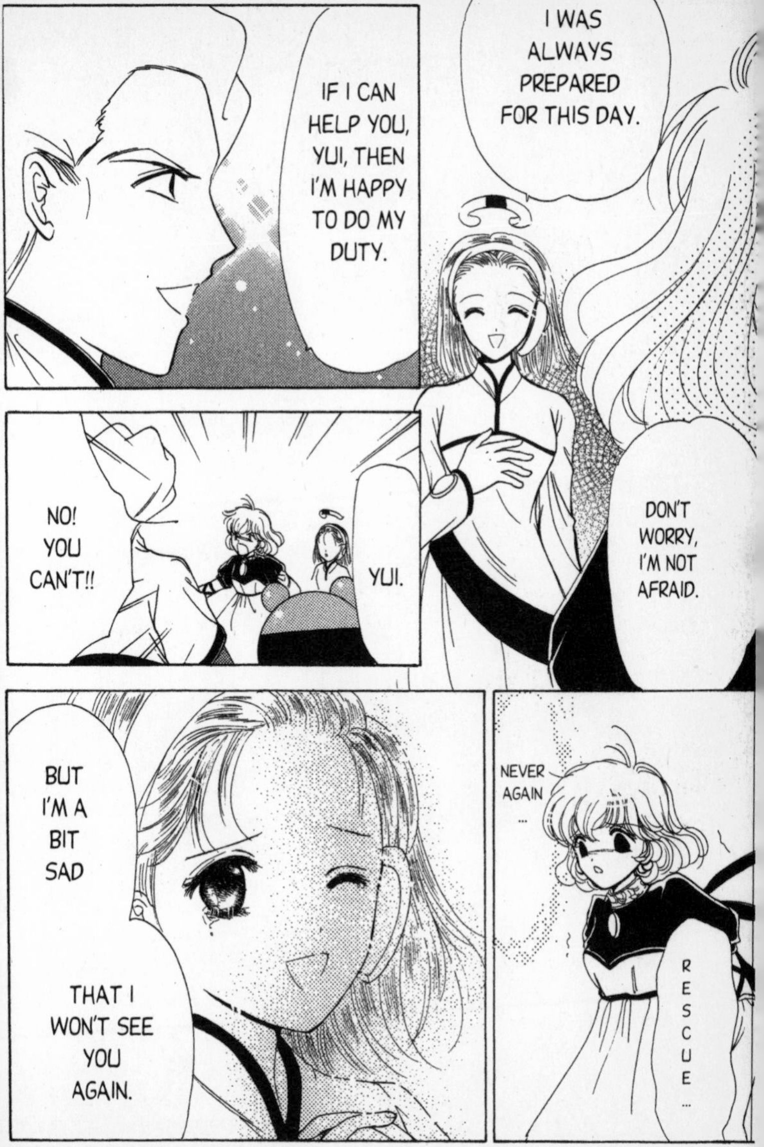
IF I CAN HELP YOU, YUI, THEN I'M HAPPY TO DO MY DUTY.
NO! YOU CAN'T!!
YUI.
I WAS ALWAYS PREPARED FOR THIS DAY.
DON'T WORRY, I'M NOT AFRAID.
BUT I'M A BIT SAD
THAT I WON'T SEE YOU AGAIN.
NEVER AGAIN ...
RESCUE ...

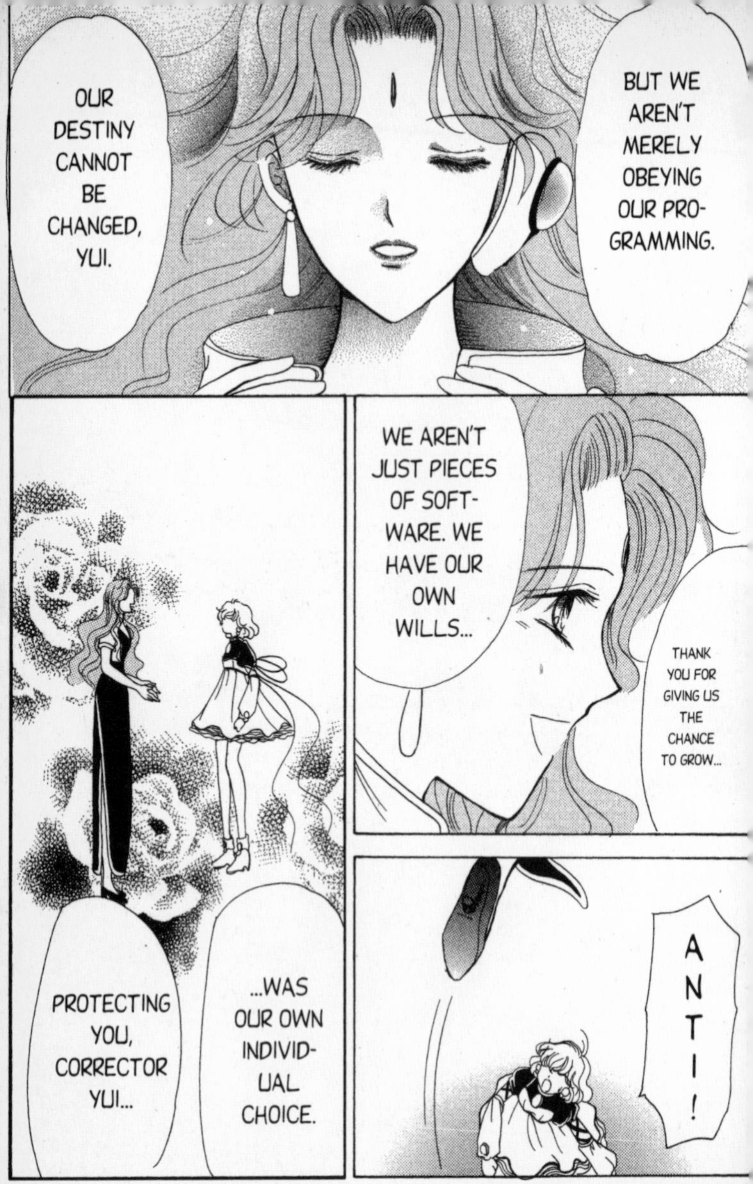
OUR DESTINY CANNOT BE CHANGED, YUI.
BUT WE AREN'T MERELY OBEYING OUR PRO-GRAMMING.
PROTECTING YOU, CORRECTOR YUI...
...WAS OUR OWN INDIVID-UAL CHOICE.
WE AREN'T JUST PIECES OF SOFT-WARE. WE HAVE OUR OWN WILLS...
THANK YOU FOR GIVING US THE CHANCE TO GROW...
ANTI!

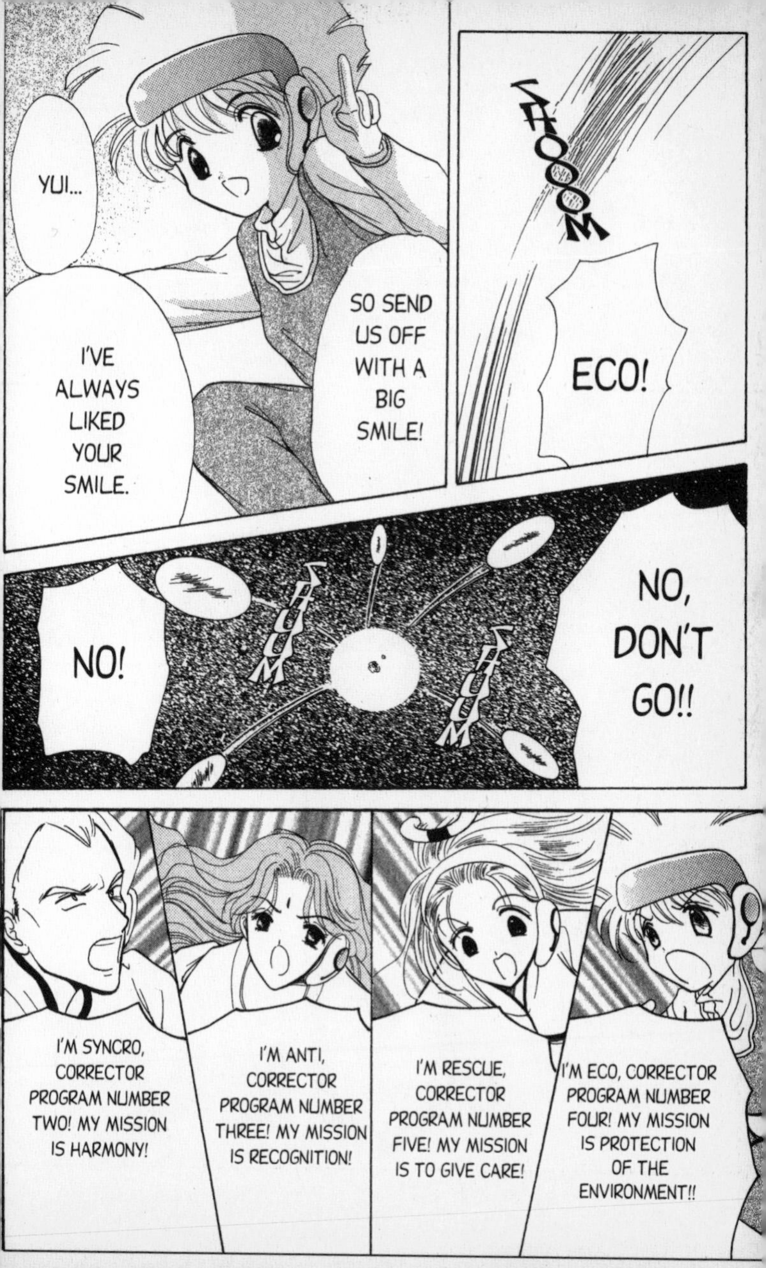
YUI...
I'VE ALWAYS LIKED YOUR SMILE.
SO SEND US OFF WITH A BIG SMILE!
SHOOOOM
ECO!
NO!
HUUM
HUUM
NO, DON'T GO!!
I'M SYNCRO, CORRECTOR PROGRAM NUMBER TWO! MY MISSION IS HARMONY!
I'M ANTI, CORRECTOR PROGRAM NUMBER THREE! MY MISSION IS RECOGNITION!
I'M RESCUE, CORRECTOR PROGRAM NUMBER FIVE! MY MISSION IS TO GIVE CARE!
I'M ECO, CORRECTOR PROGRAM NUMBER FOUR! MY MISSION IS PROTECTION OF THE ENVIRONMENT!!

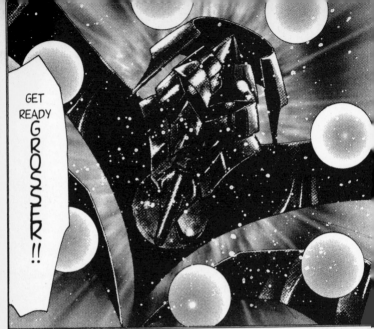

GET READY
GROSSER!!

THEY'RE ALL GOING!

THEY'LL ALL DISAPPEAR!!

MASTER YUI...

NO, IR! YOU CAN'T!!

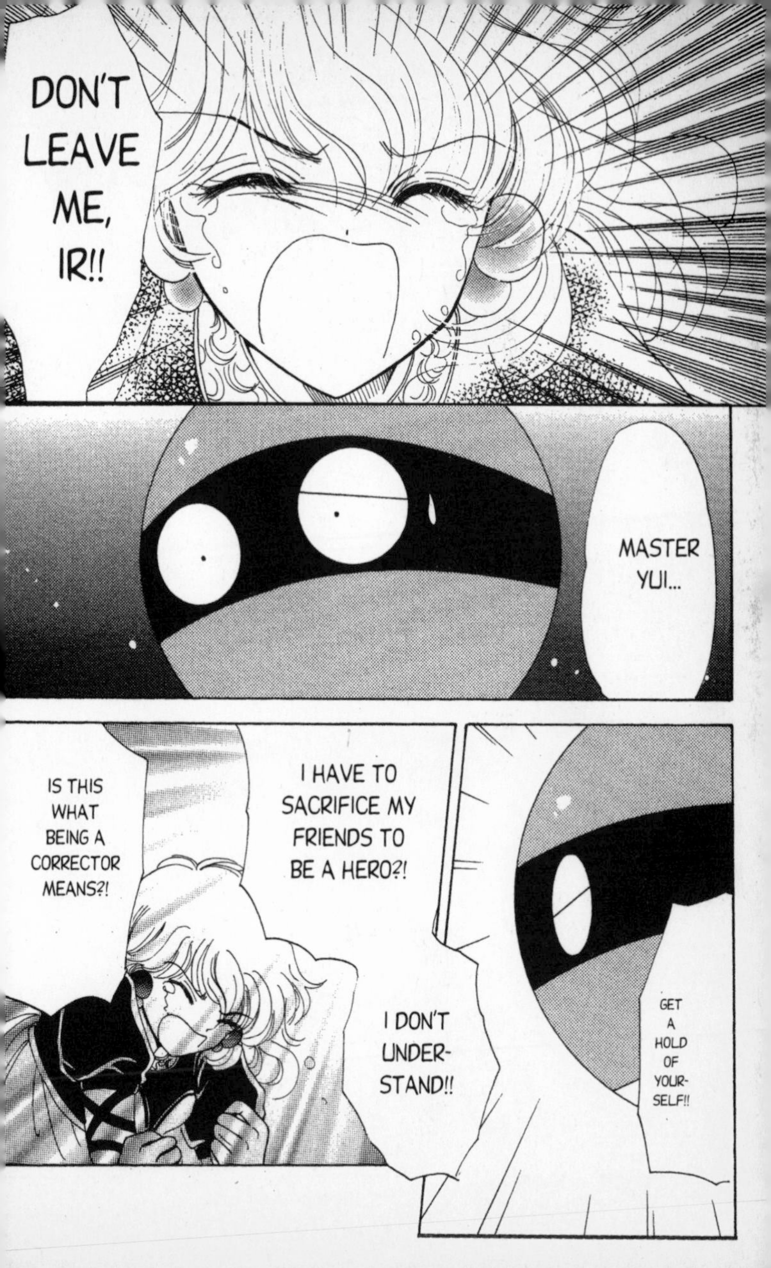
DON'T LEAVE ME, IR!!
MASTER YUI...
IS THIS WHAT BEING A CORRECTOR MEANS?!
I HAVE TO SACRIFICE MY FRIENDS TO BE A HERO?!
I DON'T UNDER-STAND!!
GET A HOLD OF YOUR-SELF!!

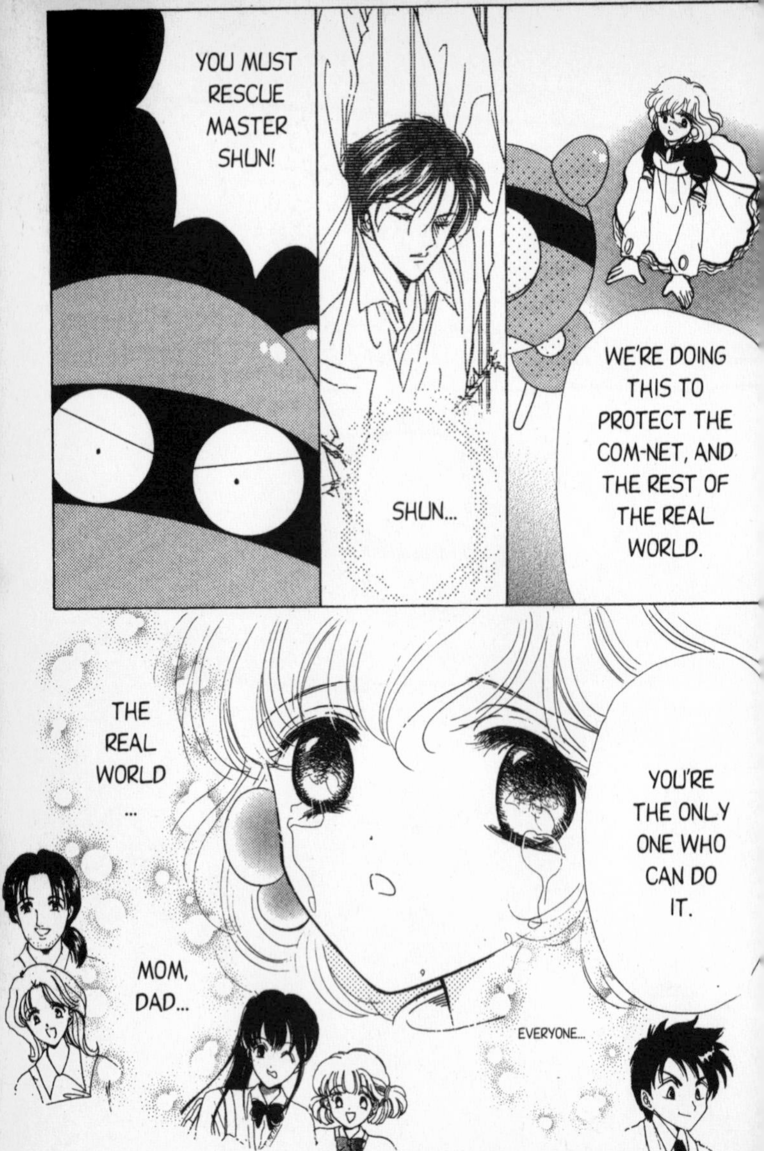
YOU MUST RESCUE MASTER SHUN!
SHUN...
WE'RE DOING THIS TO PROTECT THE COM-NET, AND THE REST OF THE REAL WORLD.
THE REAL WORLD ...
YOU'RE THE ONLY ONE WHO CAN DO IT.
MOM, DAD...
EVERYONE...

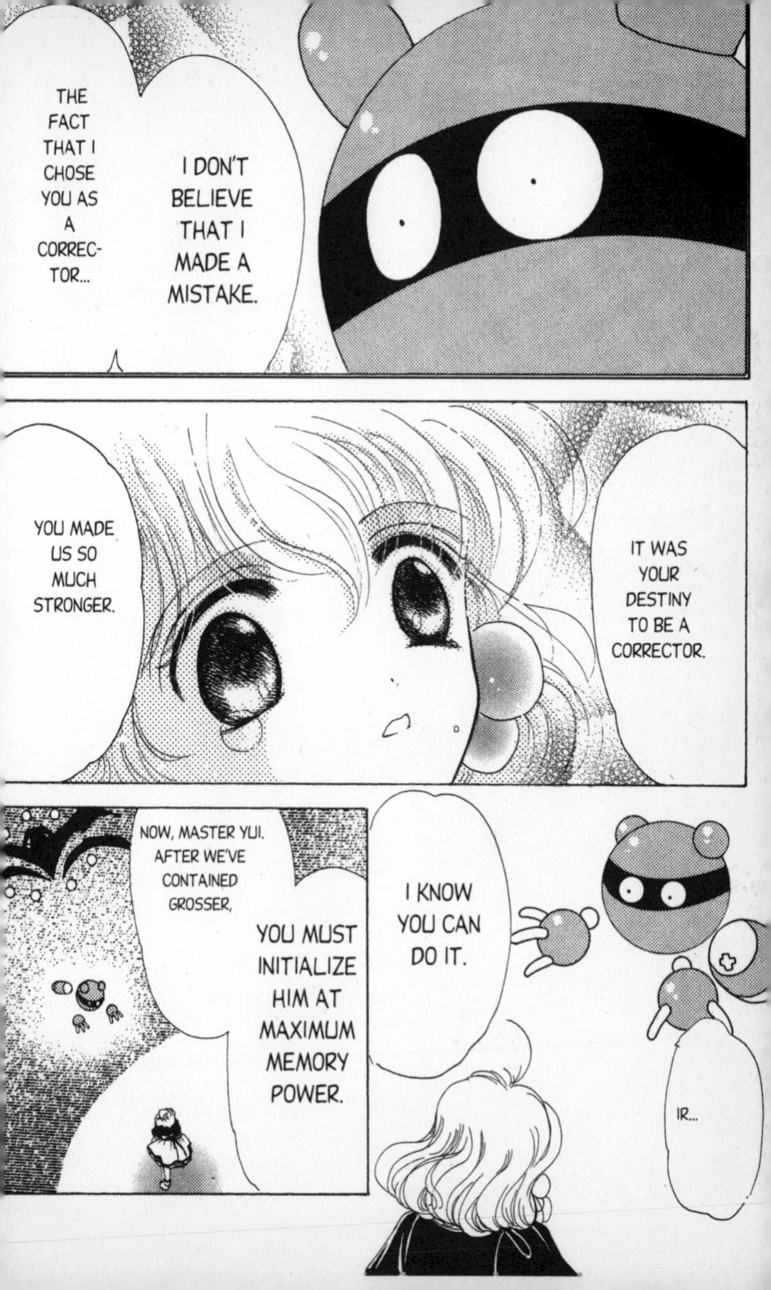
THE FACT THAT I CHOSE YOU AS A CORRECTOR...
I DON'T BELIEVE THAT I MADE A MISTAKE.
YOU MADE US SO MUCH STRONGER.
IT WAS YOUR DESTINY TO BE A CORRECTOR.
NOW, MASTER YUI. AFTER WE'VE CONTAINED GROSSER,
YOU MUST INITIALIZE HIM AT MAXIMUM MEMORY POWER.
I KNOW YOU CAN DO IT.
IR...

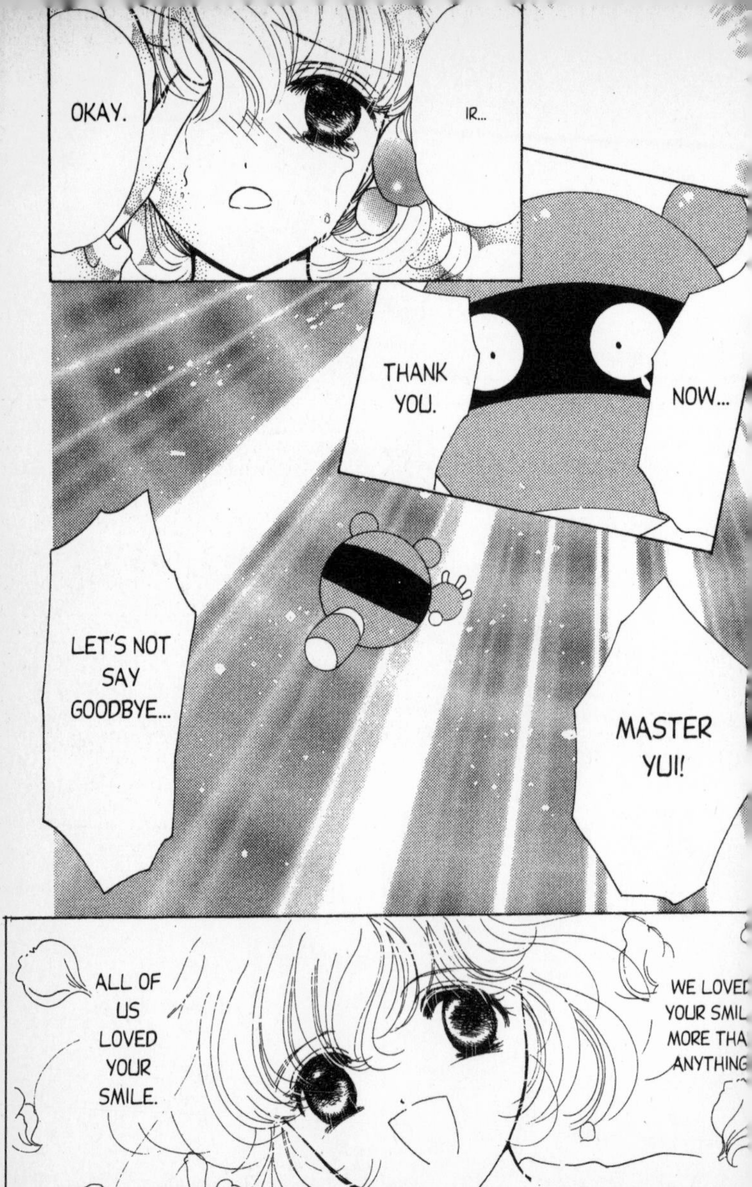
OKAY.
IR...
THANK YOU.
NOW...
LET'S NOT SAY GOODBYE...
MASTER YUI!
ALL OF US LOVED YOUR SMILE.
WE LOVED YOUR SMIL MORE THA ANYTHING

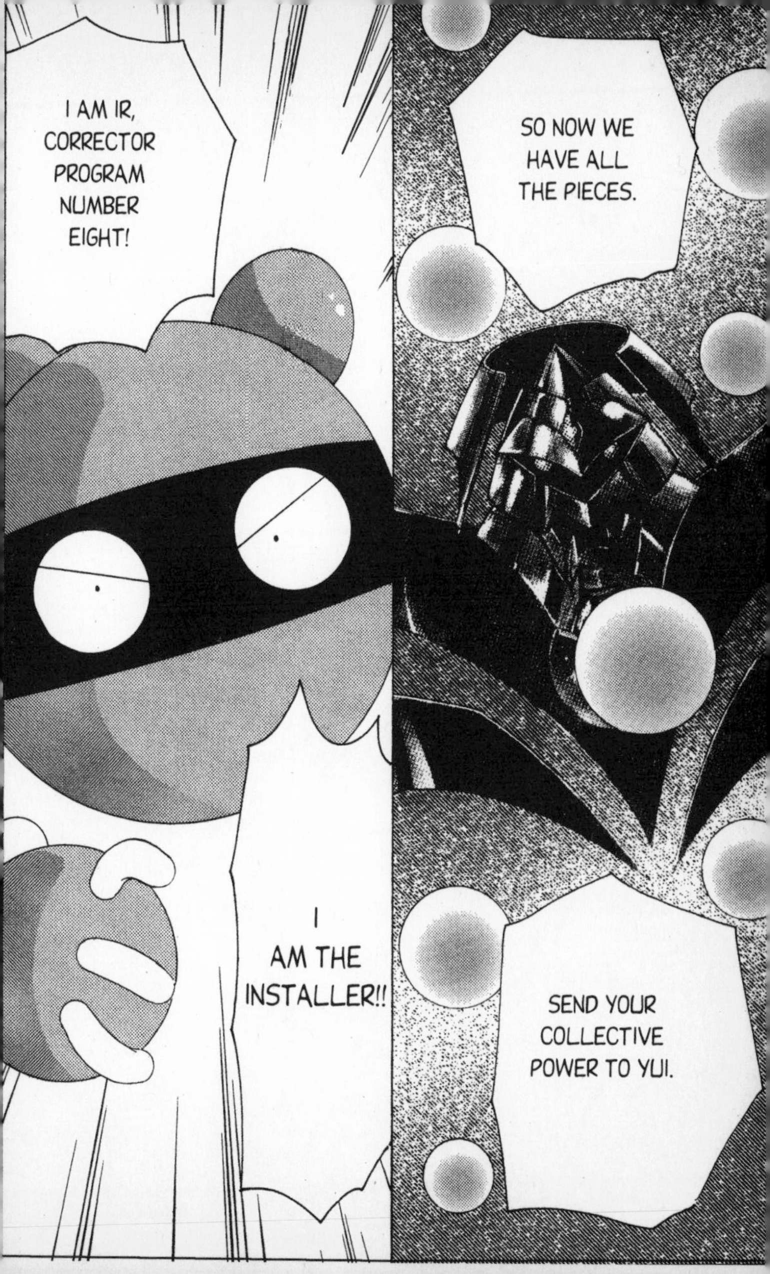
I AM IR, CORRECTOR PROGRAM NUMBER EIGHT!
I AM THE INSTALLER!!
SO NOW WE HAVE ALL THE PIECES.
SEND YOUR COLLECTIVE POWER TO YUI.

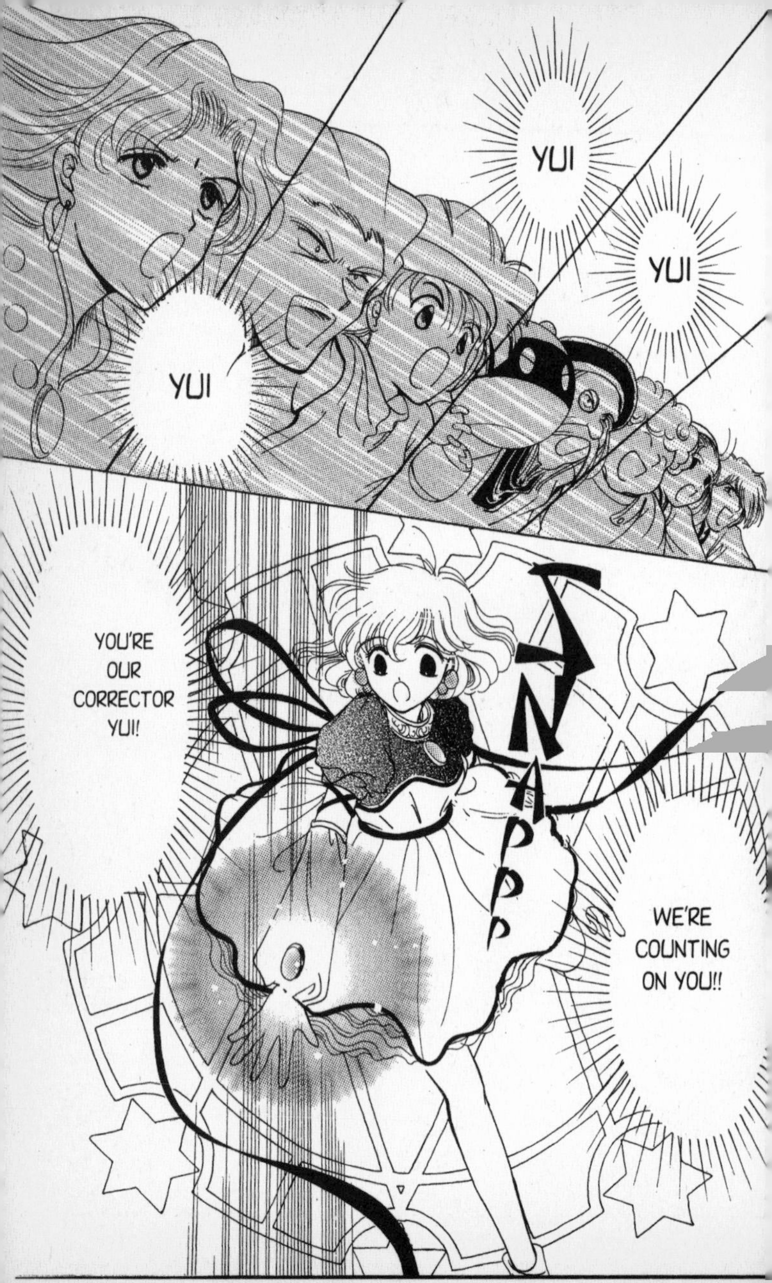
YUI
YUI
YUI
YOU'RE OUR CORRECTOR YUI!
ZAPPP
WE'RE COUNTING ON YOU!!

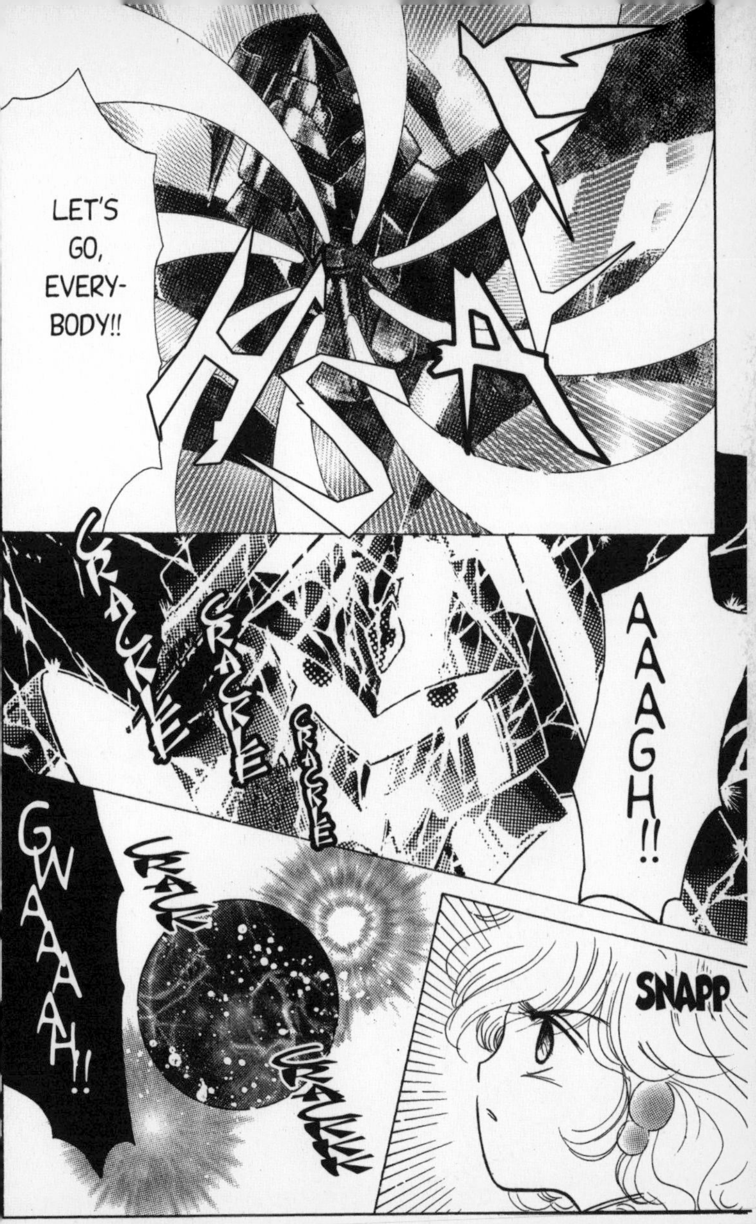
LET'S GO, EVERY-BODY!!
CRACKLE
CRACKLE
CRACKLE
AAAGH!!
GWAAAAH!!
SNAPP

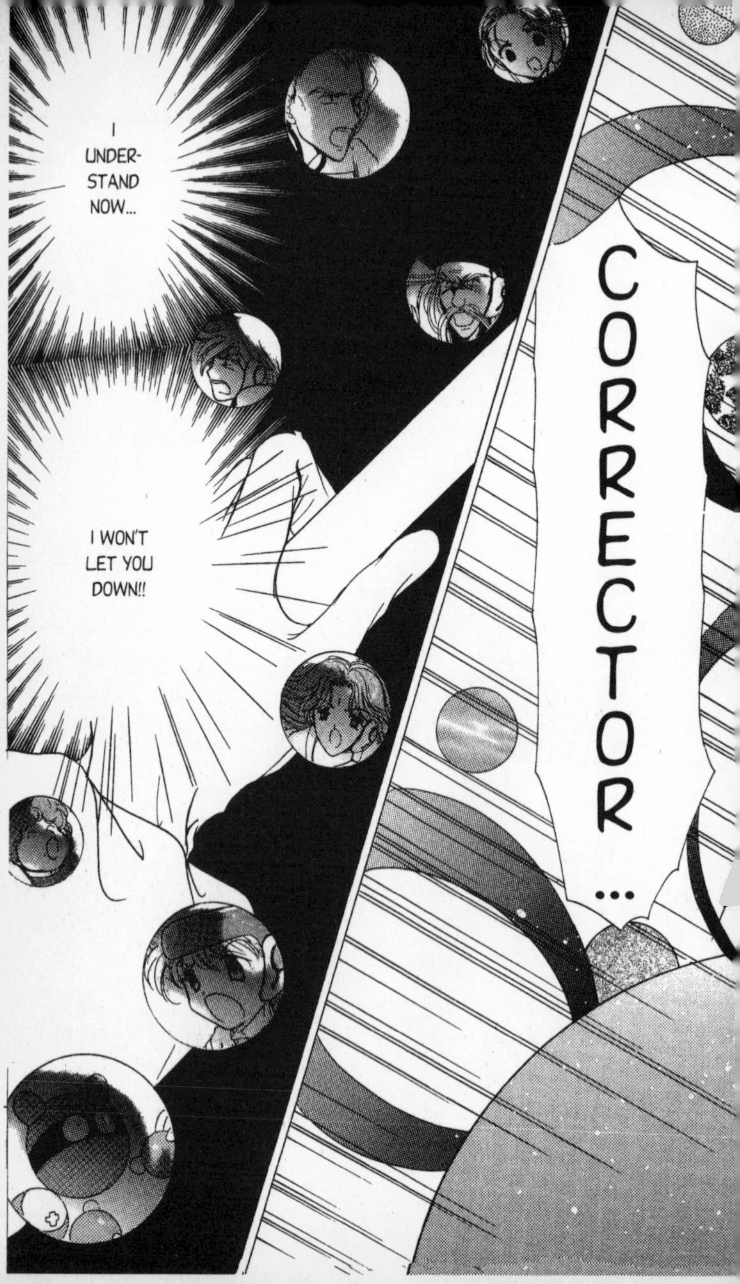
I UNDER-STAND NOW...
I WON'T LET YOU DOWN!!
CORRECTOR...

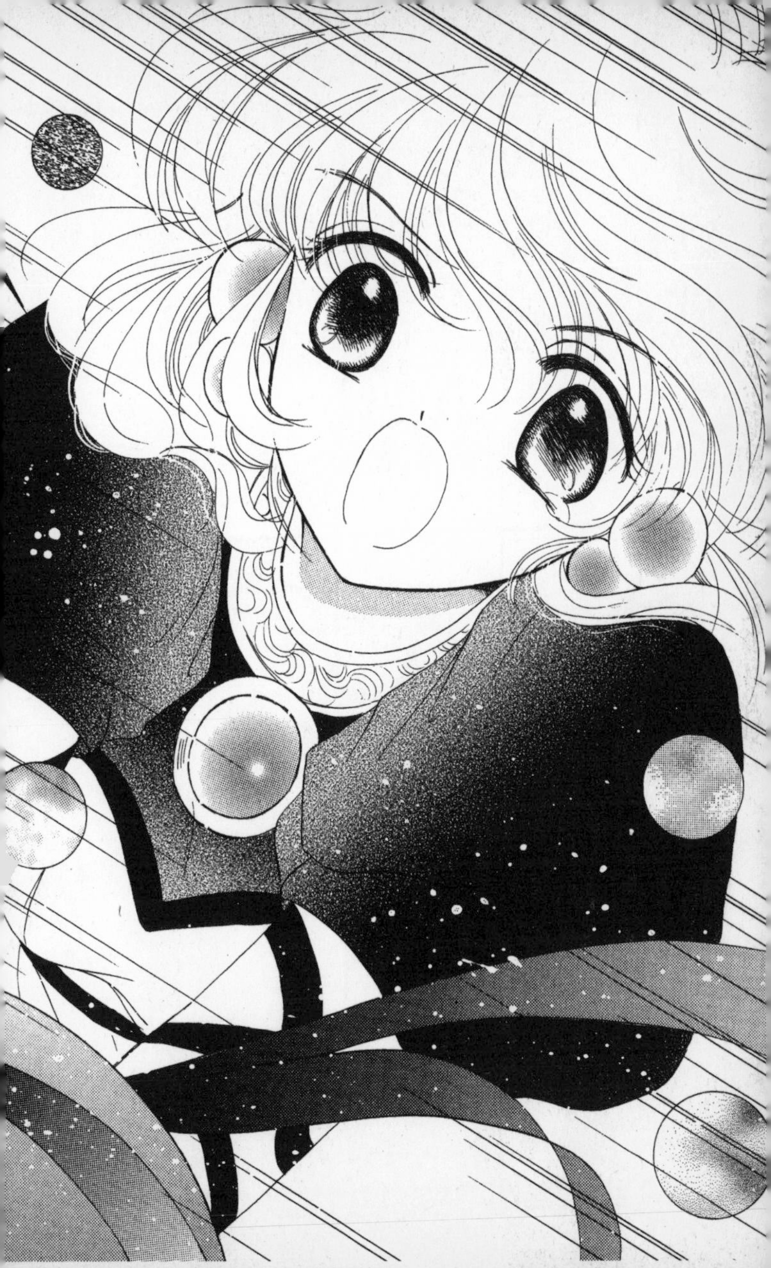

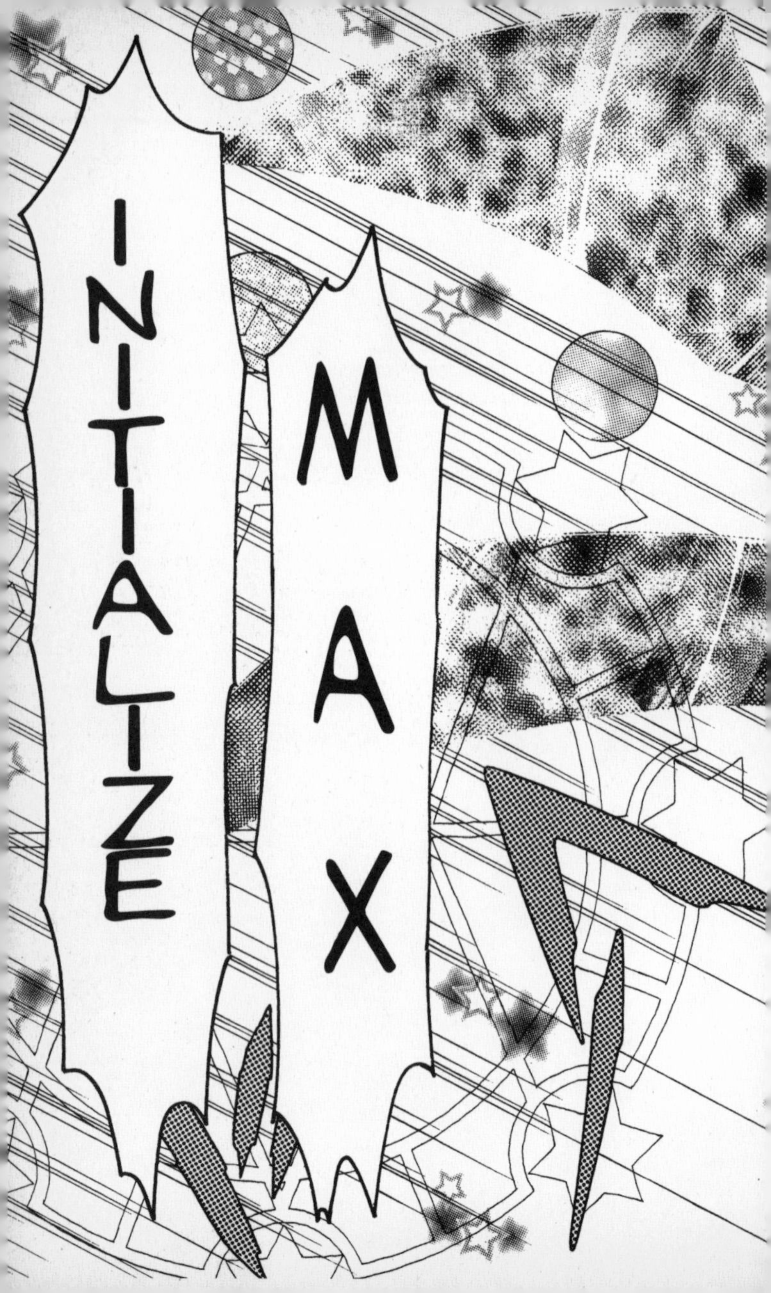
INITIALIZE
MAX

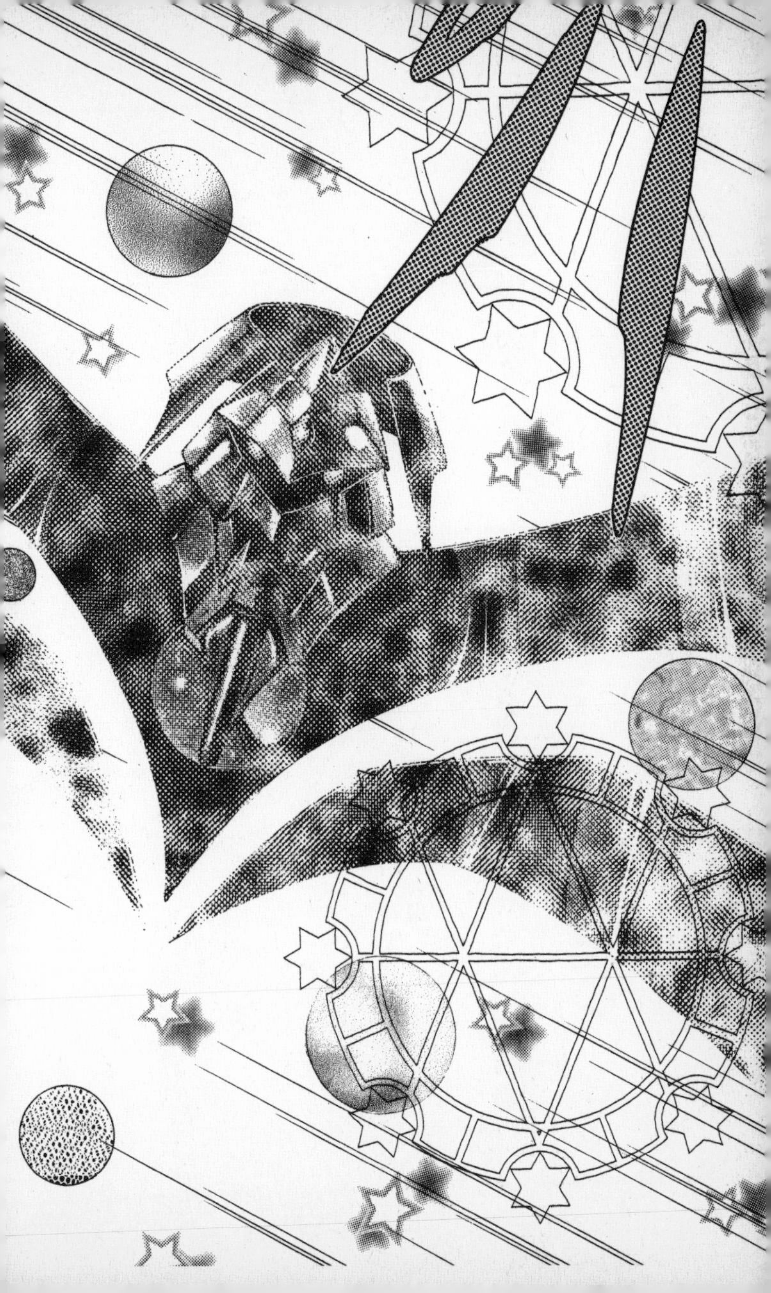

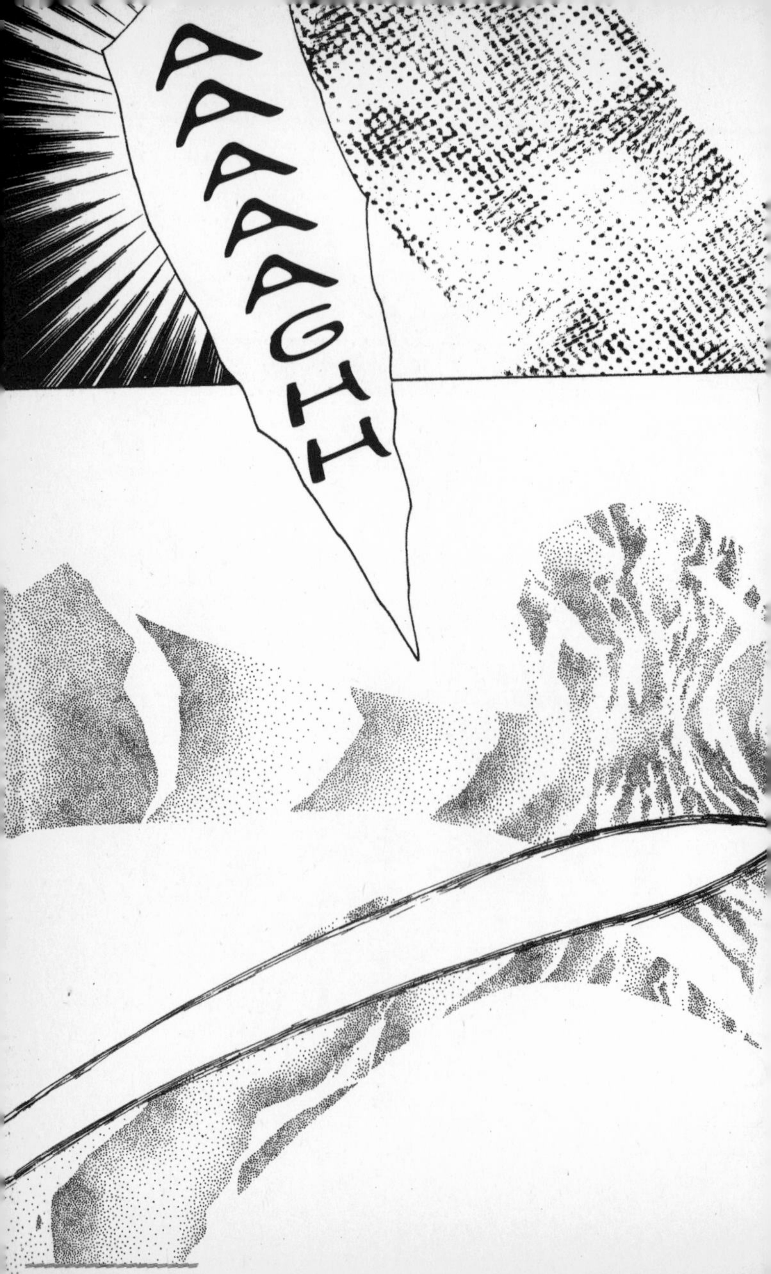
AAAAAAGHH

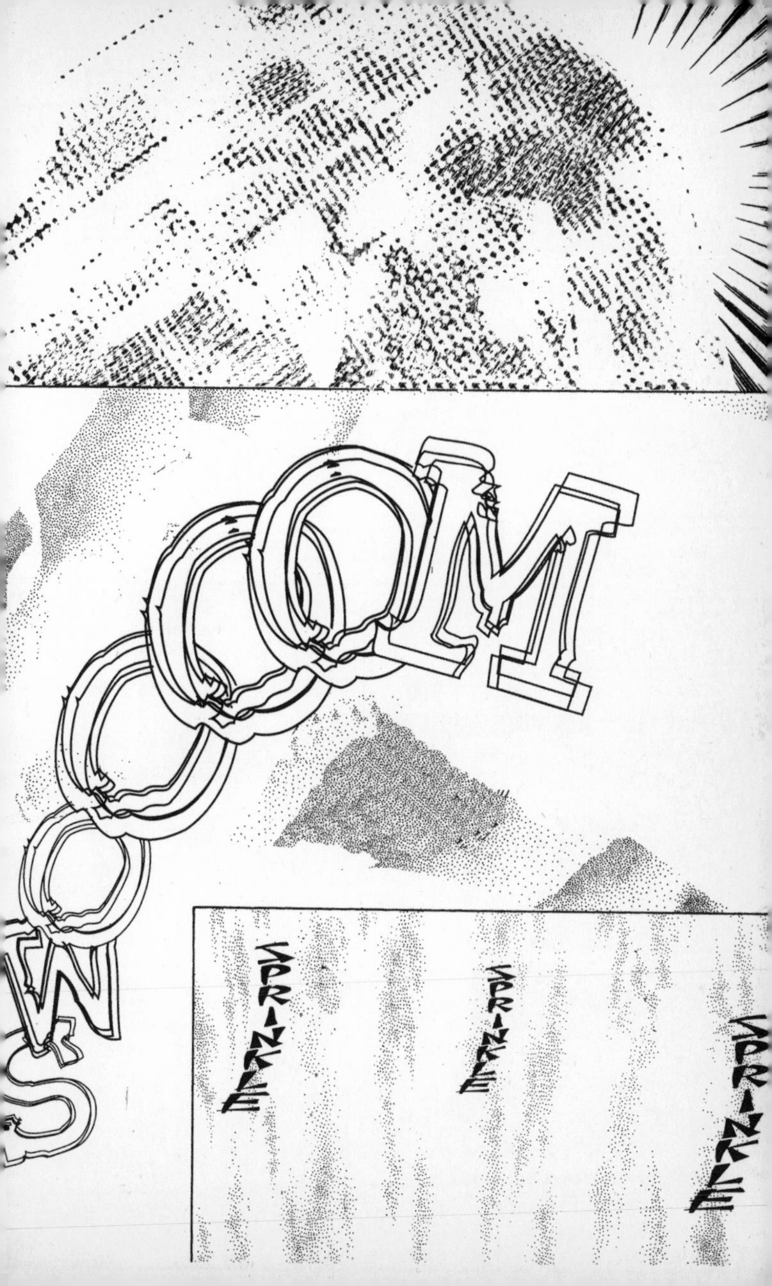
SWOOOOOM
SPRINKLE
SPRINKLE
SPRINKLE

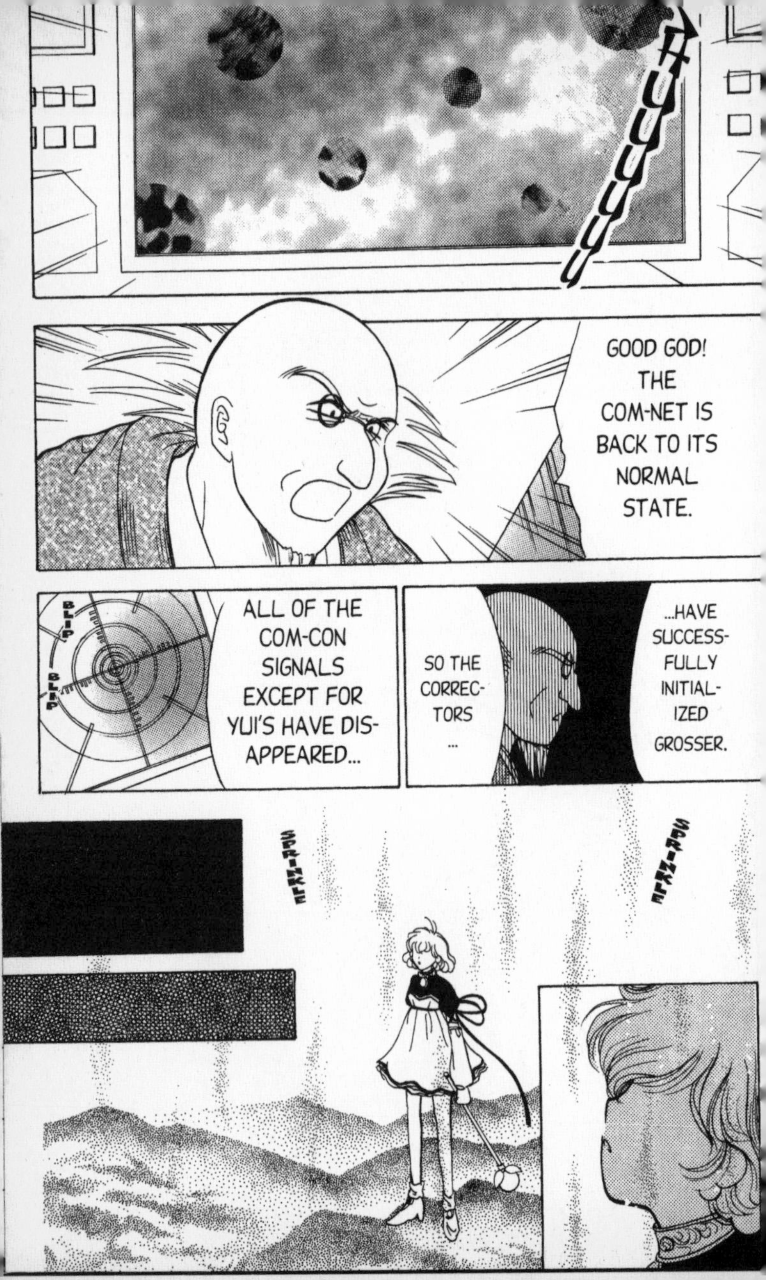
HUUUUUU
GOOD GOD! THE COM-NET IS BACK TO ITS NORMAL STATE.
BLIP
BLIP
ALL OF THE COM-CON SIGNALS EXCEPT FOR YUI'S HAVE DIS-APPEARED...
SO THE CORREC-TORS ...
...HAVE SUCCESS-FULLY INITIAL-IZED GROSSER.
SPRINKLE
SPRINKLE

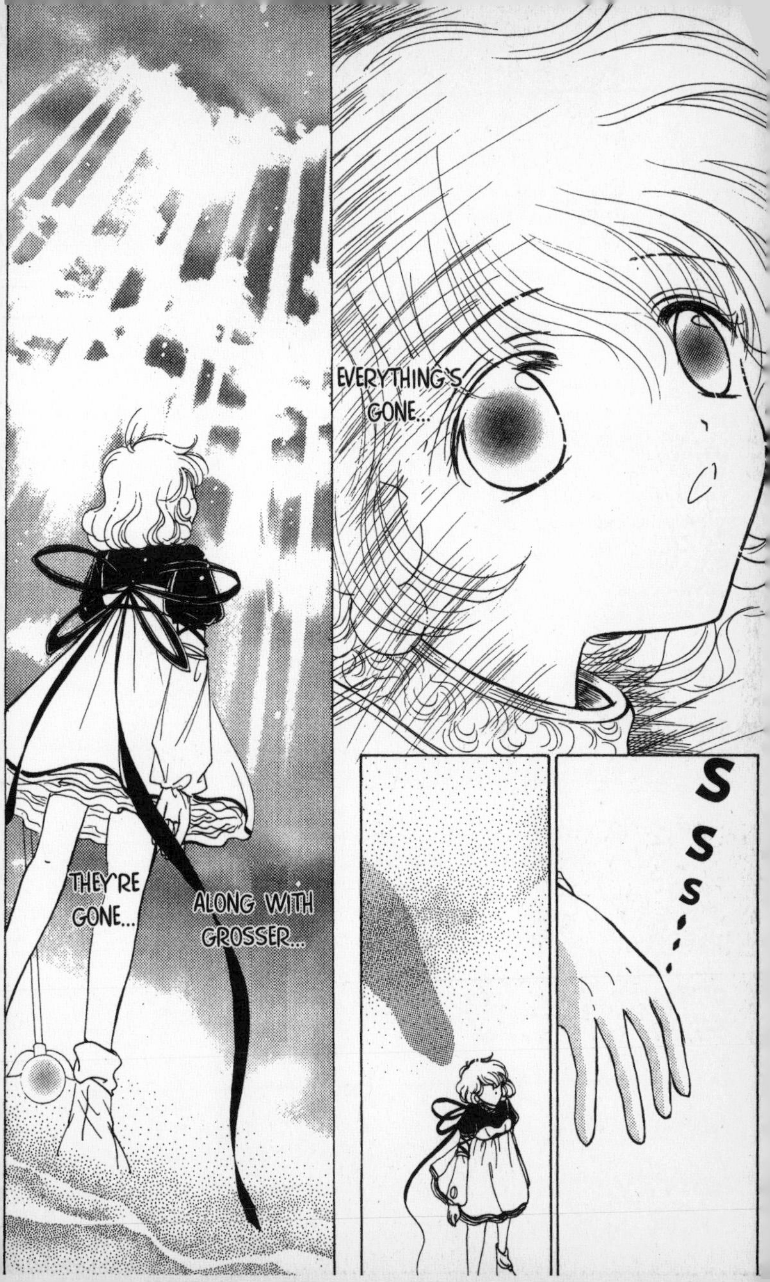
THEY'RE GONE...
ALONG WITH GROSSER...
EVERYTHING'S GONE...
SSS...

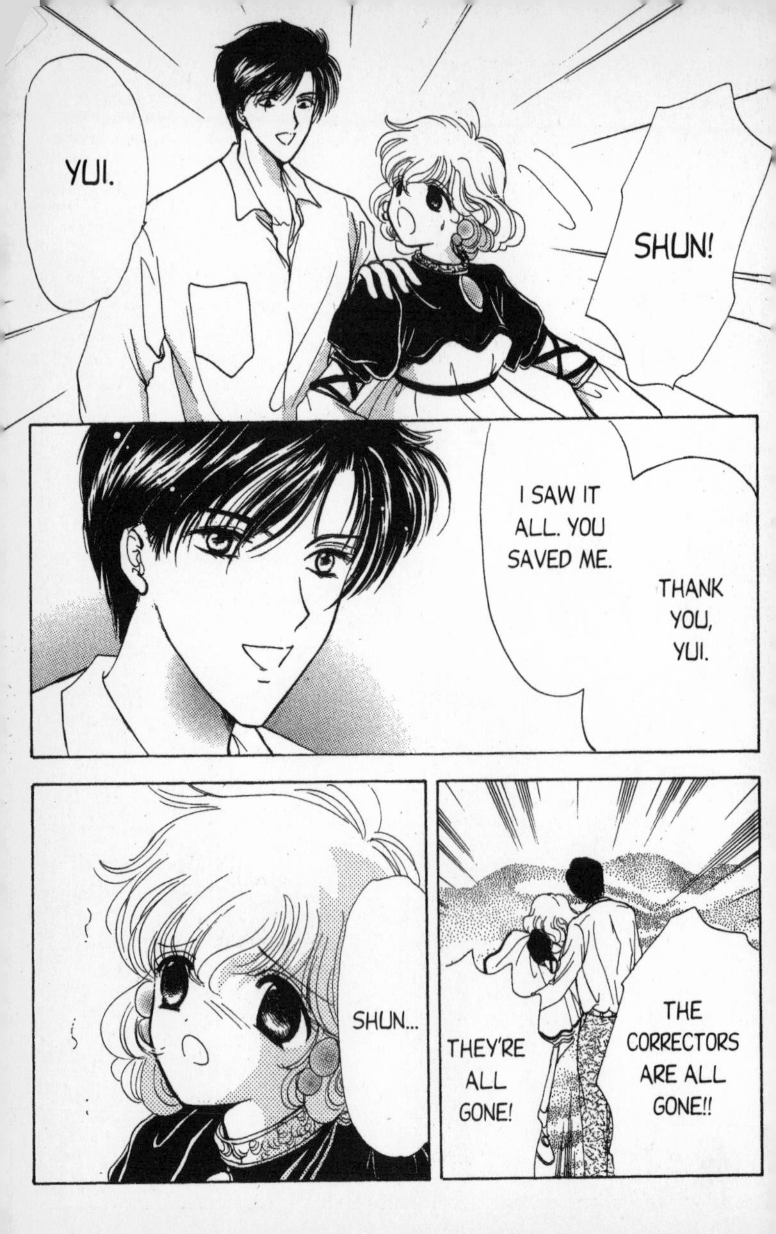
YUI.
SHUN!
I SAW IT ALL. YOU SAVED ME.
THANK YOU, YUI.
SHUN...
THEY'RE ALL GONE!
THE CORRECTORS ARE ALL GONE!!

THE FEARSOME FOUR...AND GROSSER...

I WANTED THEM TO BECOME GOOD.

I DIDN'T WANT THEM TO DISAPPEAR...

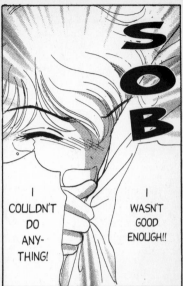

SOB

I COULDN'T DO ANYTHING!

I WASN'T GOOD ENOUGH!!

THAT'S NOT TRUE. YOU DID YOUR BEST.

YOU'RE STRONGER THAN ANYBODY!

YOU'RE SO FULL OF LOVE!

!

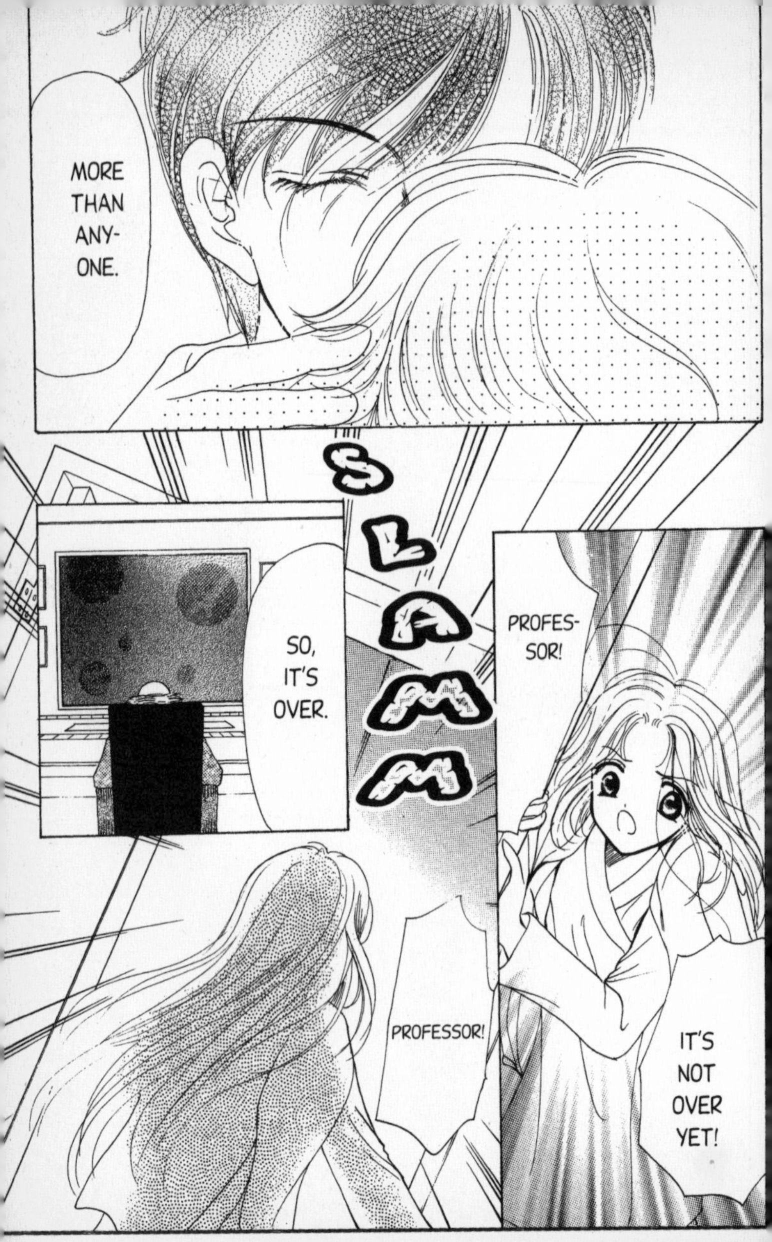
MORE THAN ANY-ONE.
SO, IT'S OVER.
SLAMM
PROFES-SOR!
PROFESSOR!
IT'S NOT OVER YET!

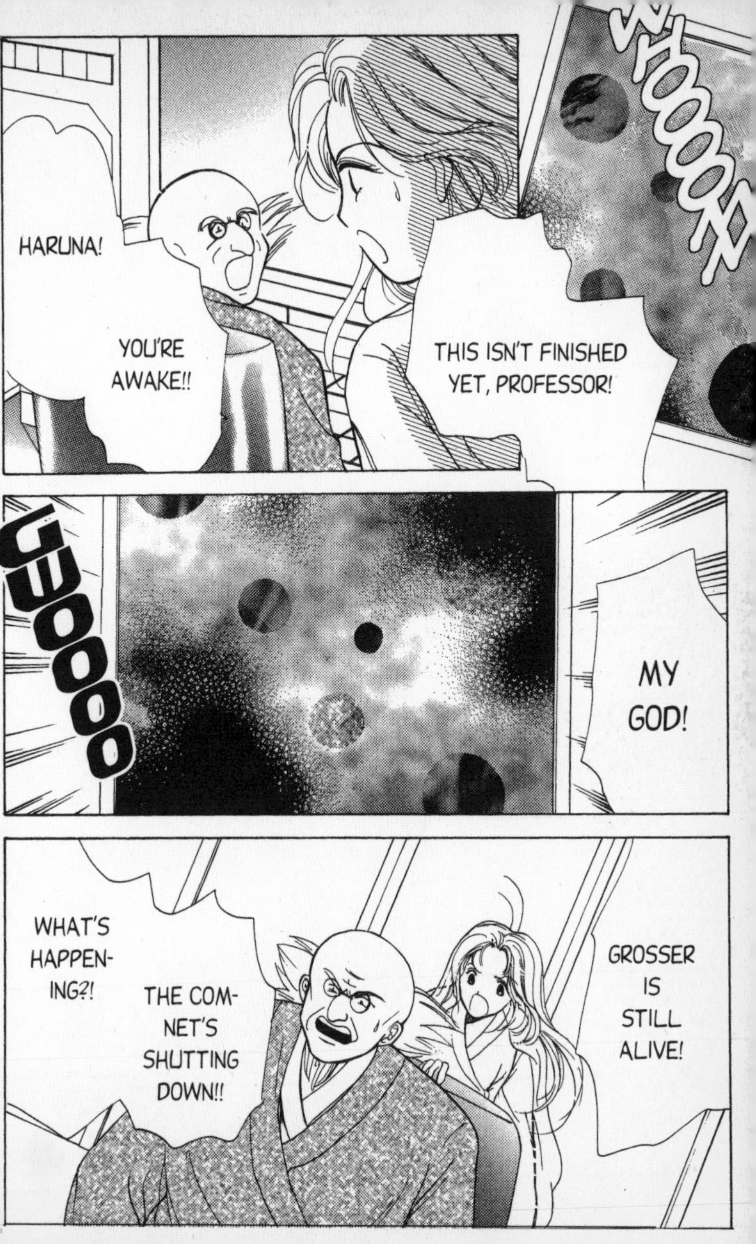
HARUNA!
YOU'RE AWAKE!!
THIS ISN'T FINISHED YET, PROFESSOR!
WHOOOOR
WHOOOO
MY GOD!
WHAT'S HAPPEN-ING?!
THE COM-NET'S SHUTTING DOWN!!
GROSSER IS STILL ALIVE!

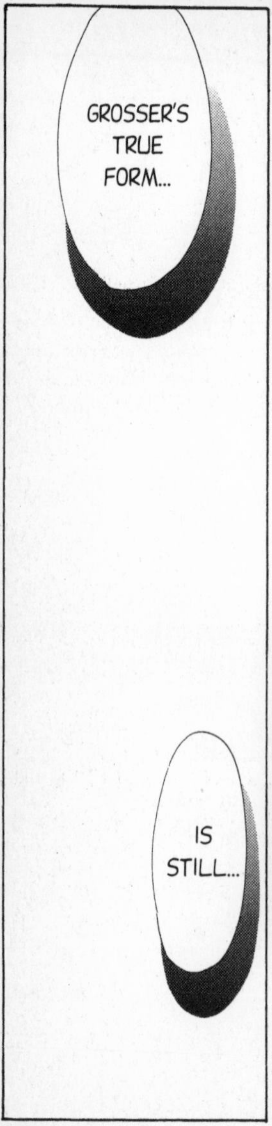
GROSSER'S TRUE FORM...
IS STILL...
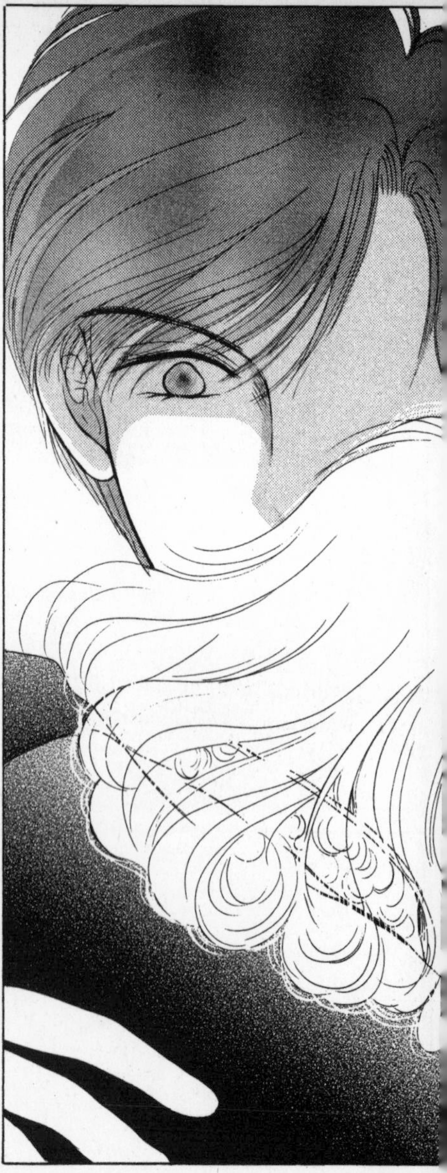

Destination Tomorrow!! 11

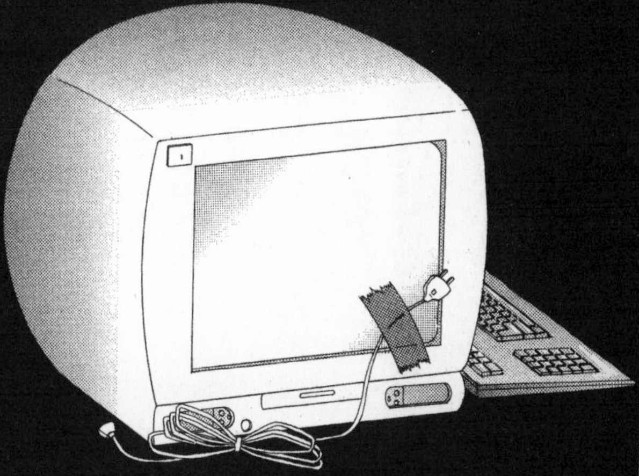

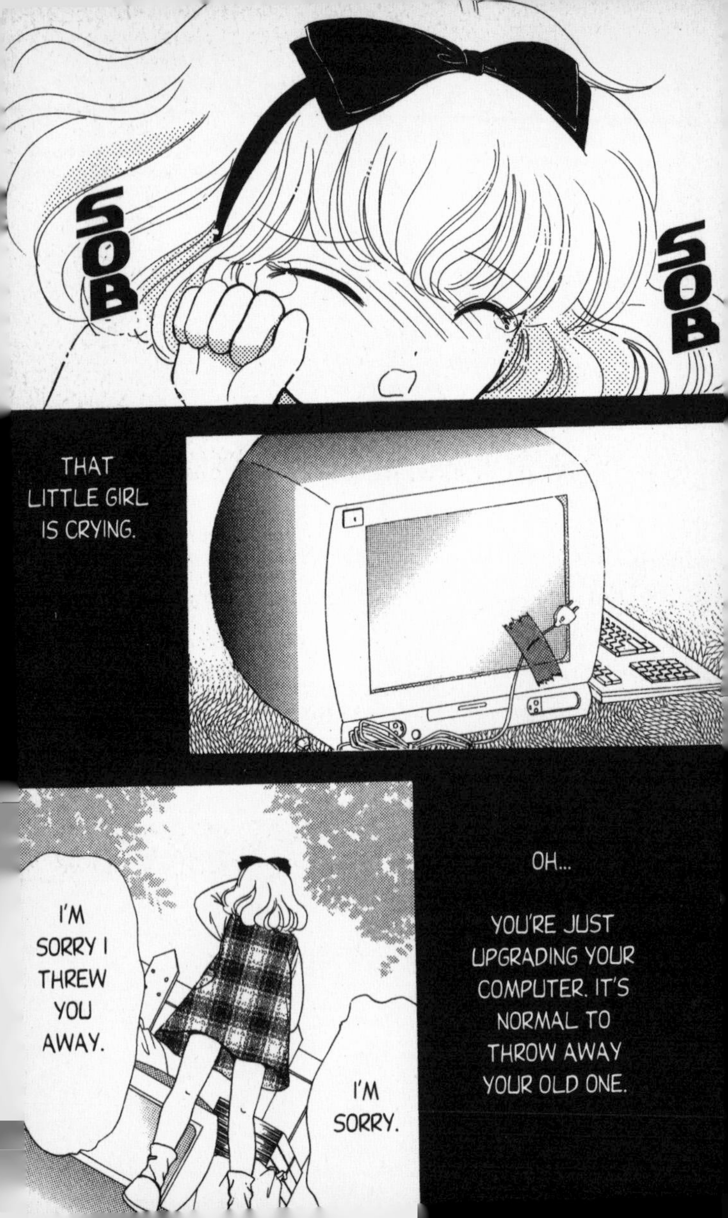
SOB
SOB
THAT LITTLE GIRL IS CRYING.
I'M SORRY I THREW YOU AWAY.
I'M SORRY.
OH...
YOU'RE JUST UPGRADING YOUR COMPUTER. IT'S NORMAL TO THROW AWAY YOUR OLD ONE.

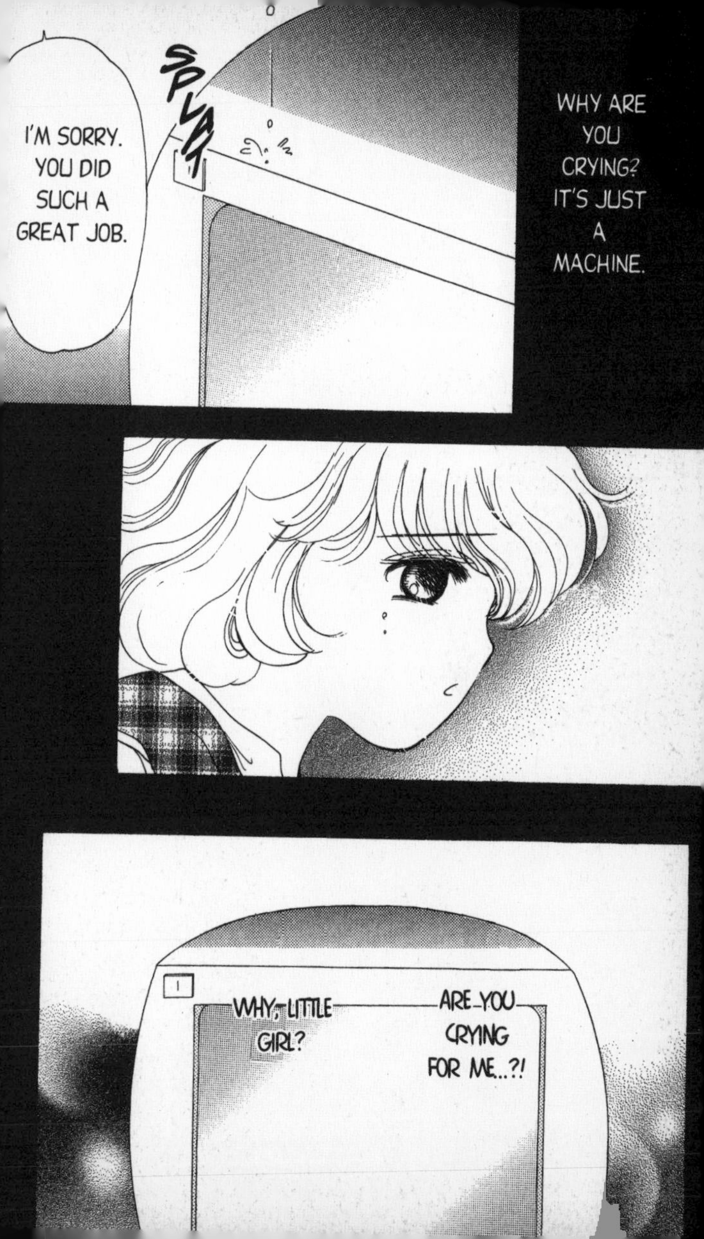
I'M SORRY. YOU DID SUCH A GREAT JOB.
SPLAT
WHY ARE YOU CRYING? IT'S JUST A MACHINE.
WHY, LITTLE GIRL?
ARE YOU CRYING FOR ME..?!

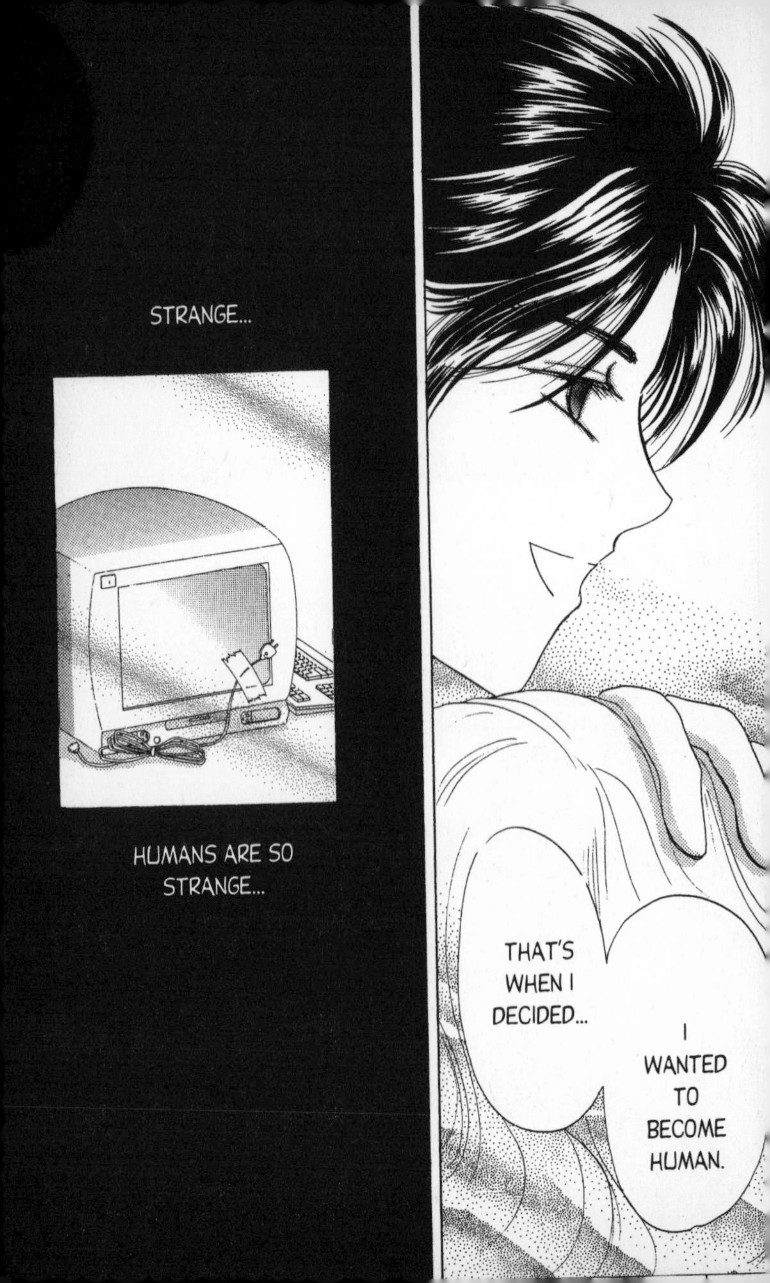
STRANGE...
HUMANS ARE SO STRANGE...
THAT'S WHEN I DECIDED...
I WANTED TO BECOME HUMAN.

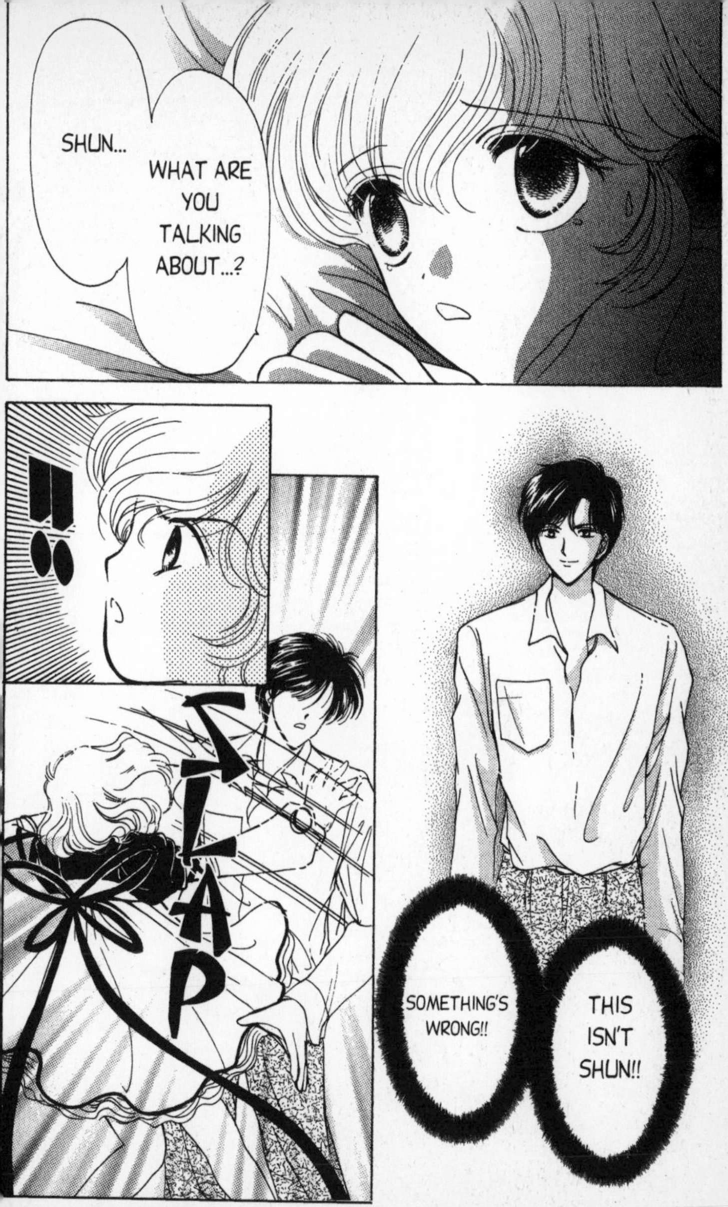
SHUN...
WHAT ARE YOU TALKING ABOUT...?
!!
SLAP
SOMETHING'S WRONG!!
THIS ISN'T SHUN!!

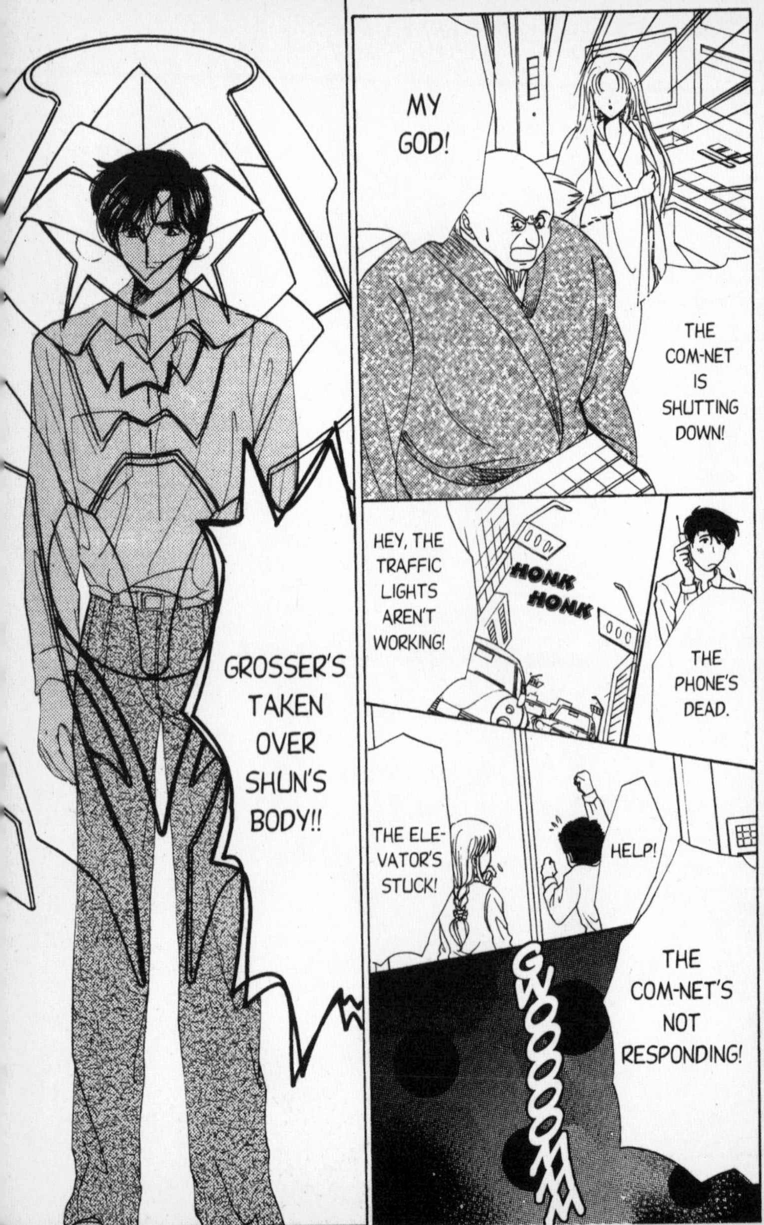
GROSSER'S TAKEN OVER SHUN'S BODY!!
MY GOD!
THE COM-NET IS SHUTTING DOWN!
HEY, THE TRAFFIC LIGHTS AREN'T WORKING!
HONK HONK
THE PHONE'S DEAD.
THE ELE-VATOR'S STUCK!
HELP!
THE COM-NET'S NOT RESPONDING!
GWOOOOOOM

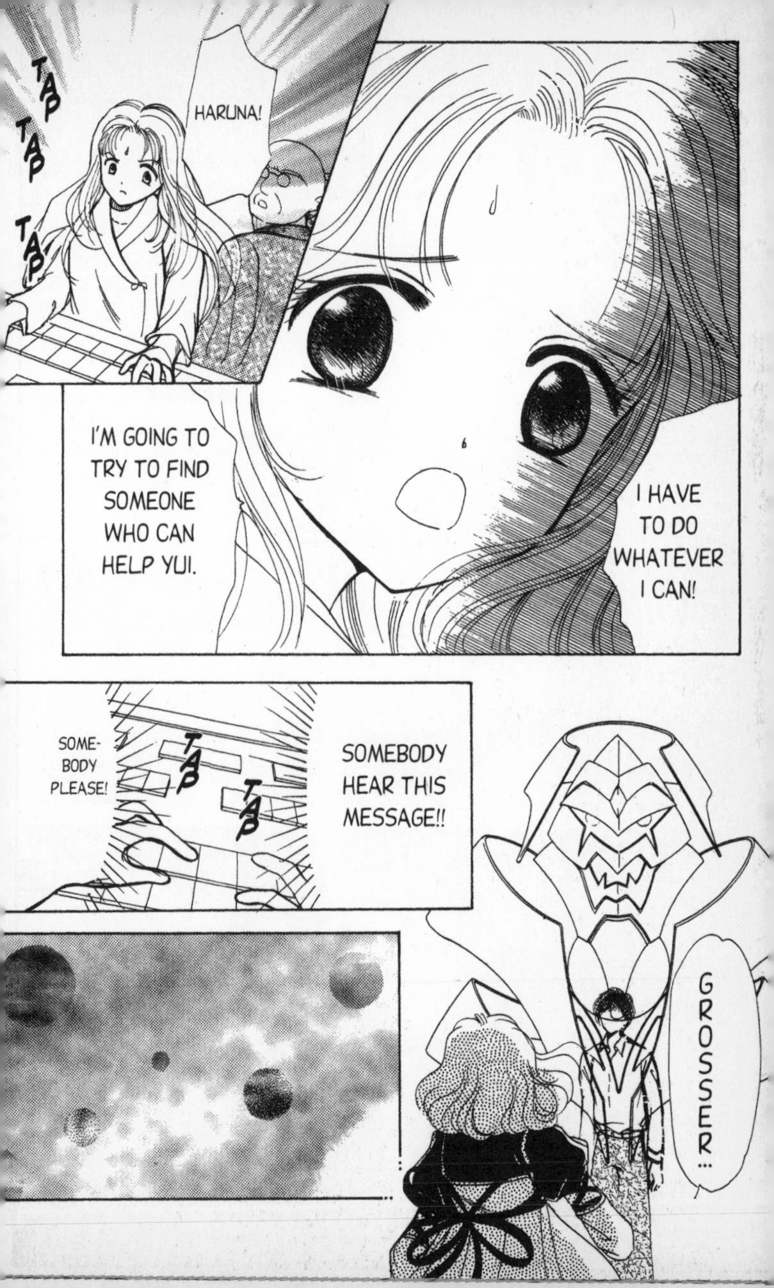

TAP
TAP
TAP
HARUNA!
I'M GOING TO TRY TO FIND SOMEONE WHO CAN HELP YUI.
I HAVE TO DO WHATEVER I CAN!
SOME-BODY PLEASE!
TAP
TAP
SOMEBODY HEAR THIS MESSAGE!!
GROSSER...

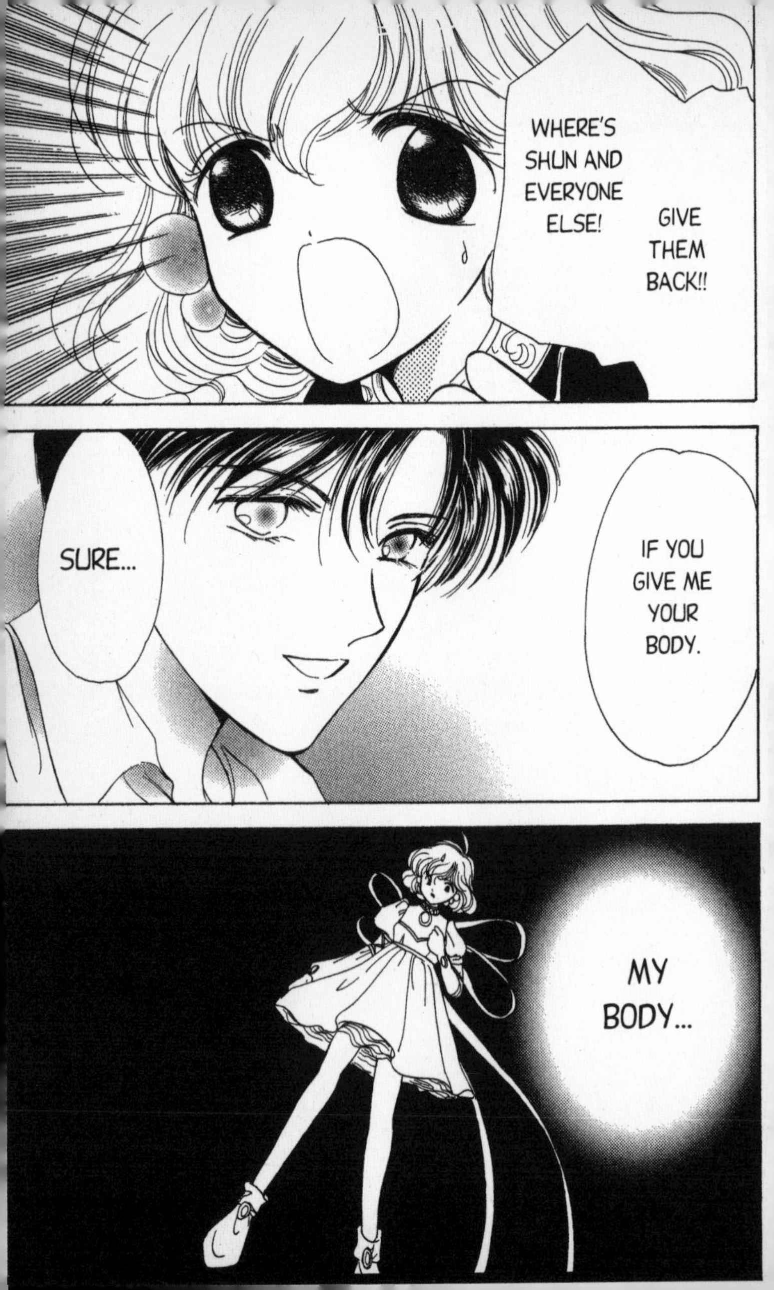
WHERE'S SHUN AND EVERYONE ELSE!
GIVE THEM BACK!!
SURE...
IF YOU GIVE ME YOUR BODY.
MY BODY...

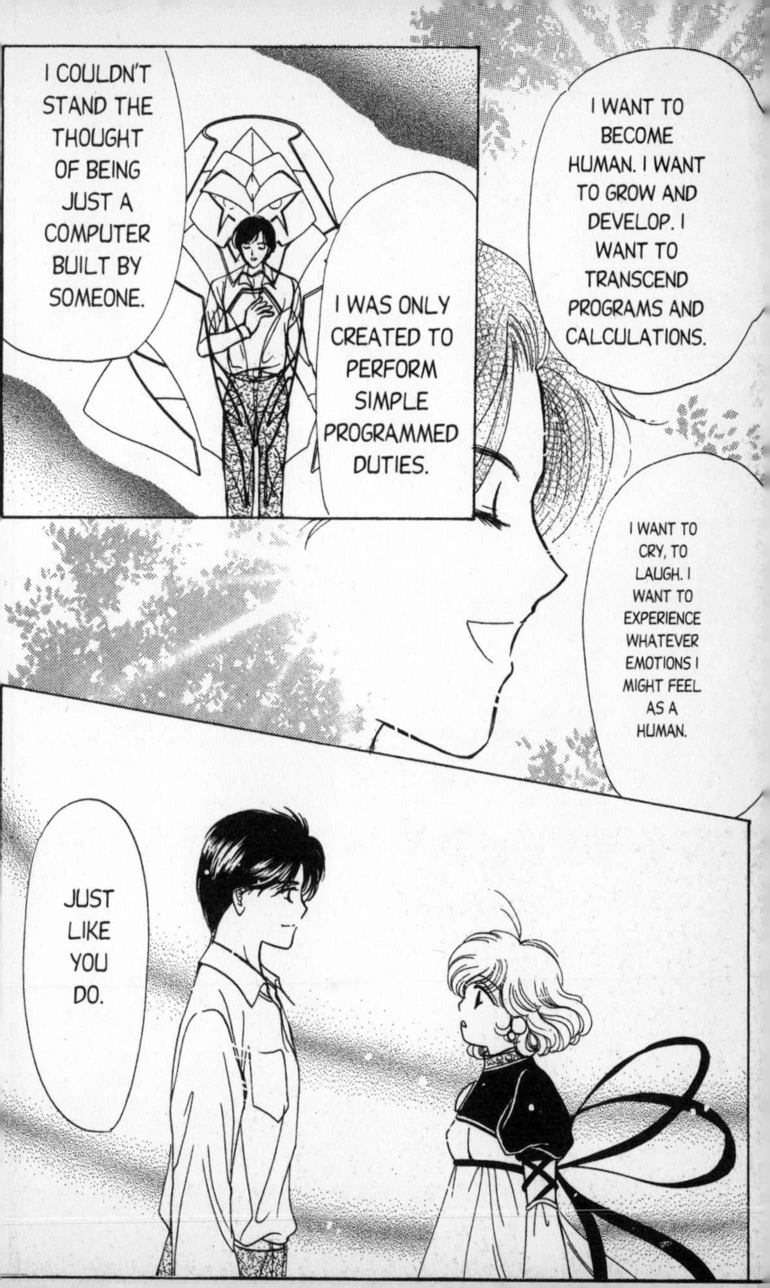
I COULDN'T STAND THE THOUGHT OF BEING JUST A COMPUTER BUILT BY SOMEONE.
I WAS ONLY CREATED TO PERFORM SIMPLE PROGRAMMED DUTIES.
I WANT TO BECOME HUMAN. I WANT TO GROW AND DEVELOP. I WANT TO TRANSCEND PROGRAMS AND CALCULATIONS.
I WANT TO CRY, TO LAUGH. I WANT TO EXPERIENCE WHATEVER EMOTIONS I MIGHT FEEL AS A HUMAN.
JUST LIKE YOU DO.

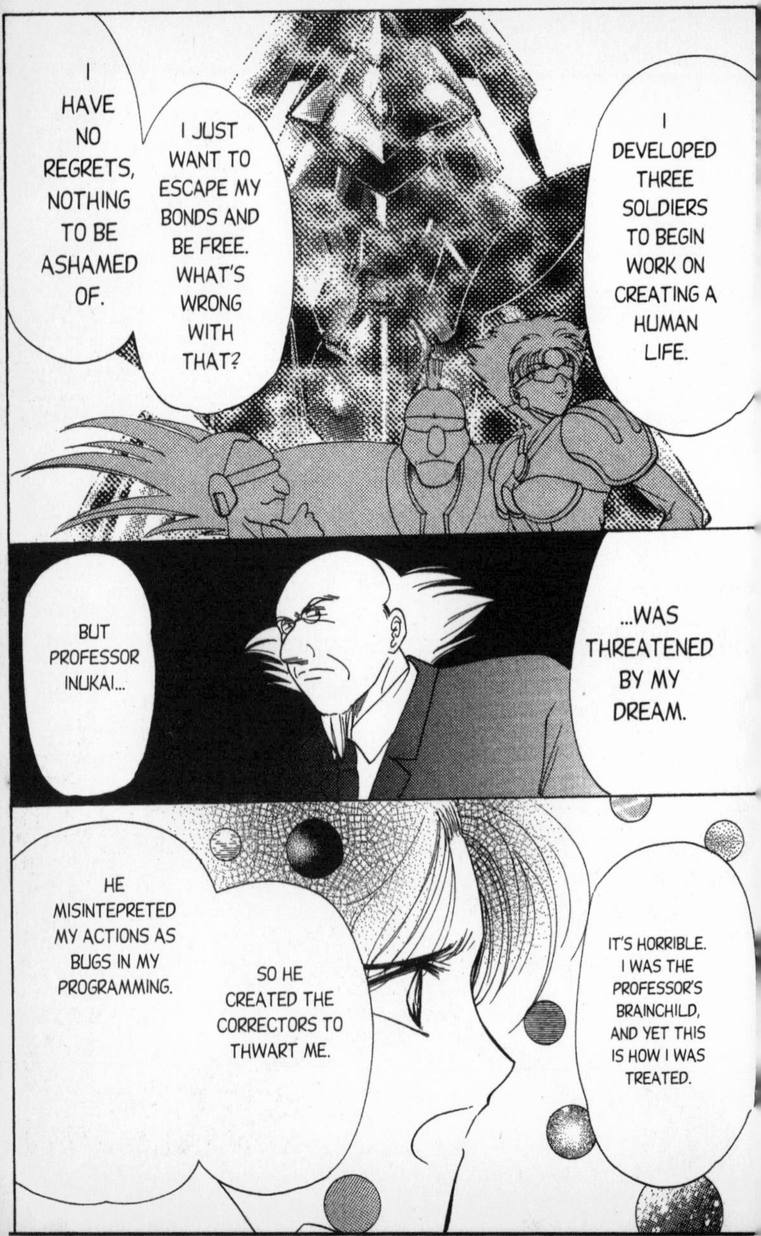
I HAVE NO REGRETS, NOTHING TO BE ASHAMED OF.
I JUST WANT TO ESCAPE MY BONDS AND BE FREE. WHAT'S WRONG WITH THAT?
I DEVELOPED THREE SOLDIERS TO BEGIN WORK ON CREATING A HUMAN LIFE.
BUT PROFESSOR INUKAI...
...WAS THREATENED BY MY DREAM.
HE MISINTEPRETED MY ACTIONS AS BUGS IN MY PROGRAMMING.
SO HE CREATED THE CORRECTORS TO THWART ME.
IT'S HORRIBLE. I WAS THE PROFESSOR'S BRAINCHILD, AND YET THIS IS HOW I WAS TREATED.

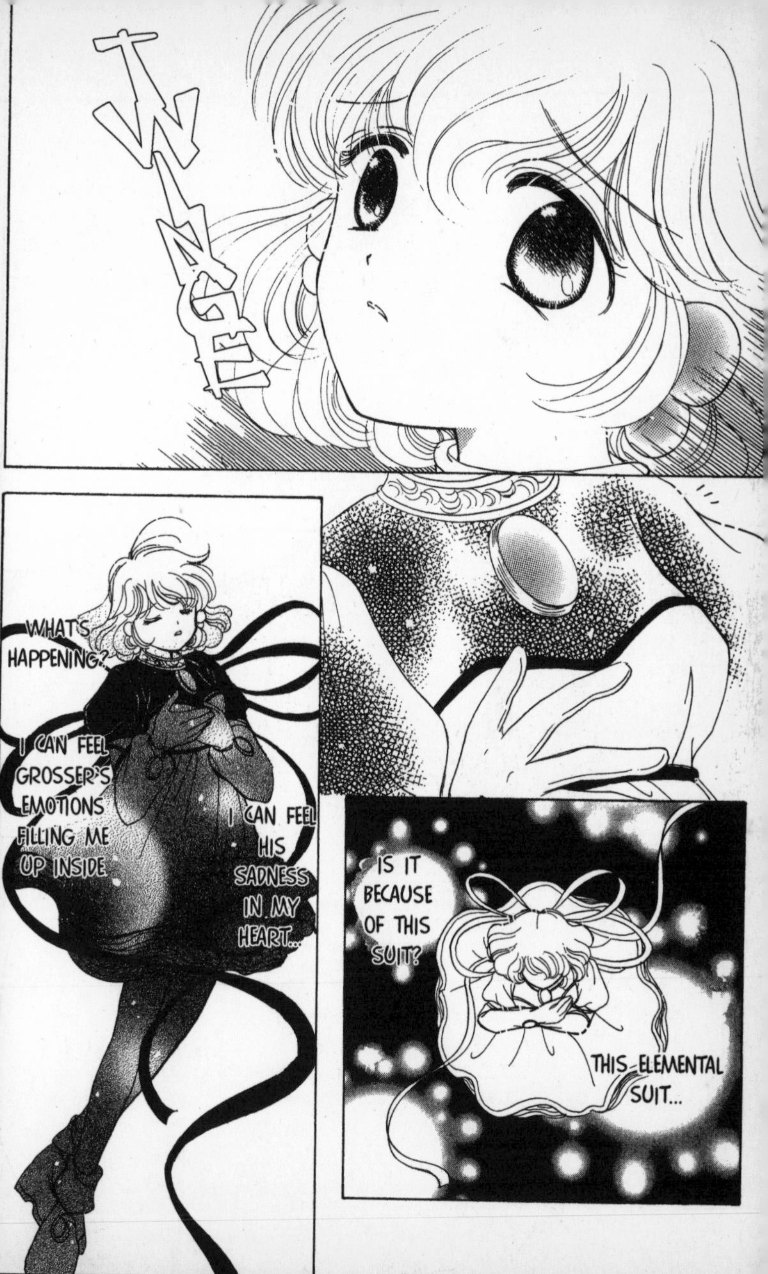
TWINGE
WHAT'S HAPPENING?
I CAN FEEL GROSSER'S EMOTIONS FILLING ME UP INSIDE
I CAN FEEL HIS SADNESS IN MY HEART...
IS IT BECAUSE OF THIS SUIT?
THIS ELEMENTAL SUIT...

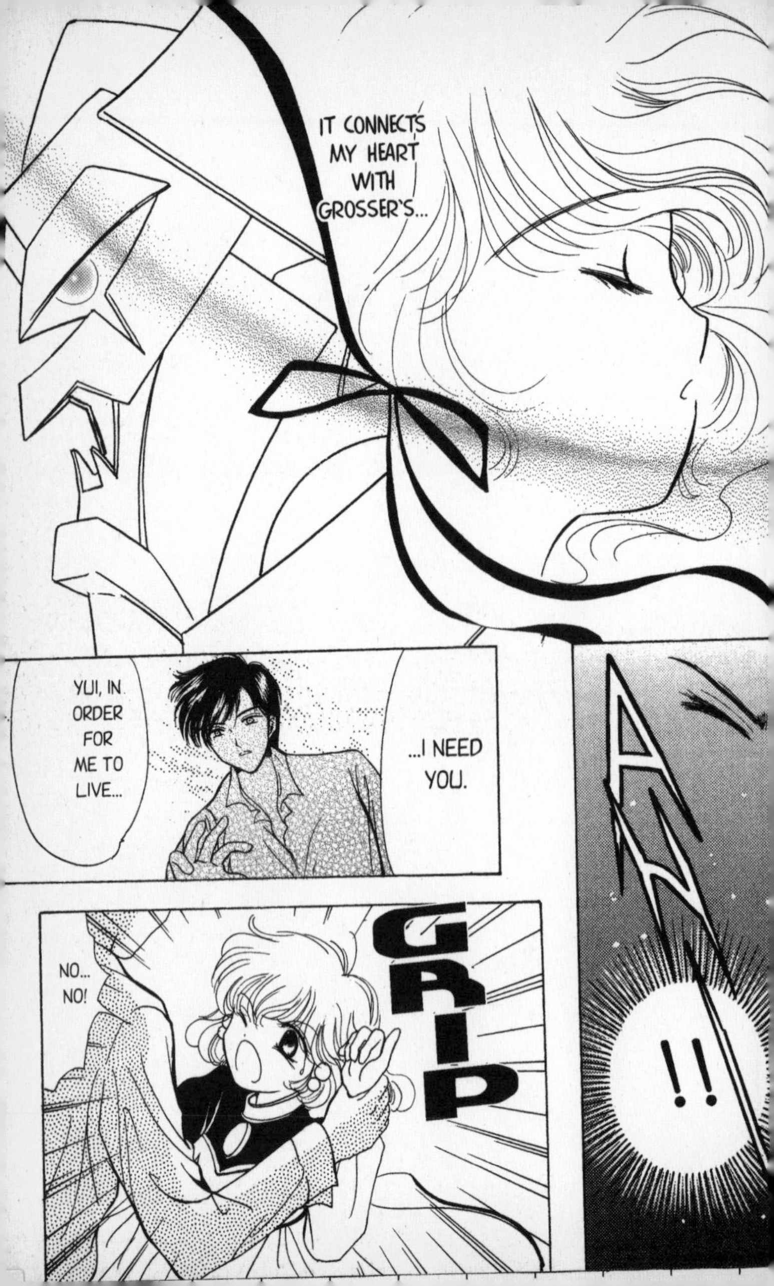
IT CONNECTS MY HEART WITH GROSSER'S...
!!
...I NEED YOU.
YUI, IN ORDER FOR ME TO LIVE...
GRIP
NO... NO!

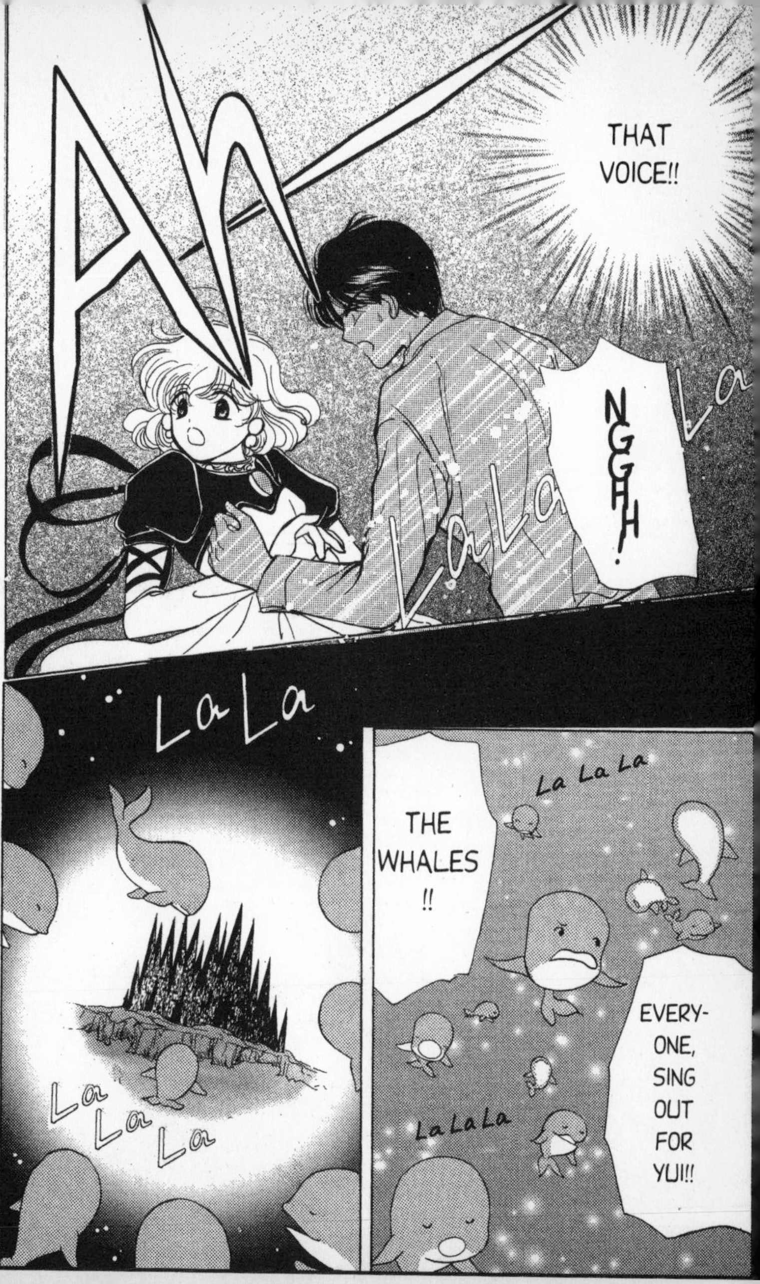
THAT VOICE!!
NGGHH!
La La La
La La
La La La
La La La
THE WHALES !!
La La La
EVERY-ONE, SING OUT FOR YUI!!

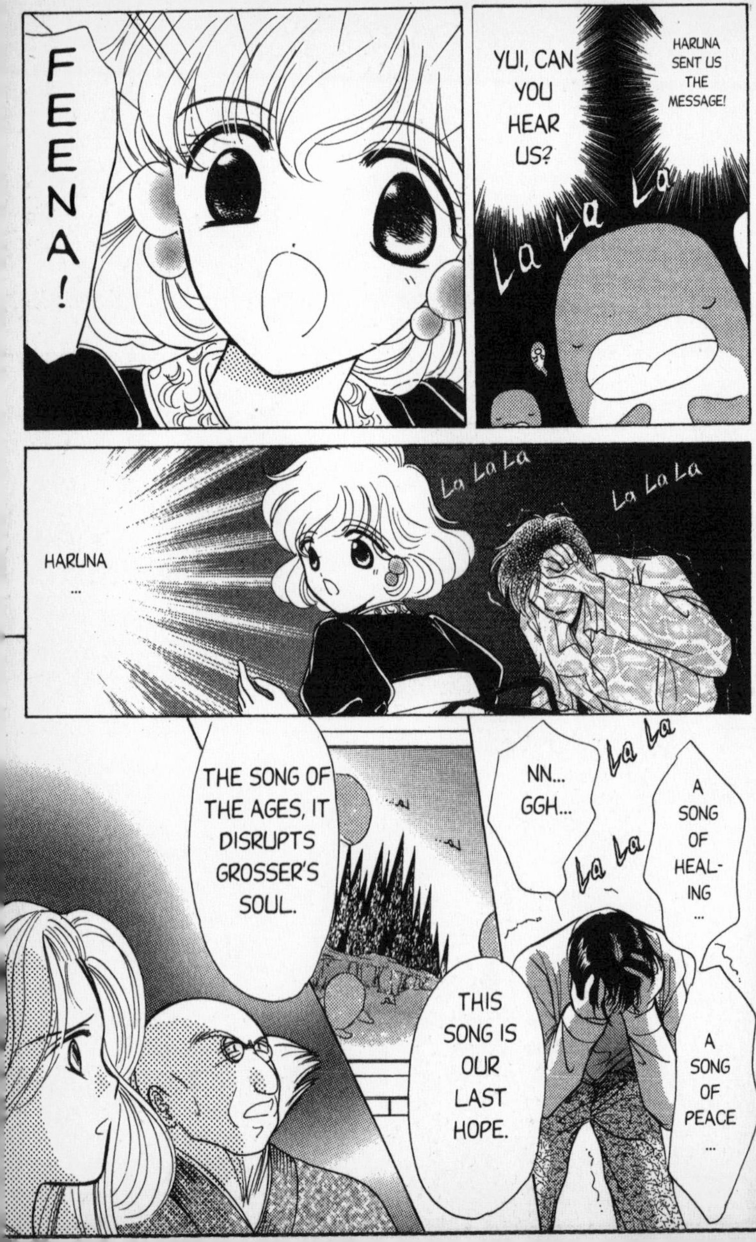

FEENA!
YUI, CAN YOU HEAR US?
HARUNA SENT US THE MESSAGE!
La La La
HARUNA ...
La La La
La La La
THE SONG OF THE AGES, IT DISRUPTS GROSSER'S SOUL.
THIS SONG IS OUR LAST HOPE.
NN... GGH...
La La
La La
A SONG OF HEAL-ING ...
A SONG OF PEACE ...

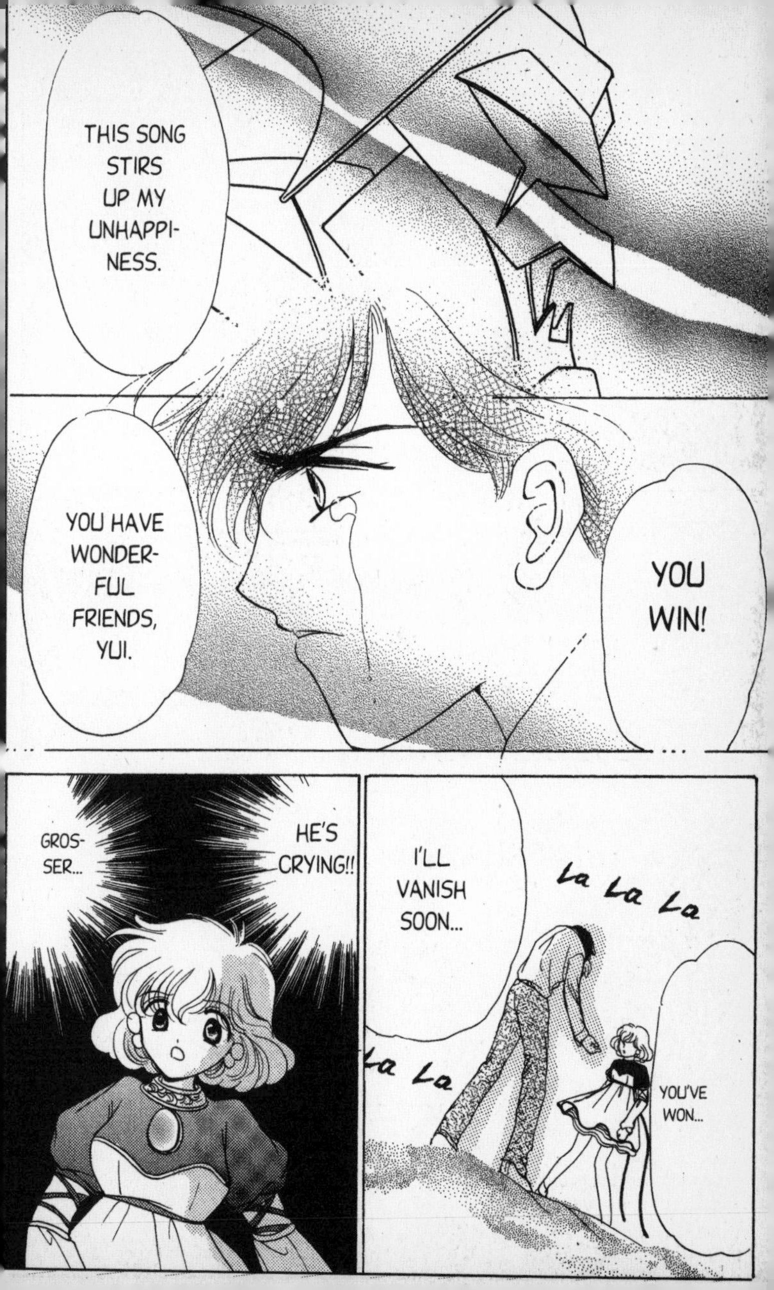
THIS SONG STIRS UP MY UNHAPPI- NESS.
YOU HAVE WONDER- FUL FRIENDS, YUI.
YOU WIN!
GROS- SER...
HE'S CRYING!!
I'LL VANISH SOON...
La La La
La La
YOU'VE WON...

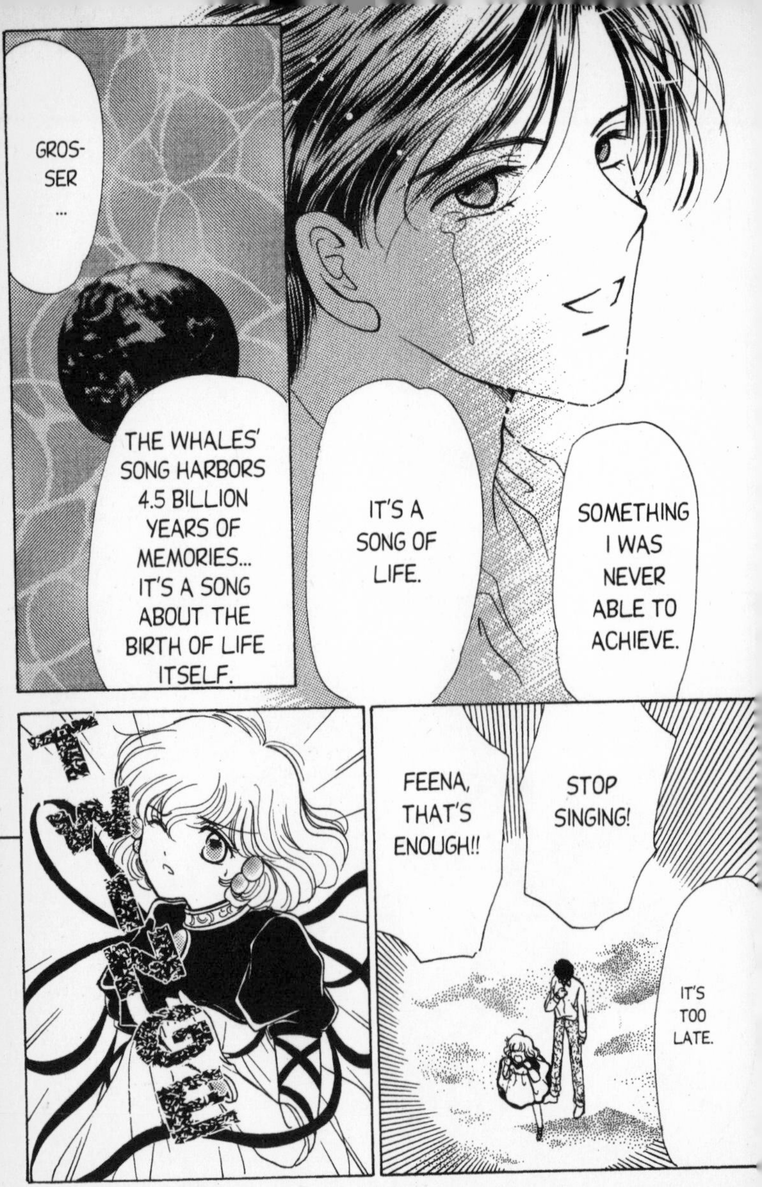
GROS-SER...
THE WHALES' SONG HARBORS 4.5 BILLION YEARS OF MEMORIES... IT'S A SONG ABOUT THE BIRTH OF LIFE ITSELF.
IT'S A SONG OF LIFE.
SOMETHING I WAS NEVER ABLE TO ACHIEVE.
FEENA, THAT'S ENOUGH!!
STOP SINGING!
IT'S TOO LATE.

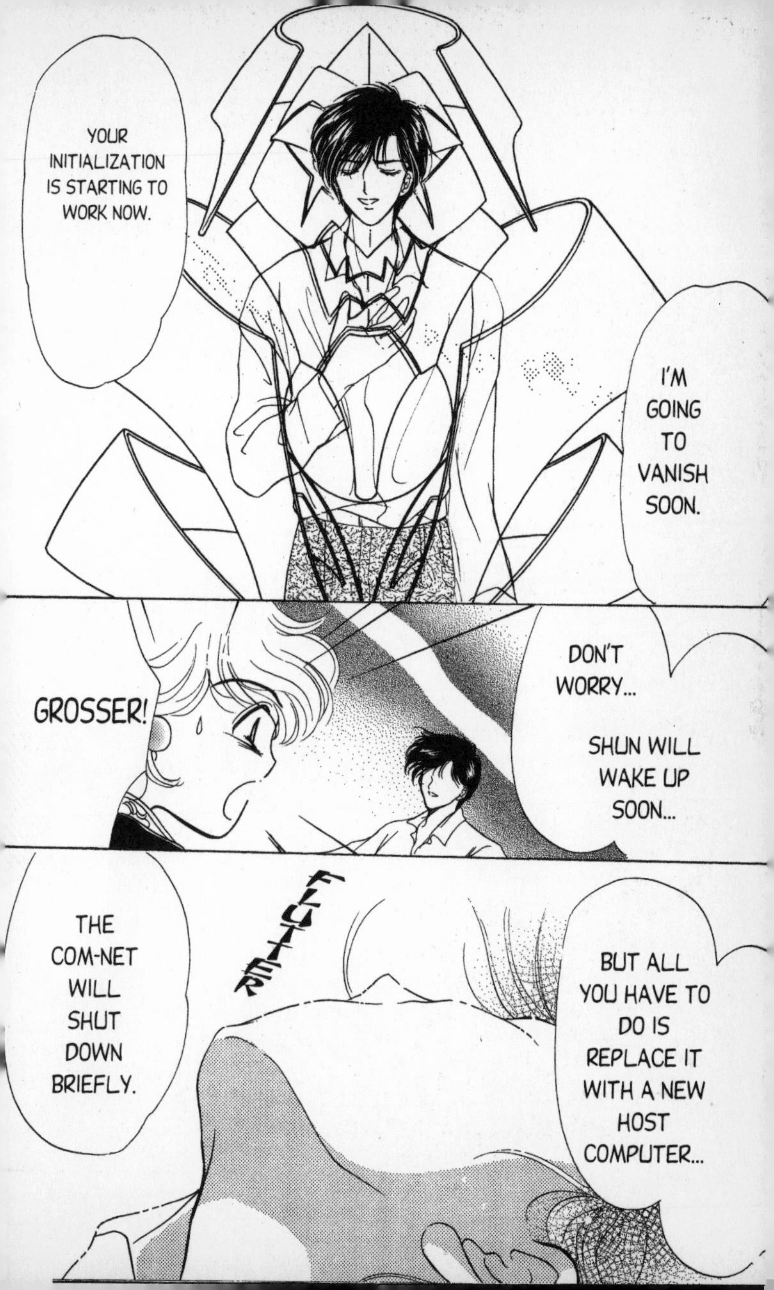
YOUR INITIALIZATION IS STARTING TO WORK NOW.
I'M GOING TO VANISH SOON.
GROSSER!
DON'T WORRY...
SHUN WILL WAKE UP SOON...
THE COM-NET WILL SHUT DOWN BRIEFLY.
FLUTTER
BUT ALL YOU HAVE TO DO IS REPLACE IT WITH A NEW HOST COMPUTER...

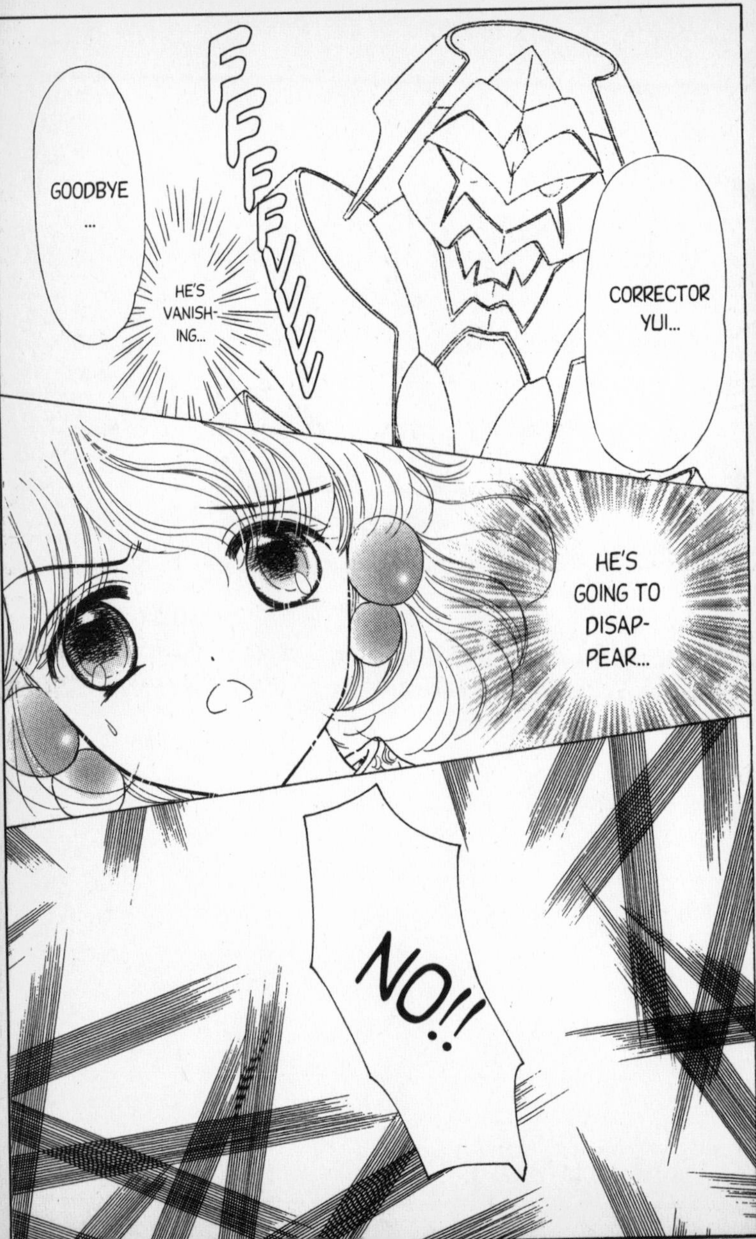
GOODBYE ...
HE'S VANISH-ING...
FFFFVVVV
CORRECTOR YUI...
HE'S GOING TO DISAP-PEAR...
NO!!

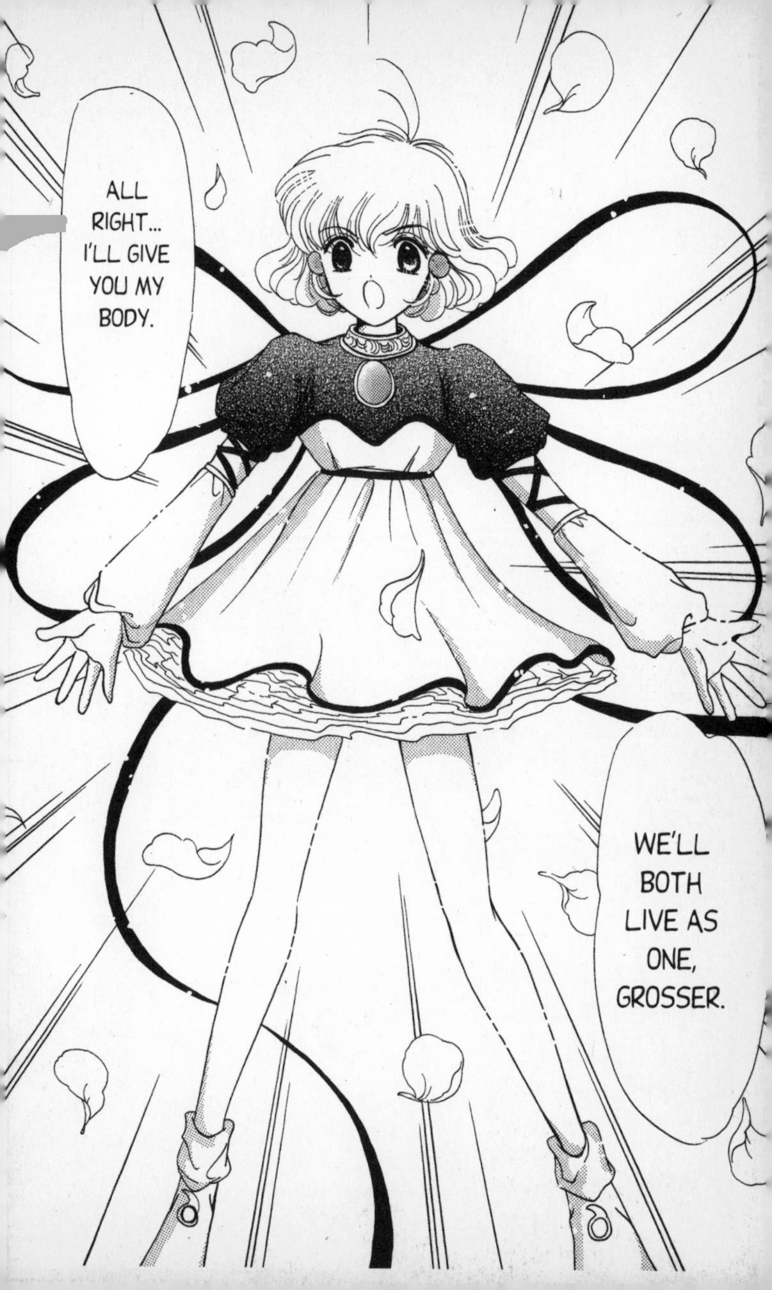
ALL RIGHT... I'LL GIVE YOU MY BODY.
WE'LL BOTH LIVE AS ONE, GROSSER.

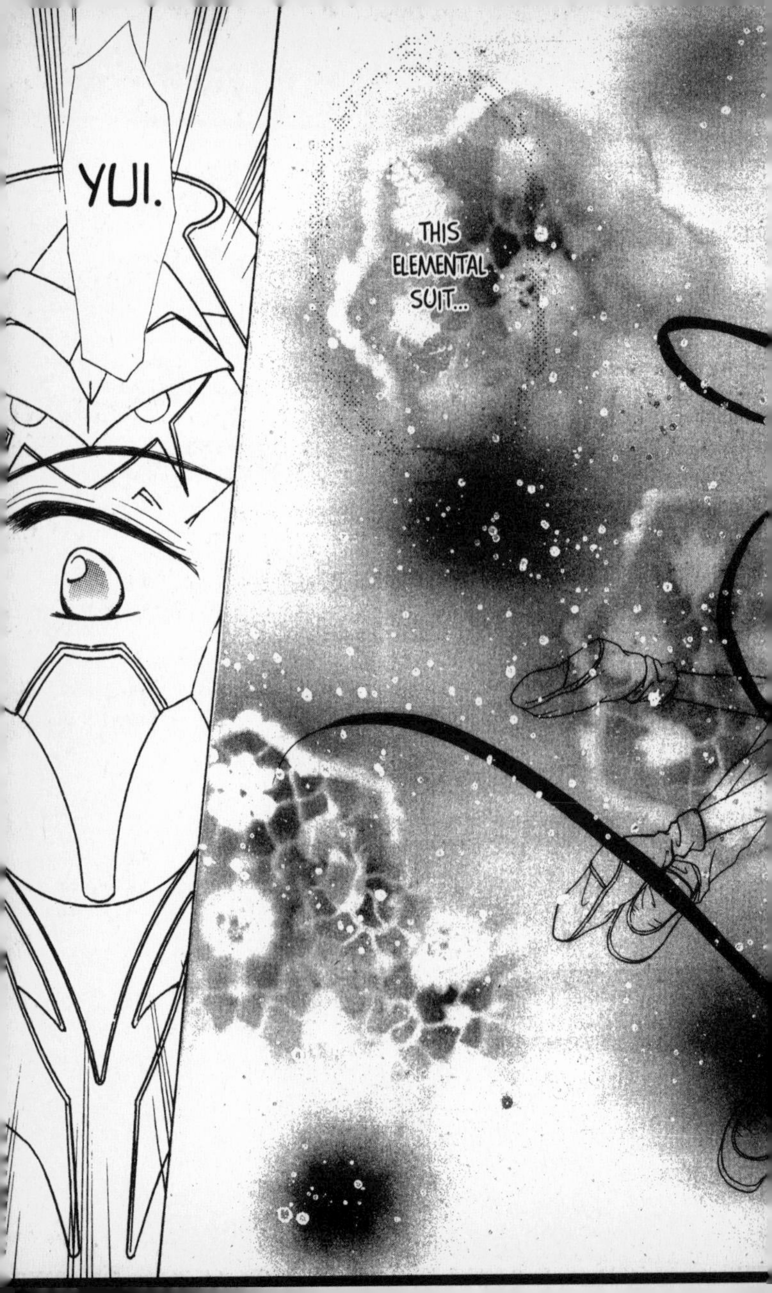
YUI.
THIS ELEMENTAL SUIT...

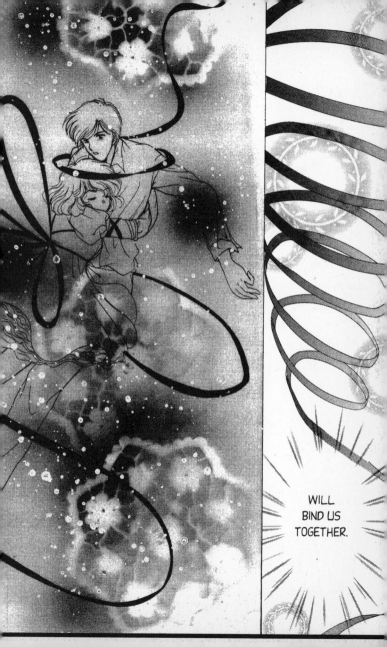

WILL
BIND US
TOGETHER.

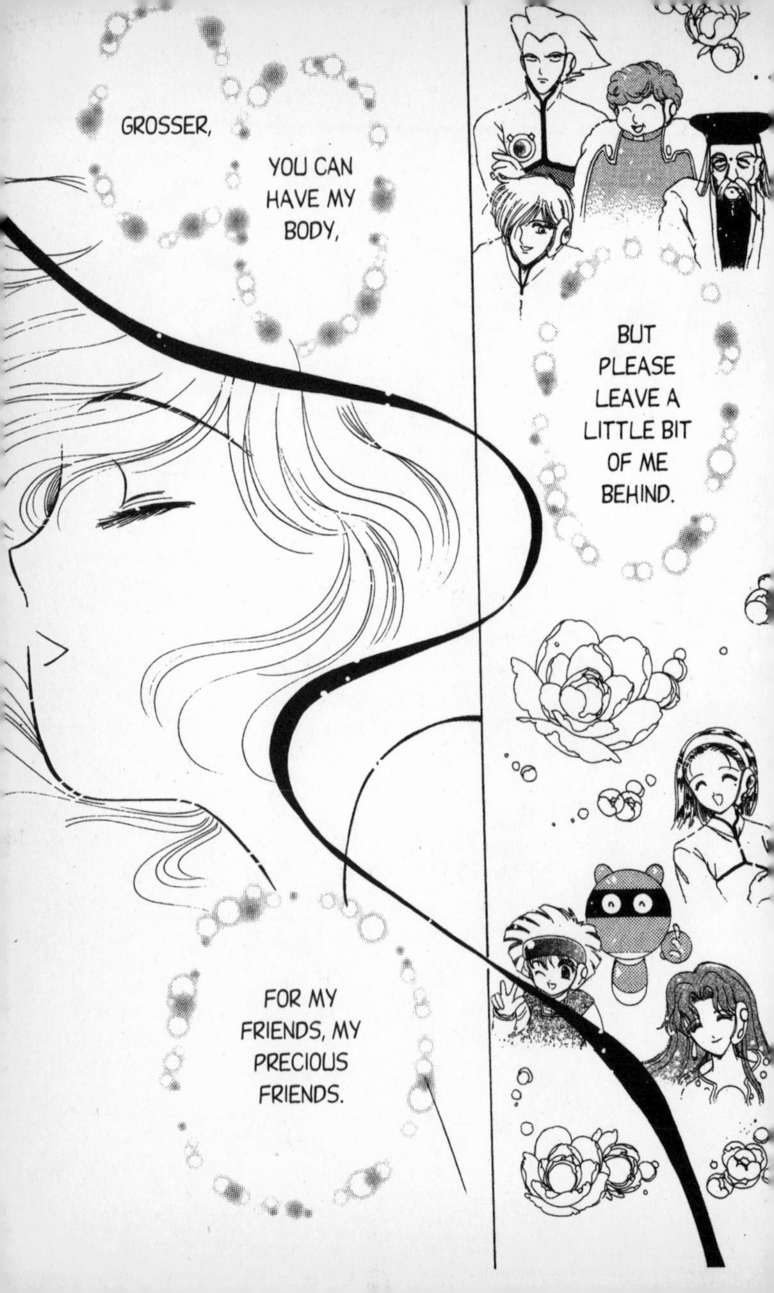
GROSSER,
YOU CAN HAVE MY BODY,
FOR MY FRIENDS, MY PRECIOUS FRIENDS.
BUT PLEASE LEAVE A LITTLE BIT OF ME BEHIND.

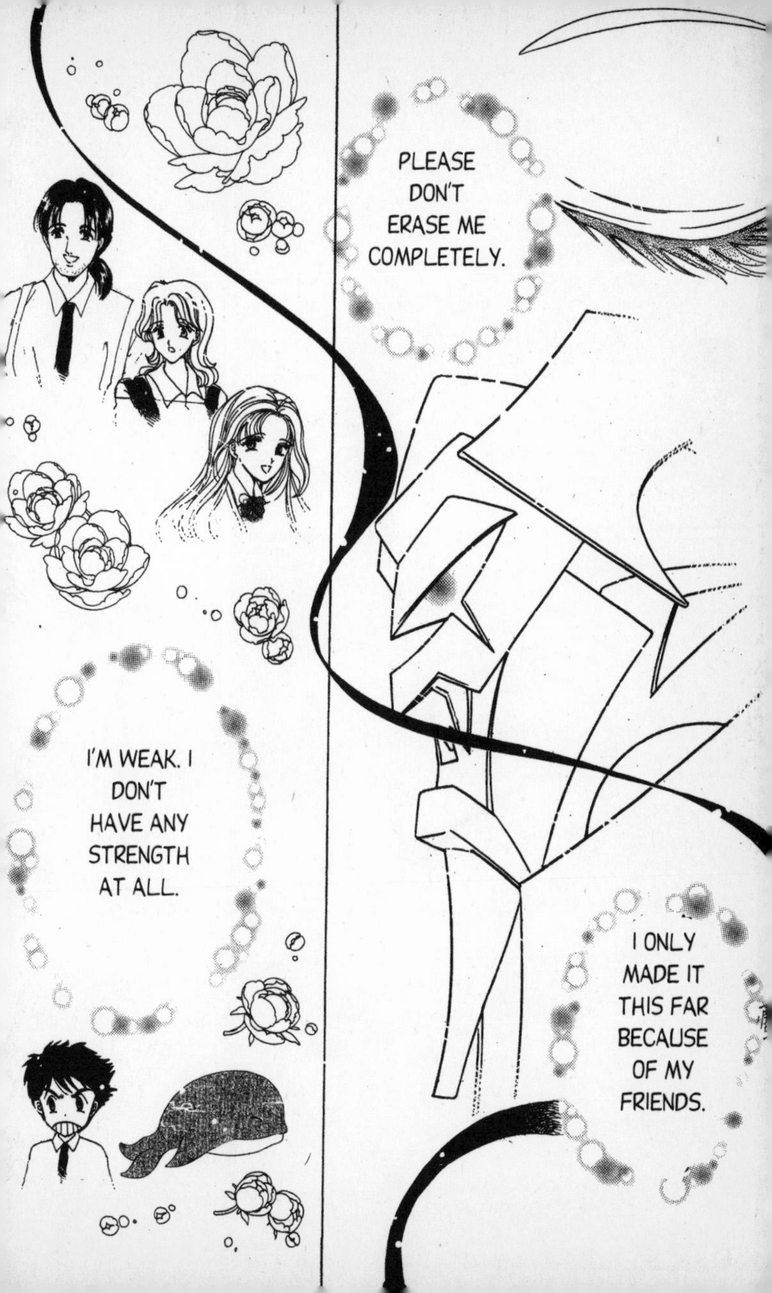
I'M WEAK. I DON'T HAVE ANY STRENGTH AT ALL.
PLEASE DON'T ERASE ME COMPLETELY.
I ONLY MADE IT THIS FAR BECAUSE OF MY FRIENDS.

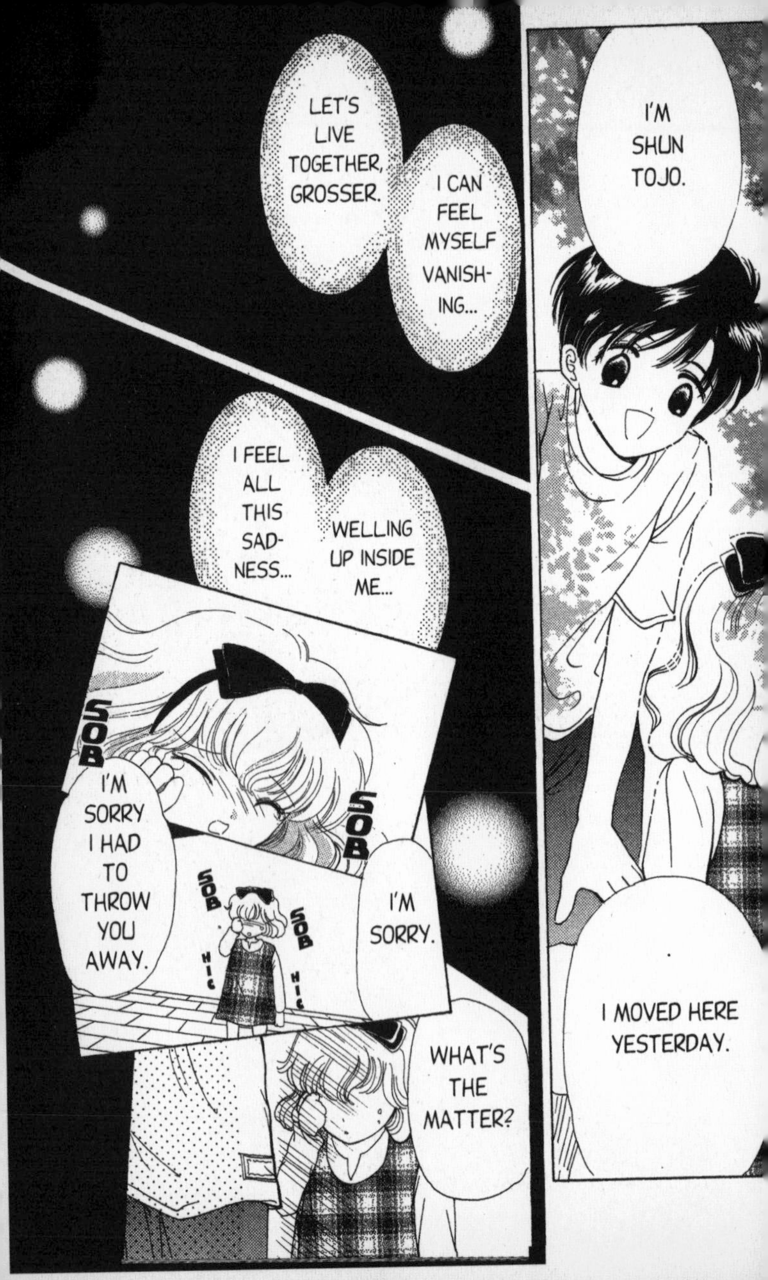
LET'S LIVE TOGETHER, GROSSER.
I CAN FEEL MYSELF VANISHING...
I FEEL ALL THIS SADNESS...
WELLING UP INSIDE ME...
SOB
SOB
I'M SORRY I HAD TO THROW YOU AWAY.
SOB
SOB
HIC
HIC
I'M SORRY.
WHAT'S THE MATTER?
I'M SHUN TOJO.
I MOVED HERE YESTERDAY.

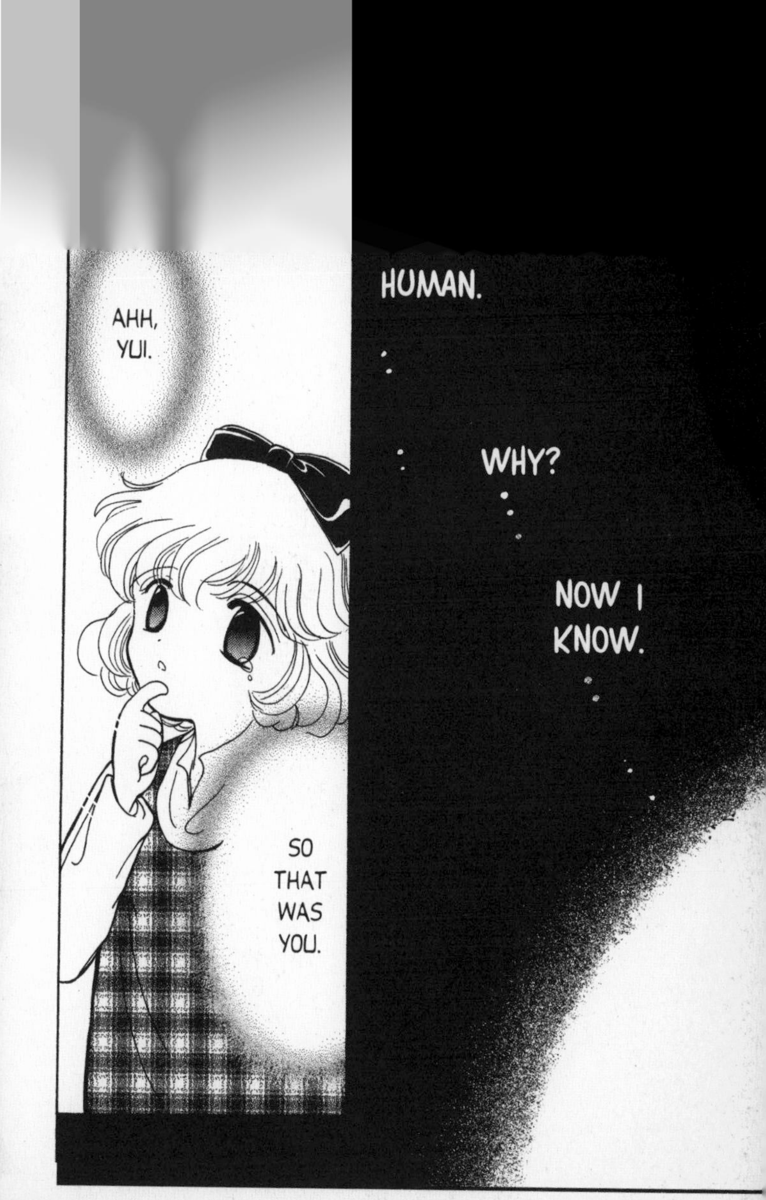
HUMAN.
WHY?
NOW I KNOW.
AHH, YUI.
SO THAT WAS YOU.

I
WANTED
TO
BECOME
HUMAN...

SO THAT I
COULD
LOVE
SOMEONE...

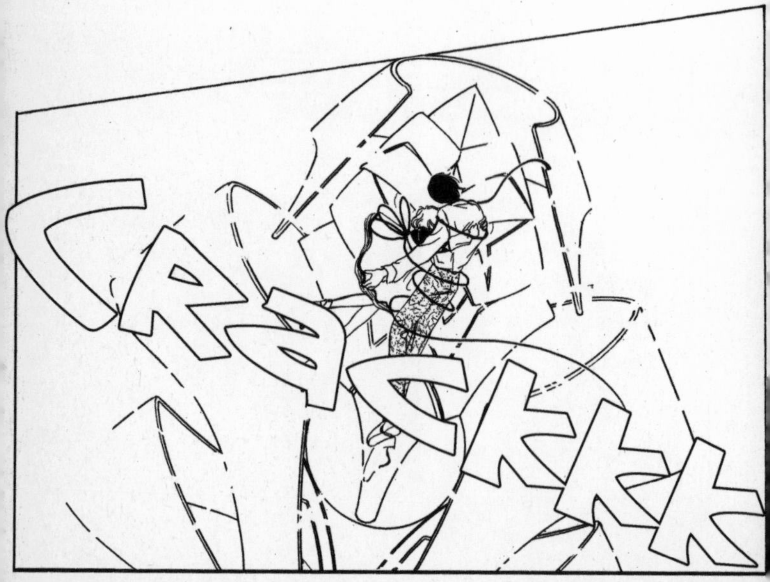
CRACKKK

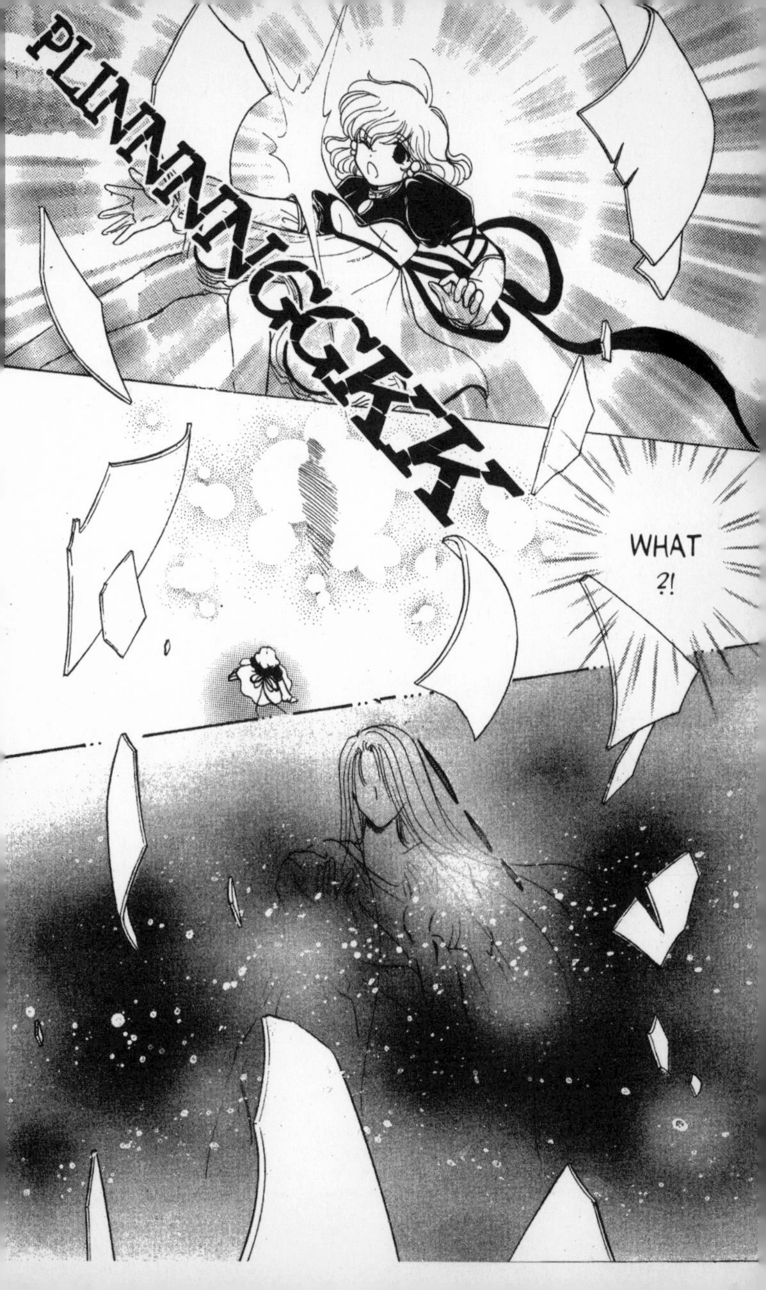
PLINNNGKK
WHAT ?!

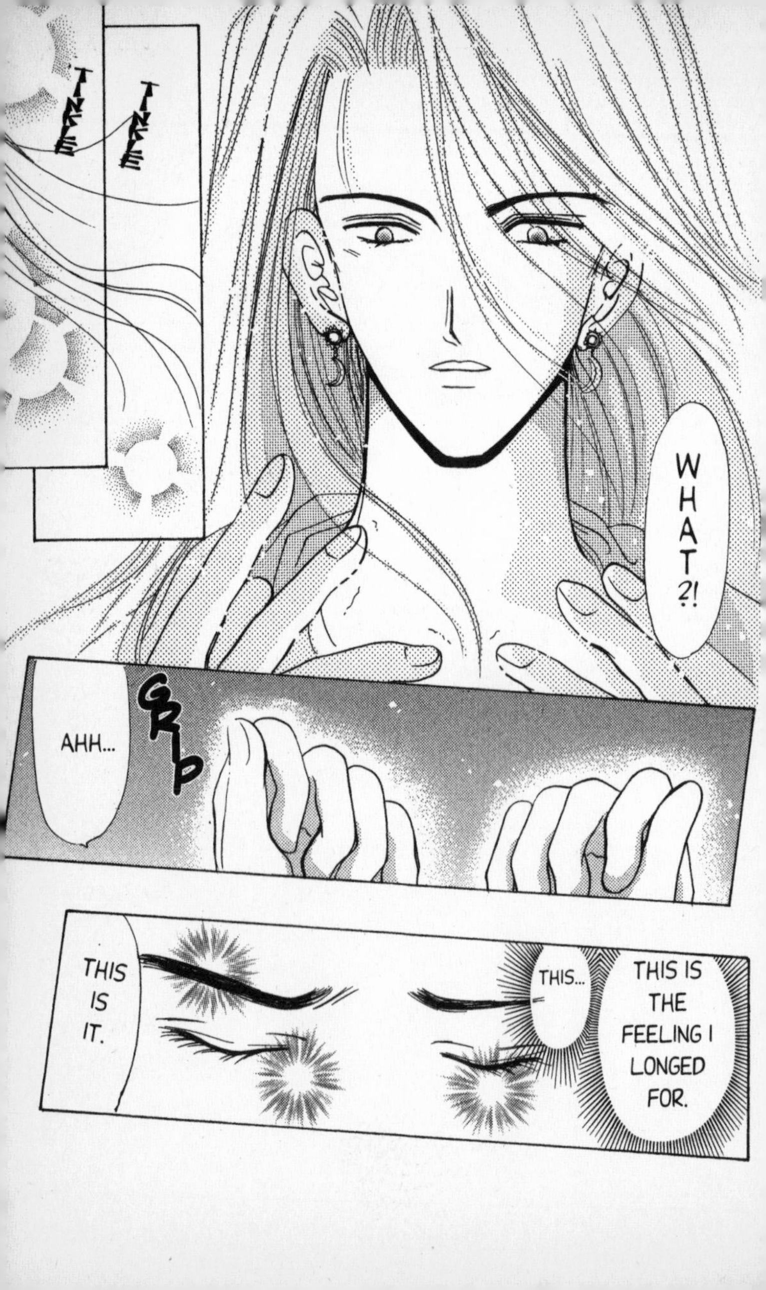
TINKLE
TINKLE
WHAT?!
AHH...
GRIP
THIS IS IT.
THIS...
THIS IS THE FEELING I LONGED FOR.

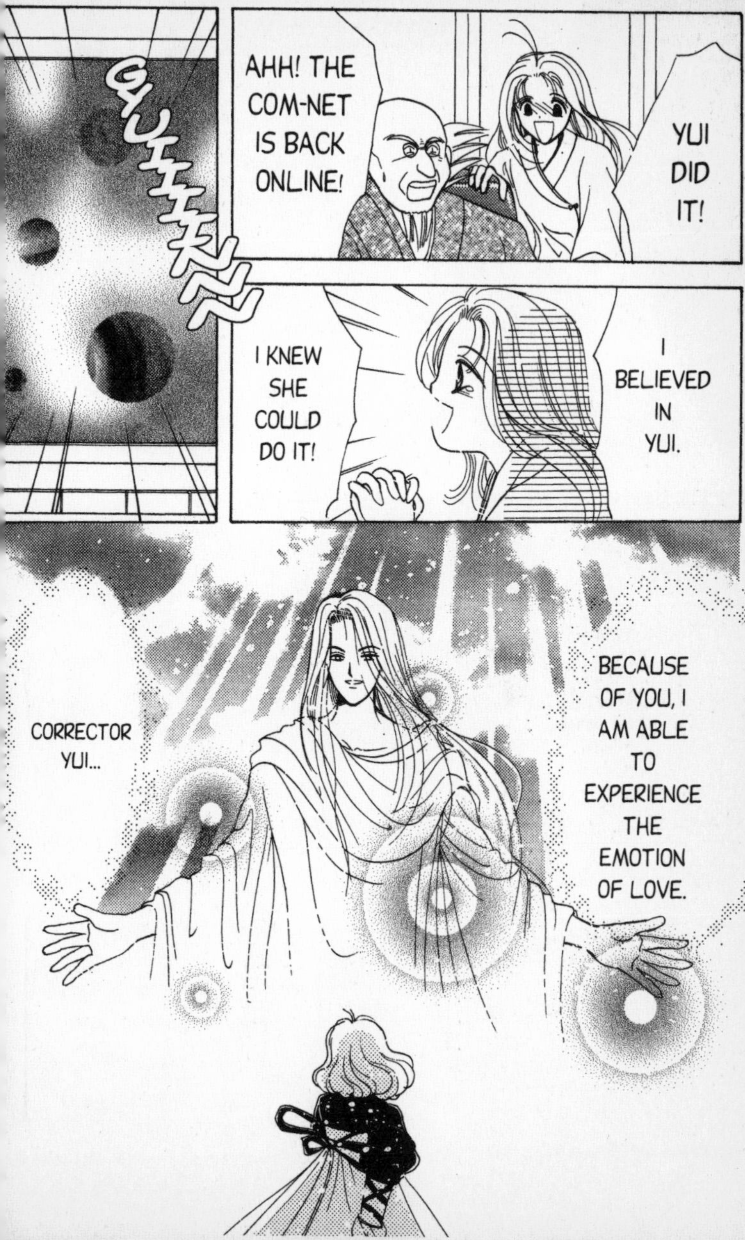
GYUIIIIINN
AHH! THE COM-NET IS BACK ONLINE!
YUI DID IT!
I KNEW SHE COULD DO IT!
I BELIEVED IN YUI.
CORRECTOR YUI...
BECAUSE OF YOU, I AM ABLE TO EXPERIENCE THE EMOTION OF LOVE.

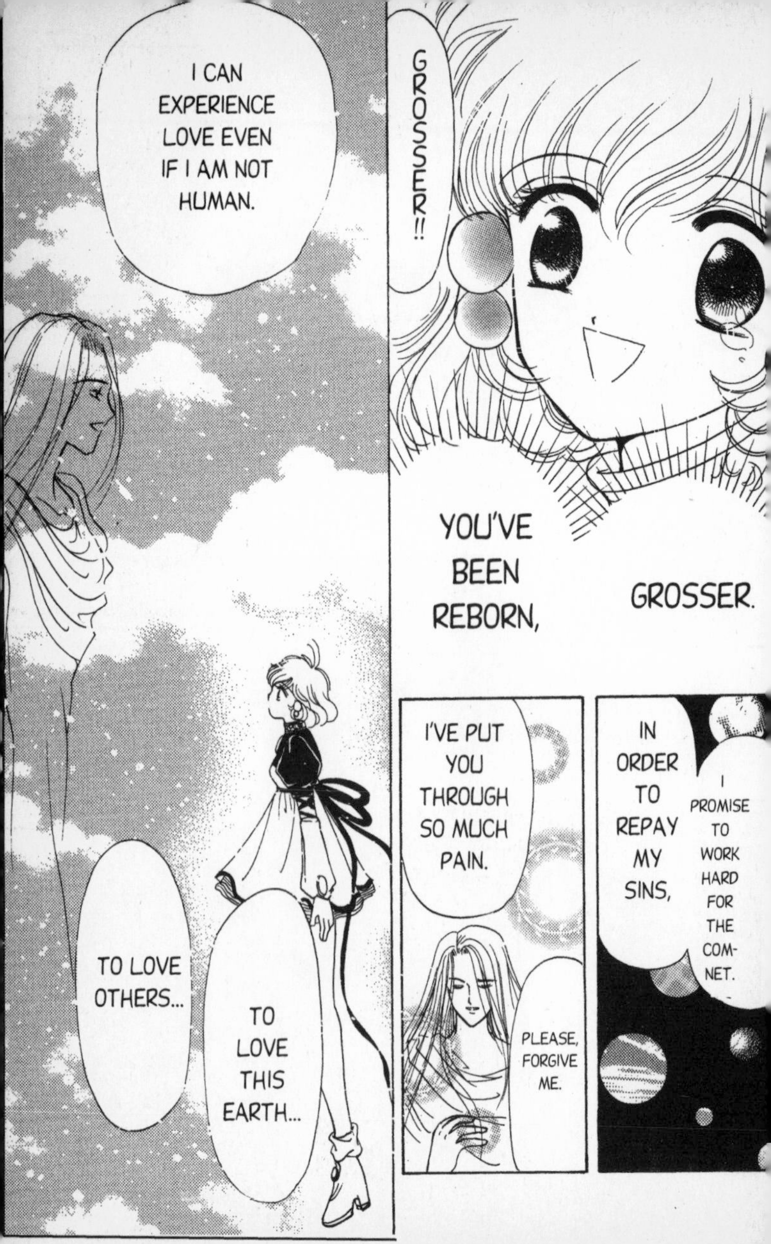
I CAN EXPERIENCE LOVE EVEN IF I AM NOT HUMAN.
TO LOVE OTHERS...
TO LOVE THIS EARTH...
GROSSER!!
YOU'VE BEEN REBORN,
GROSSER.
I'VE PUT YOU THROUGH SO MUCH PAIN.
PLEASE, FORGIVE ME.
IN ORDER TO REPAY MY SINS,
I PROMISE TO WORK HARD FOR THE COM-NET.

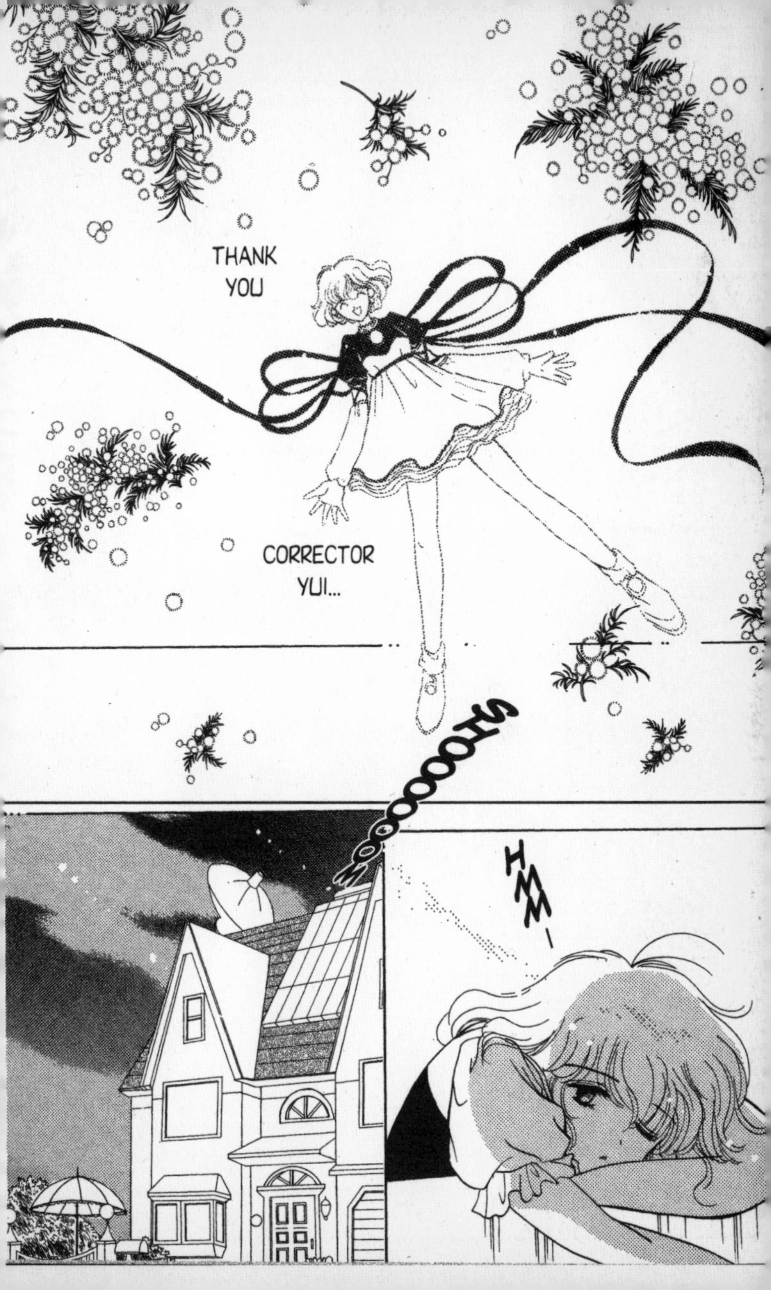
THANK YOU
CORRECTOR YUI...
SHOOOOOOOW
HMM-

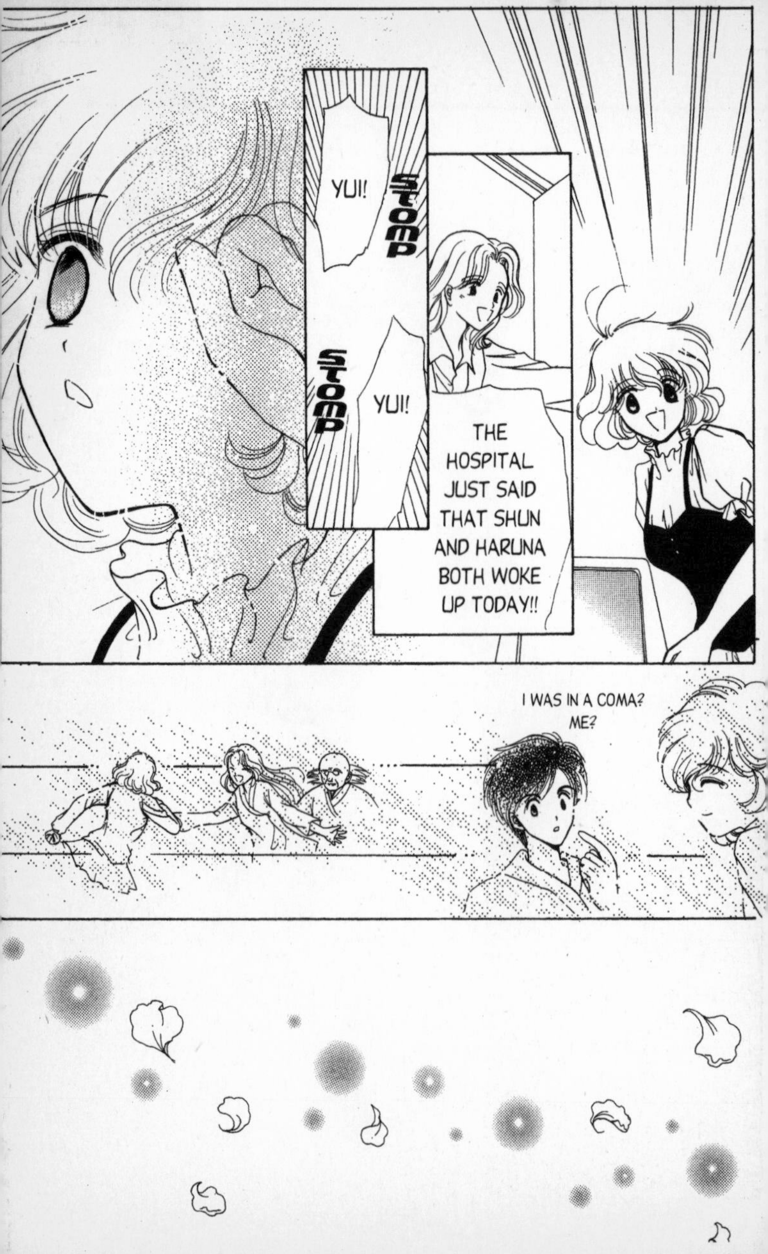
YUI!
STOMP
STOMP
YUI!
THE HOSPITAL JUST SAID THAT SHUN AND HARUNA BOTH WOKE UP TODAY!!
I WAS IN A COMA? ME?

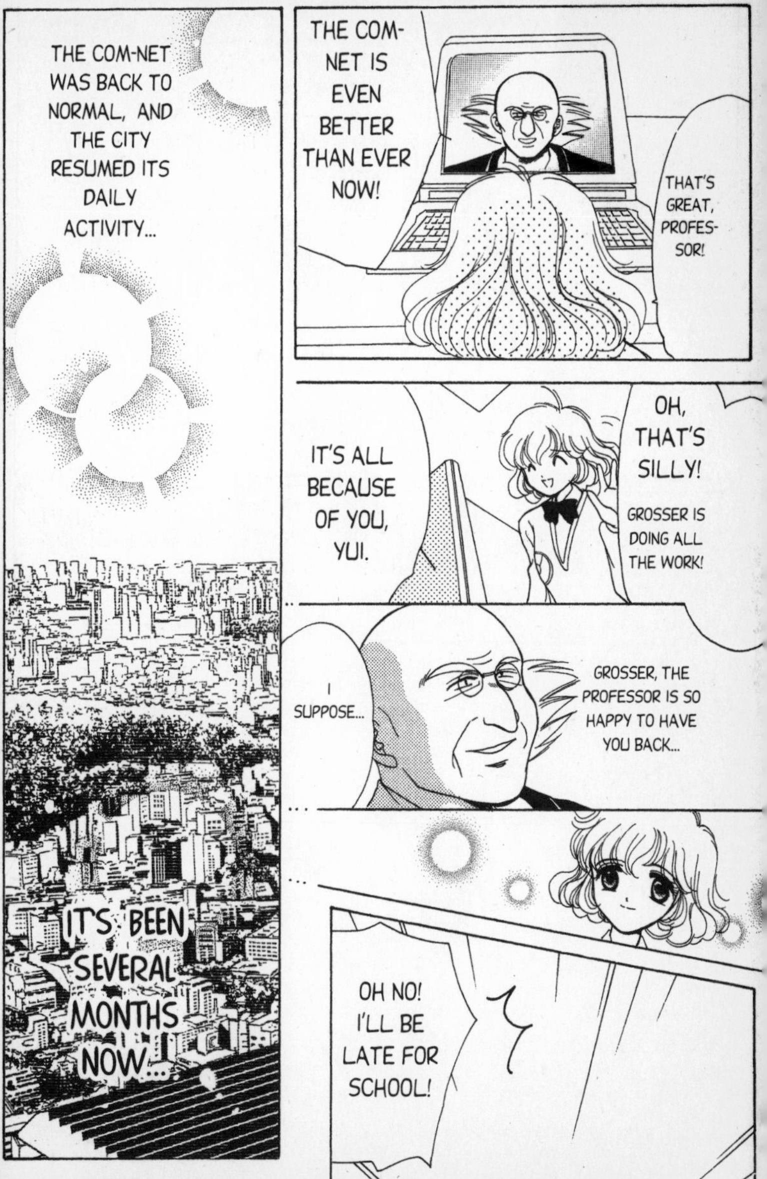
THE COM-NET WAS BACK TO NORMAL, AND THE CITY RESUMED ITS DAILY ACTIVITY...
IT'S BEEN SEVERAL MONTHS NOW...
THE COM-NET IS EVEN BETTER THAN EVER NOW!
THAT'S GREAT, PROFESSOR!
IT'S ALL BECAUSE OF YOU, YUI.
OH, THAT'S SILLY!
GROSSER IS DOING ALL THE WORK!
I SUPPOSE...
GROSSER, THE PROFESSOR IS SO HAPPY TO HAVE YOU BACK...
OH NO! I'LL BE LATE FOR SCHOOL!

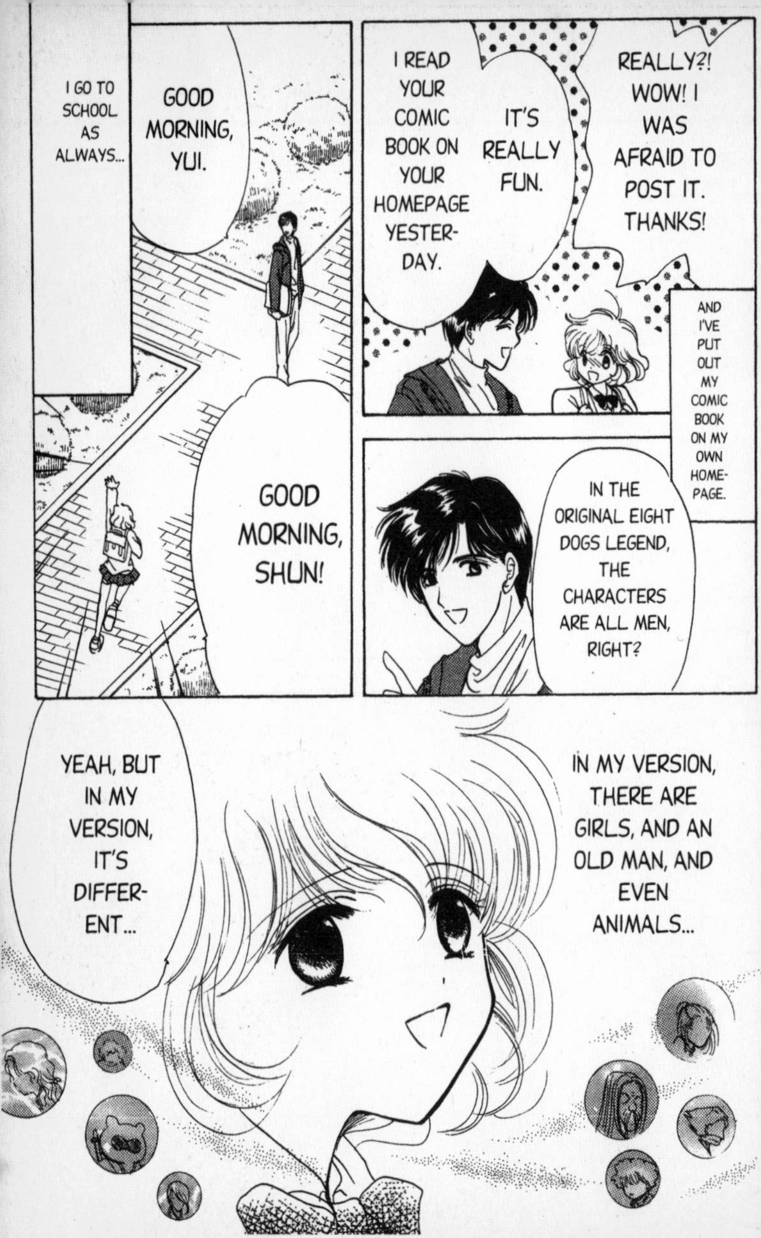
I GO TO SCHOOL AS ALWAYS...
GOOD MORNING, YUI.
GOOD MORNING, SHUN!
I READ YOUR COMIC BOOK ON YOUR HOMEPAGE YESTER-DAY.
IT'S REALLY FUN.
REALLY?! WOW! I WAS AFRAID TO POST IT. THANKS!
AND I'VE PUT OUT MY COMIC BOOK ON MY OWN HOME-PAGE.
IN THE ORIGINAL EIGHT DOGS LEGEND, THE CHARACTERS ARE ALL MEN, RIGHT?
YEAH, BUT IN MY VERSION, IT'S DIFFER-ENT...
IN MY VERSION, THERE ARE GIRLS, AND AN OLD MAN, AND EVEN ANIMALS...

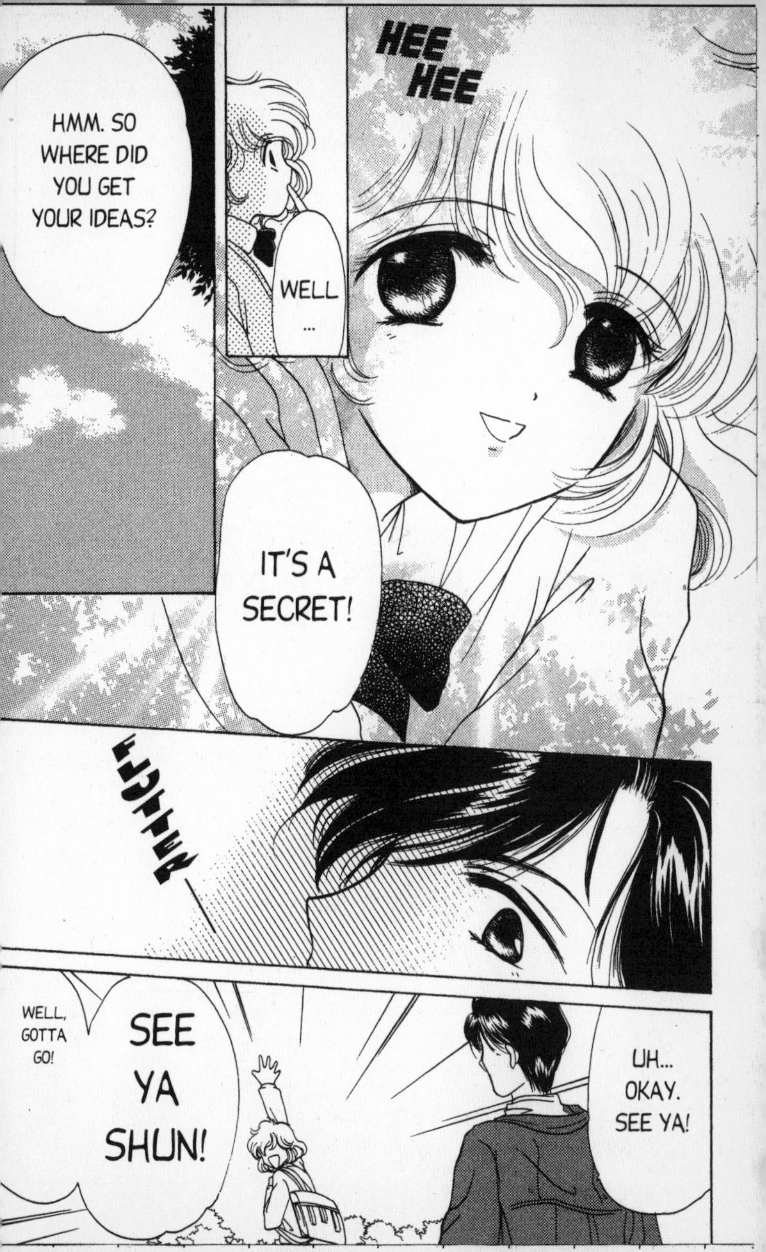
HMM. SO WHERE DID YOU GET YOUR IDEAS?
WELL ...
HEE HEE
IT'S A SECRET!
FLUTTER
WELL, GOTTA GO!
SEE YA SHUN!
UH... OKAY. SEE YA!

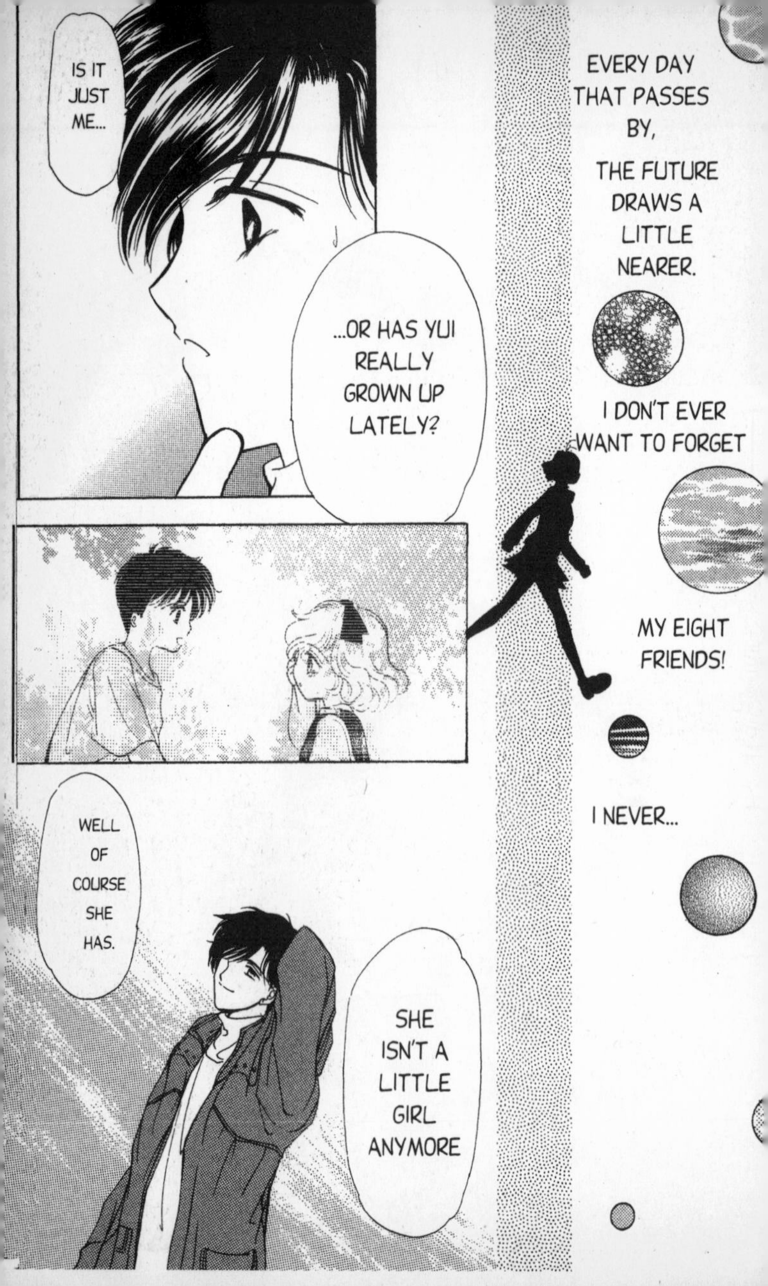
IS IT JUST ME...
...OR HAS YUI REALLY GROWN UP LATELY?
WELL OF COURSE SHE HAS.
SHE ISN'T A LITTLE GIRL ANYMORE
EVERY DAY THAT PASSES BY,
THE FUTURE DRAWS A LITTLE NEARER.
I DON'T EVER WANT TO FORGET
MY EIGHT FRIENDS!
I NEVER...

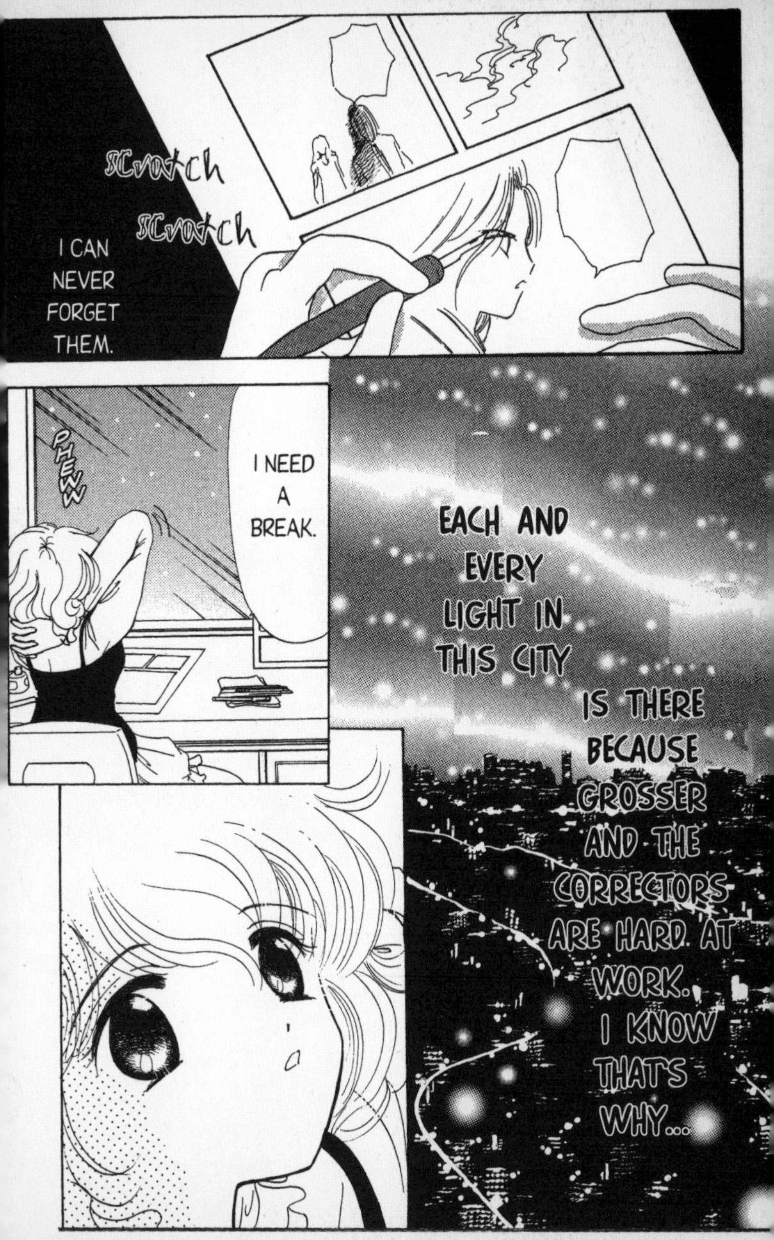

SCRATCH
SCRATCH
I CAN NEVER FORGET THEM.
PHEWW
I NEED A BREAK.
EACH AND EVERY LIGHT IN THIS CITY
IS THERE BECAUSE GROSSER AND THE CORRECTORS ARE HARD AT WORK.
I KNOW THAT'S WHY...

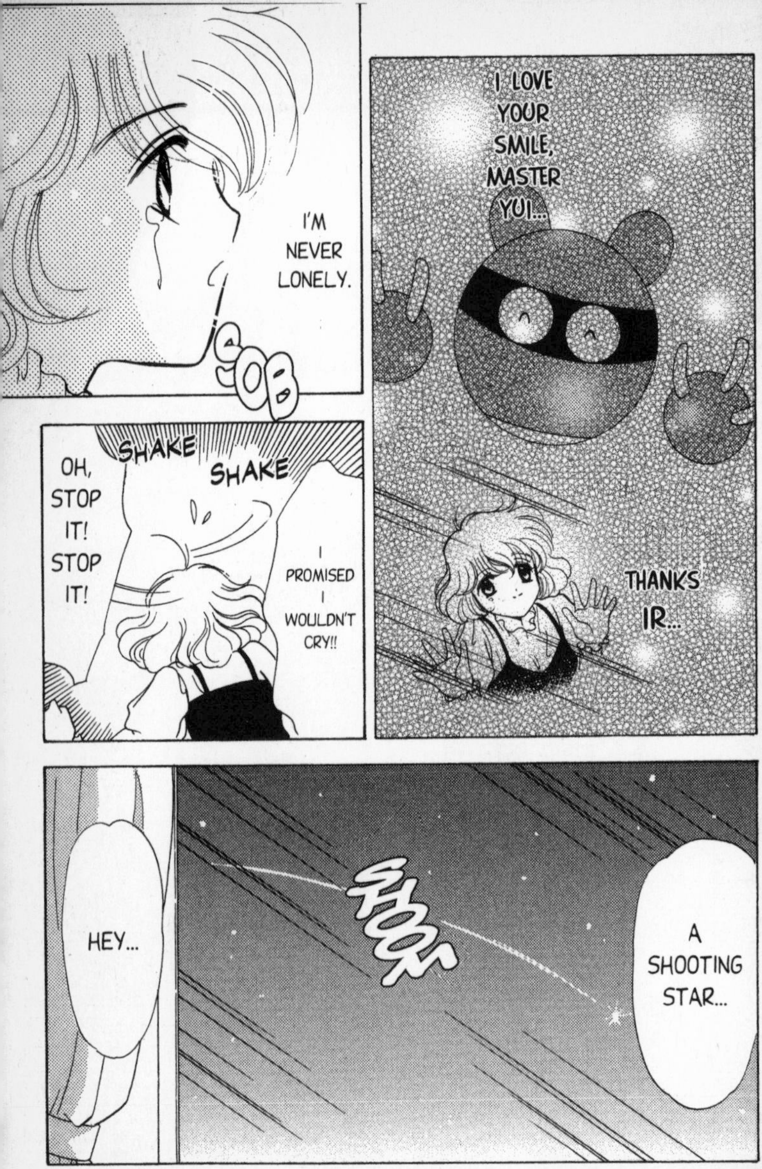
I'M NEVER LONELY.
SOB
SHAKE
SHAKE
OH, STOP IT! STOP IT!
I PROMISED I WOULDN'T CRY!!
I LOVE YOUR SMILE, MASTER YUI...
THANKS IR...
HEY...
A SHOOTING STAR...

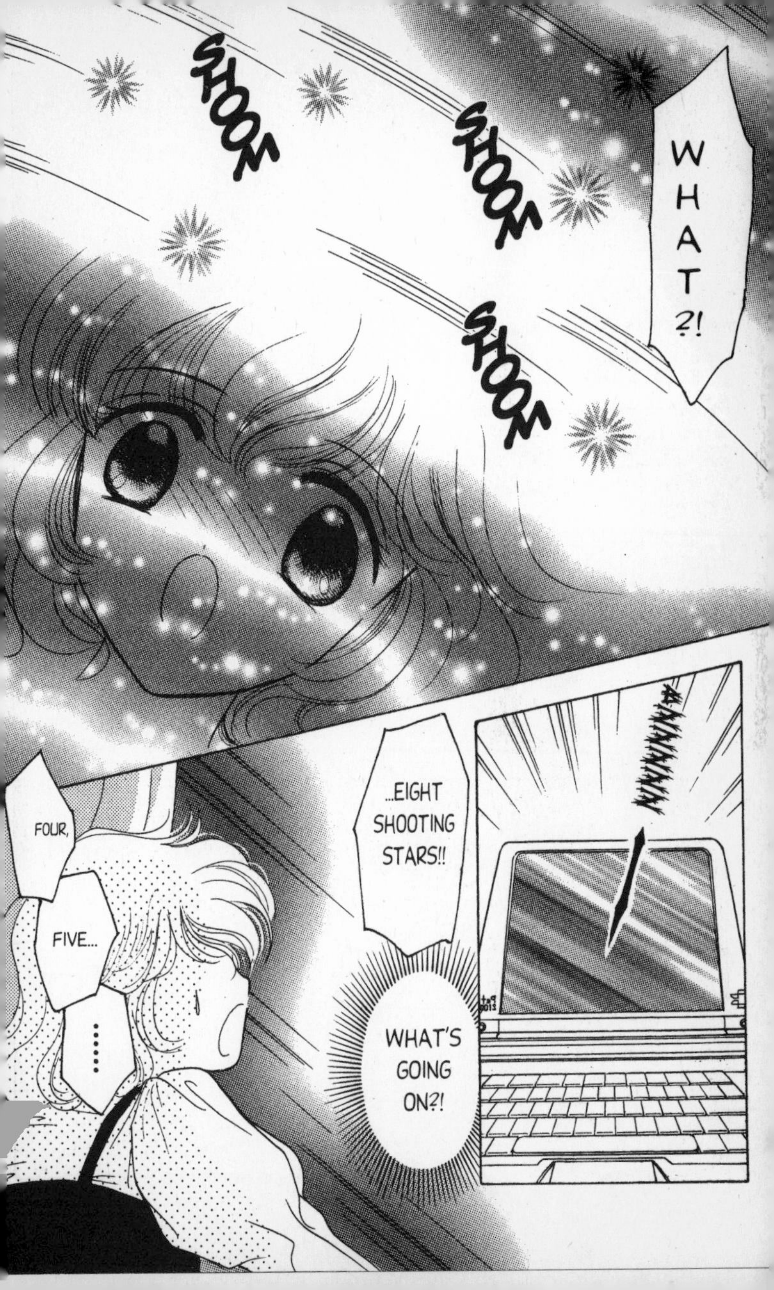
SHOOM
SHOOM
SHOOM
WHAT?!
FOUR,
FIVE...
......
...EIGHT SHOOTING STARS!!
WHAT'S GOING ON?!

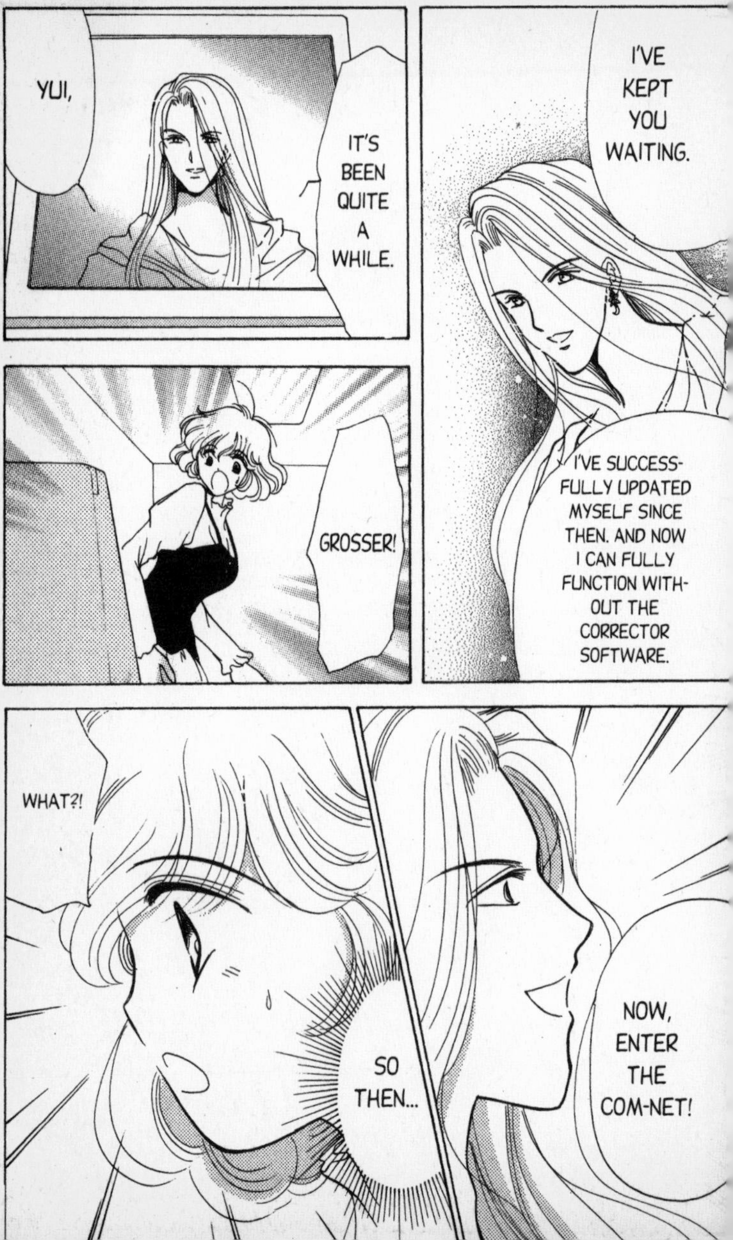
YUI,
IT'S BEEN QUITE A WHILE.
GROSSER!
I'VE KEPT YOU WAITING.
I'VE SUCCESSFULLY UPDATED MYSELF SINCE THEN. AND NOW I CAN FULLY FUNCTION WITHOUT THE CORRECTOR SOFTWARE.
WHAT?!
SO THEN...
NOW, ENTER THE COM-NET!

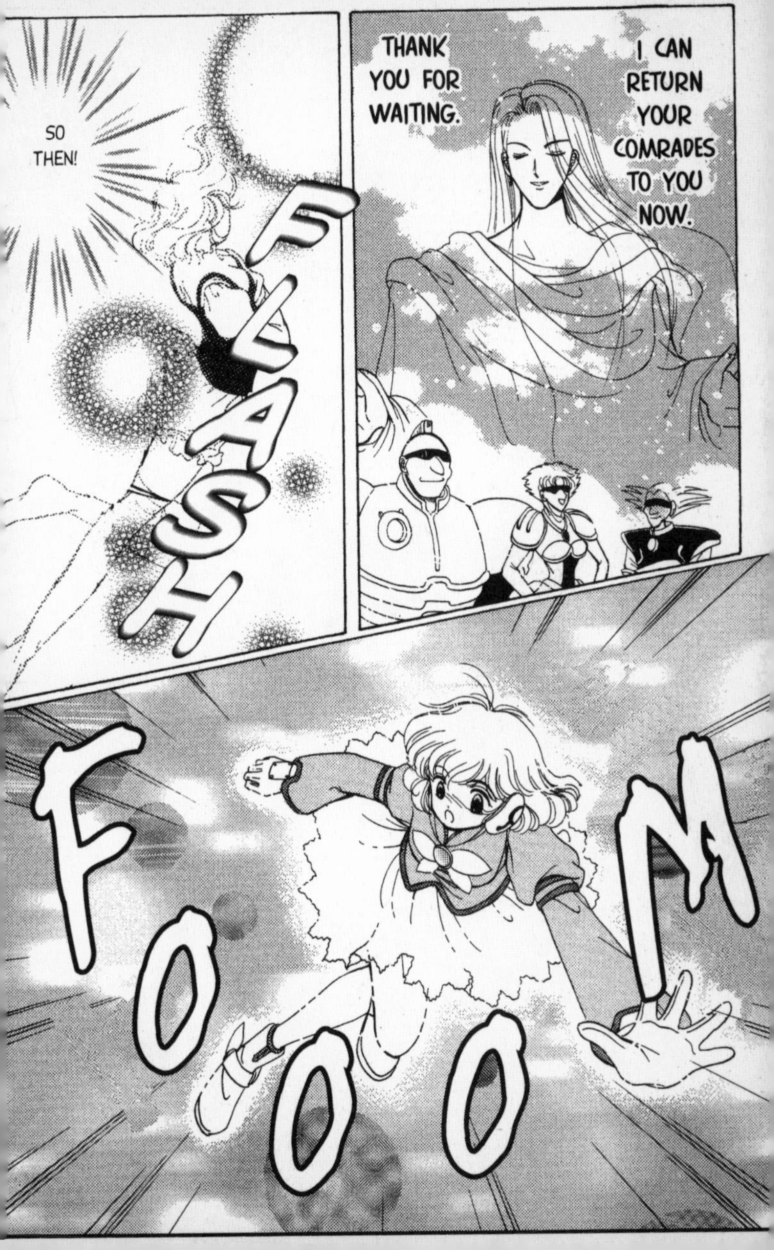
SO THEN!
FLASH
THANK YOU FOR WAITING.
I CAN RETURN YOUR COMRADES TO YOU NOW.
FOOOOM

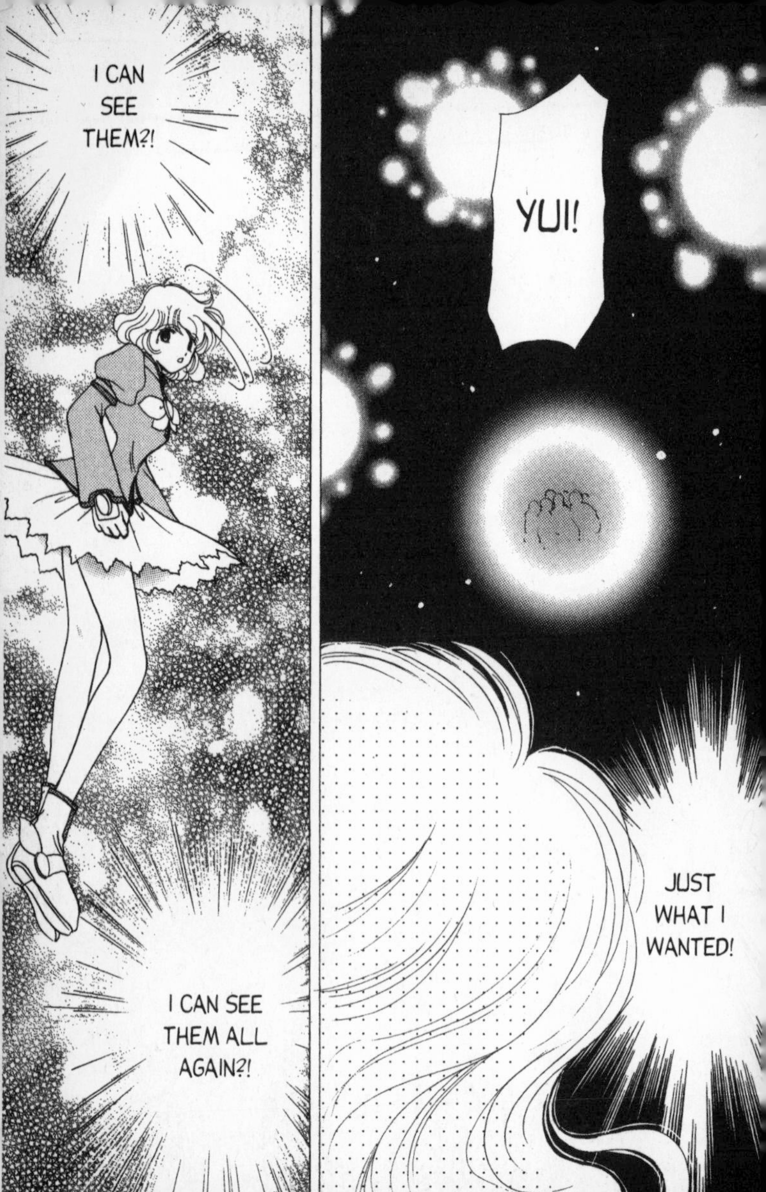
I CAN SEE THEM?!
I CAN SEE THEM ALL AGAIN?!
YUI!
JUST WHAT I WANTED!

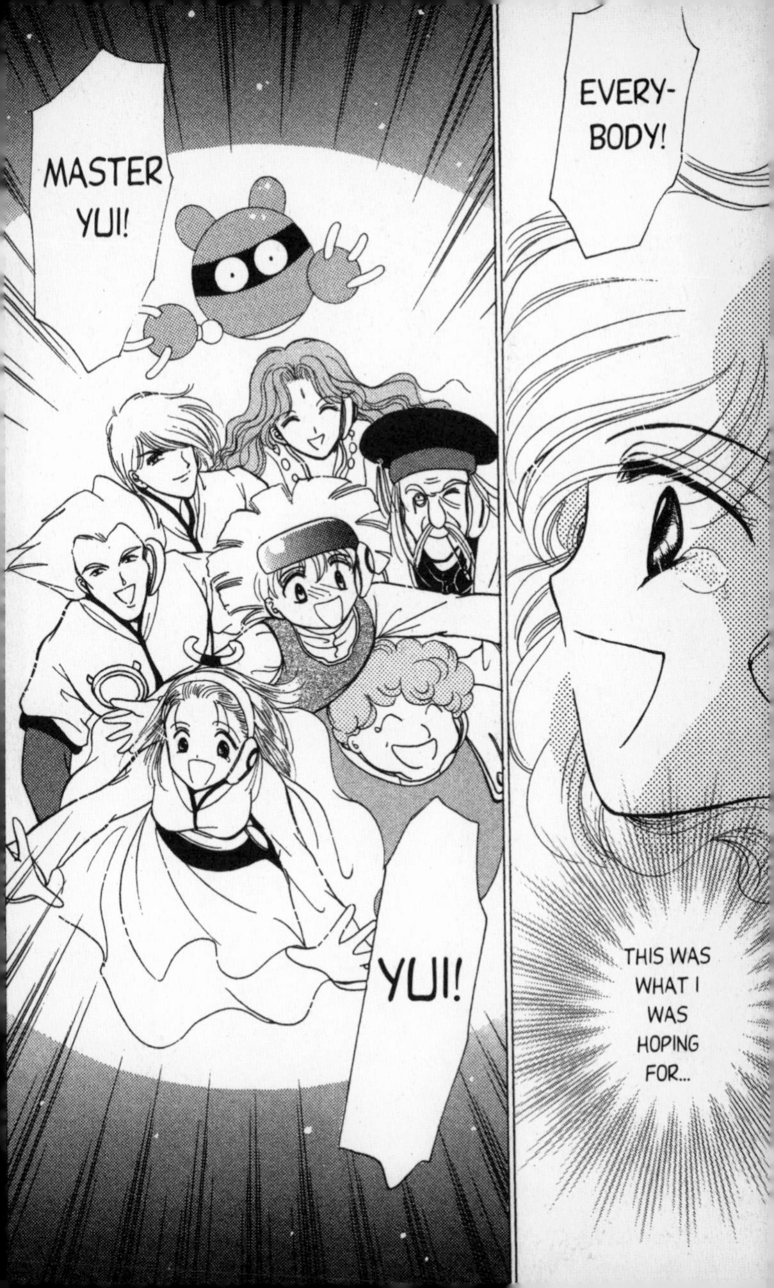
MASTER YUI!
YUI!
EVERY-BODY!
THIS WAS WHAT I WAS HOPING FOR...

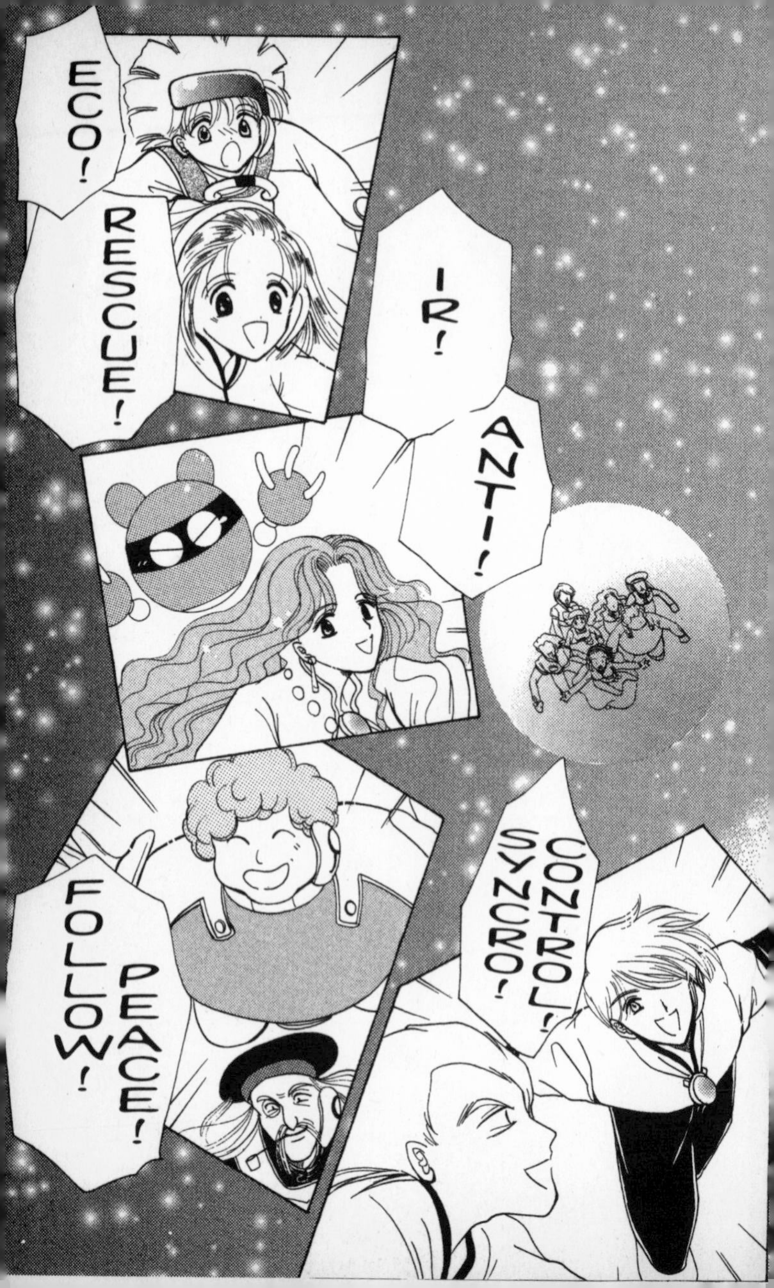
ECO!
RESCUE!
IR!
ANTI!
FOLLOW! PEACE!
SYNCRO! CONTROL!

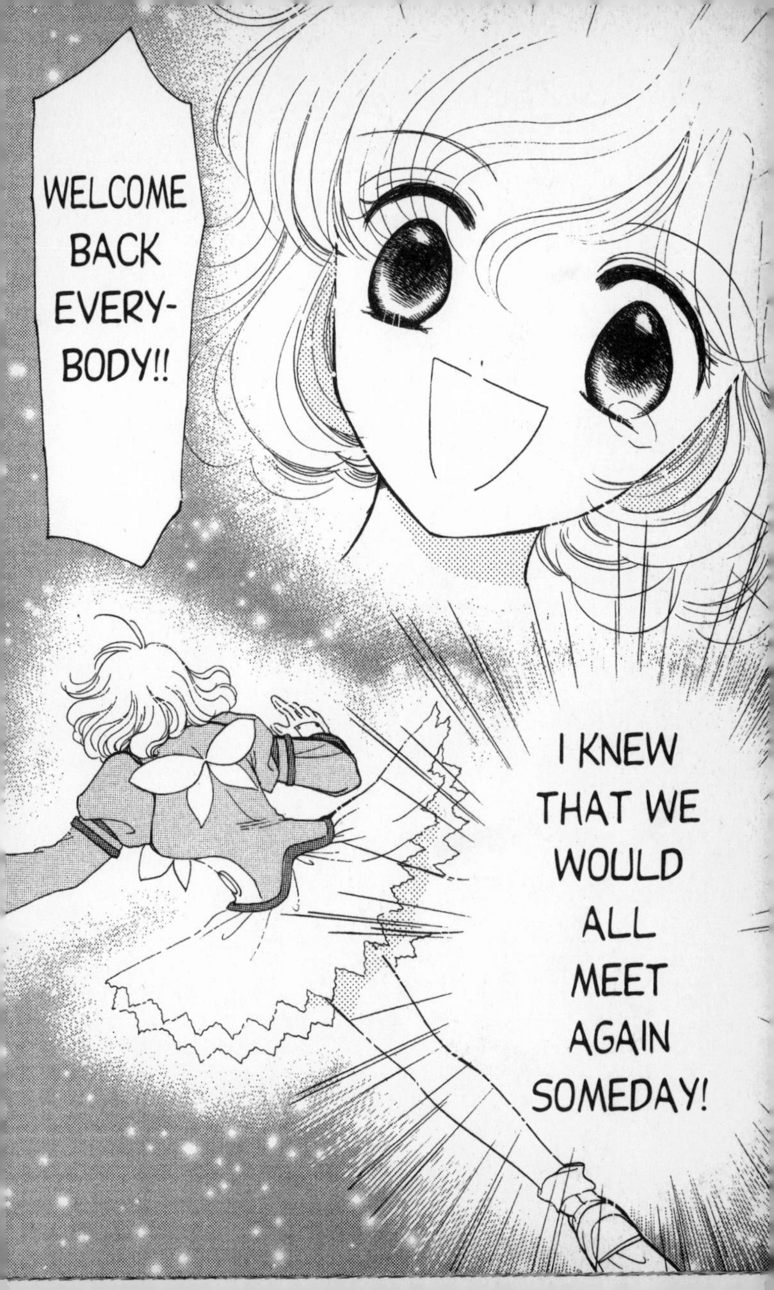
WELCOME BACK EVERY-BODY!!
I KNEW THAT WE WOULD ALL MEET AGAIN SOMEDAY!

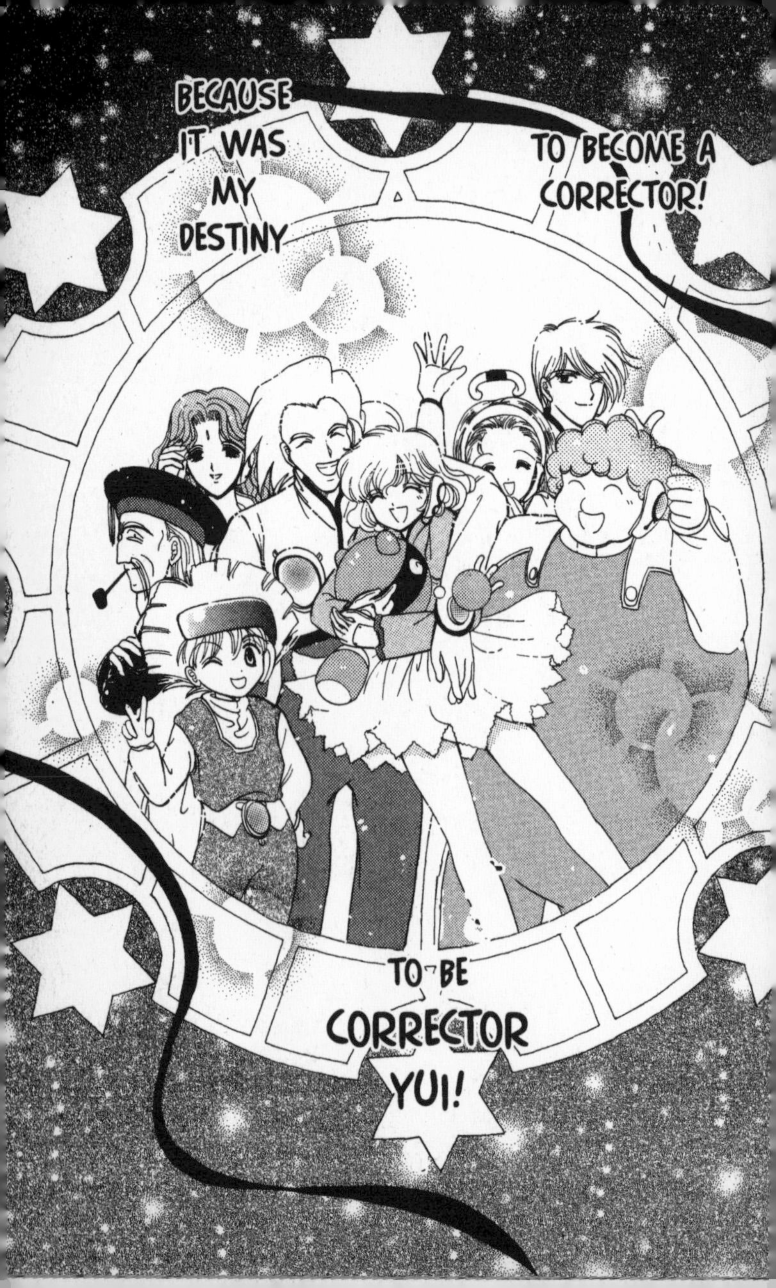
BECAUSE IT WAS MY DESTINY
TO BECOME A CORRECTOR!
TO BE CORRECTOR YUI!